Insurgency through Culture and Religion

Insurgency through Culture and Religion

The Islamic Revolution of Iran

M. M. Salehi

PRAEGER

New York
Westport, Connecticut
London

Library of Congress Cataloging-in-Publication Data

Salehi, M. M.
    Insurgency through culture and religion.

    Bibliography: p.
    Includes index.
    1. Iran—Politics and government—20th century.
2. Islam and politics—Iran.   I. Title.
DS316.32.S25   1988   955'.05   88-5943
ISBN 0-275-92902-7 (alk. paper)

Library of Congress Catalog Card Number: 88-5943
ISBN: 0-275-92902-7

First published in 1988

Praeger Publishers, One Madison Avenue, New York, NY 10010
A division of Greenwood Press, Inc.

Printed in the United States of America

The paper used in this book complies with the
Permanent Paper Standard issued by the National
Information Standards Organization (Z39.48-1984).

10 9 8 7 6 5 4 3 2 1

To all Iranians
who sacrificed their lives
for the sake of their ideals

Contents

Acknowledgments

This book is the result of what I have learned from many different people and sources. Two groups must be specifically named. The first is the people of Iran who, by their heroic acts now as in the past, have set records of wisdom and bravery in their struggle against injustice. Because they are located in a place where the propensity toward dictatorial rule and foreign domination has always been high, they may not have yet fully reaped the fruits of their struggles. Nevertheless, they have not given up and will continue this struggle to preserve their dignity as a proud and self-sovereign nation.

Second, I must mention the faculty of the Department of Sociology at Michigan State University where I received my sociological training. This excellent intellectual center was, and still is, gifted with some of America's most brilliant scholars. I will mention a few with whom I have been in more frequent contact; nevertheless, all others are at the same level of excellence.

First, I salute Professor William H. Form, as an example of a scholar and a studious intellectual. I associated with Dr. Form, who is no longer teaching at Michigan State, all through my graduate work. He has taught me much of what I have learned.

I also thank Dr. B. Anderson, Dr. D. Morrison, Dr. F. Waisanen, and Dr. J. McKee. Dr. Waisanen read the manuscript of this book and offered several suggestions.

I owe a special acknowledgment to Dr. C. Vanderpool, whom I have known since we were both graduate students, and who is now a professor of Sociology at Michigan State University. He has been a source of encouragement ever since I started writing this book. He read the manuscript and provided me with numerous suggestions. Dr. Vanderpool is a brilliant sociologist, a humane individual, and an American who understands other societies as well as his own.

I also thank Ms. Kathleen A. O'Connor, who worked with me as editor and typist. I am grateful for her indispensable treatment of my work in terms of my written English and her wide familiarity with concepts that ordinarily would have been unfamiliar to an editor. She has treated this work as that of her own.

Last, but not least, I thank my parents, whose ideal was that they provide their seven children with the best educational services that they could find.

Insurgency through Culture and Religion

Introduction

The purpose of our lives is never to cease the struggle.
We are like waves—
  our calmness is in our fading away.
               A slogan of Iranian college students in the 1970s

The 1978 political turbulence that put an end to the millennium-old monarchy in Iran has become known as the "Iranian Revolution." Officially, it is called the "Islamic Revolution," a notion emphasized by the new sovereigns and their loyal supporters in order to justify the rule of the Shiia clergymen and their Islamic principles.

The "Revolution" replaced the existing political order with a theocracy, a development incongruent with trends prevalent elsewhere in contemporary history wherever there has been a revolution. The incongruency is apparent not merely because a revolution had taken place, but because it had occurred under the leadership of a traditionalist Moslem clergy, who were striving to materialize their long term objective: the establishment of a theocracy.

In fact, it is surprising to note that until the early 1970s Iran was undergoing a transition toward a more secular society, with the role of religion diminishing in regard to political affairs. The outspoken revolutionary and reformist opposition forces were mainly secular in their orientation. Their domain of influence was expanding, making them a likely candidate to replace the existing regime. Then, in the 1970s, a renewed Shiia revitalization movement began. This movement gained momentum and penetrated almost every segment of the population. It conquered certain social territories that had been the stronghold of the former secular political groups. Simultaneously, it strengthened and expanded its influence among the lower classes and rural people.

1

This movement even found access to those members of the middle class who were better educated than most other Iranians. It was a great success for the proponents of Islamic rule, for now they had easy access to the group with the most significant political potential in the country—the urban middle class. This stratum included most of Iran's politically hotheaded college students, younger white-collar employees, and young officers in the administration of Iran's growing industrial system. These groups included most of Iran's long-time opponents of the regime, who were thoroughly experienced in radical activities under repressive rule. They were people with the knowledge and skills of political persuasion. It was not, therefore, the size of this stratum that was significant, but its political potential.

It became increasingly apparent that a redirection of the national struggle was in the process and that events were moving in favor of Islamic activists. Building upon this movement, different Moslem groups were encouraged to expand their activities, both in political and nonpolitical affairs. Some groups attempted to appeal to all classes with their political objectives and demands for a national uprising against the regime. As the struggle proceeded, during 1977-78, the Shiia groups under Ayatollah Khomeini's leadership managed to unify the major opposition forces over the objective of pushing the Shah out of office. This objective brought nearly all the opposition groups under a single leadership. As a result, the leading clergy who commanded the alliance of the insurgent masses rose to the position of leader of the opposition groups, speaking with a national voice. This promotion was not only political; simultaneously, it imposed the clergy's objectives and preferences upon the people.

Such activities at the leadership level were complemented by the entrance into the movement of millions of people who had very little previous political experience. A power was created that could easily crush any resistance, could silence any other alternative suggestions, and was obedient to the clergymen who had established themselves as the leaders of the uprising. The contribution and power of the small, but highly influential, new middle class was becoming insignificant compared to that of the urban lower class and the rural people. These earlier activists found themselves powerless to exert any determining influence upon the new course of social change. The energies that now moved the masses were beyond the control or command of the new middle class. The slogans, for example, during the early wave of the uprising in the winter of 1978, were "Freedom and Independence." By the end of the year, they had become "Freedom, Independence, and the Islamic Republic." The former reflects the earlier phase when secularists were still in the lead, and the latter reflects the time when the clergy leaders and their supporters had become a dominant force. The original political demands, for which the secularists had fought for years and to which they had tried to educate the populace, were fading away in the uproar of escalating revolution. Those demands were overstepped by an Islamic fundamentalist revitalization movement that had attracted millions of newcomers to the realm of revolutionary politics. Ideologically, the secular group found themselves to be like a gust of wind lost in a hurricane. They had helped the genie out of the bottle only to find themselves caught in his vise-like grip. The movement was entering a new phase.

In this phase, the demands of nearly all political forces that did not belong to the clergy-led groups were either removed from the agenda or pushed down on the list. Very little opportunity remained for secular demands, even if they were made by Moslem intellectuals. The revolution of the secular groups and the consequences of the earlier activists' efforts were swallowed up by the Shiia revitalization movement. The immense national power was now invested in a clerical leadership. Millions of devoted Shiia Iranians listened eagerly to these leaders as both political commanders and religious authorities. Millions of others obeyed them, at least as a political leadership. In this way, it was possible for the Shiia activists to elevate Ayatollah Khomeini to a leading position as a personification of the "People's Revolution," as both its spokesman and commander. Thus, a theocracy was born.

The observation of these historic events reinforced some of my earlier social theoretical concerns and interests. Ever since the 1960s' cultural movements among American college students, I have addressed myself to the following questions: How far may cultural and ideological movements go in changing the political order? and How far may these movements spread within different strata of the society? These kinds of questions were coupled with theoretical discussions about the role of culture and religion in modern society.

Later, in Iran of the 1970s, I was amazed by my observations of the ongoing cultural and ideological developments that were then gaining momentum and developing into revolutionary political movements. They fit well within the mainstream of some of my sociological, as well as personal, concerns about the country and its future. Having such interests for close to a decade, I kept an open eye on what was occurring in the country. As a professor of sociology, I was in a position to gain easy access to informed people and sources of material that would reveal hard-to-find facts about political events in Iran. The present book has emerged out of these participant observations.

The motivations for writing this book are numerous. Included are some social theoretical concerns that will be reflected in some brief concluding remarks in the final chapter. No doubt, viewing this historic experience from different perspectives may not only further one's understanding of the events in Iran and why they occurred, but the different points of view may also shed some light on the rather minor, but potentially significant, unrest and turbulence occurring in other Middle Eastern countries.

This book is basically addressed to an American audience. Ever since the Iranian Revolution, American people have had occasional involvement with what has been happening in Iran. Some of these experiences, such as the taking of the American Embassy hostages or other events in Lebanon that the media has reported as being linked to Iranians, may not have been pleasant to the majority of Americans or to their government. A more recent example of this might be the intensification of American involvement in the Persian Gulf.

In all such events, what may have seemed confusing to many Americans was the complication of political issues by the religious and cultural features of Iranian society. Americans, being used to thinking in terms of the separation of church and state, may have been led to wonder how they might clearly understand the Iranian case—at least in order to deal with it properly. This is why, in this book, prior to an explanation of the recent Iranian Revolution, a number of chapters will be devoted to an analysis of historical proceedings, cultural events, and the religious and psychological make-up of the Iranian people. This knowledge of the past and of the fabric of Iranian society is crucial to understanding and analyzing contemporary behavior.

I have tried to limit any bias in my analysis, which is designed to sharpen the reader's attention on a number of specific points, including the following items:

a) For many political analysts, political events, and even contemporary revolutions, are of primary concern because of the stability of a region, rivalries of the superpowers, the dominance of certain regions and potential markets, etc. These are the political concerns of the more powerful nations. The real need is to explain why people actually do revolt. What causes do they find worthy enough for which to risk the loss of their lives?

b) People are a great source of power. If organized properly, they can create such a tremendous force that the organized systems of oppression and control are unable to contain them.

c) For many decades, Iran's intellectuals and politically minded middle class have contributed toward preparing the people for an eventual alteration of the regime. Mass media coverage of a revolution, just like any other news item, focuses more on current events than on those events preceding them. This is especially so in the case of the Iranian intellectuals and the dissentive secularly oriented middle class that strove for democracy.

d) For decades, thousands of Iranians endured long prison sentences, torture-inflicted scars on both body and soul, firing squads, and the loss of precious lives in their revolutionary action. It was not due to insanity that these people decided to endure such difficulties. They dared to take action against a despotic order; even though they knew they might be persecuted. Despite earlier anticipations that the Iranian Revolution was to create a more humane political environment, i.e., a society with the promises of peace and compassion, events did not occur as expected. The post-revolutionary society became a major source of discouragement for many people, including a large number of those who had contributed greatly to its planning and enactment.

e) This study is intended to open a window on the inside world of the people who made a revolution—the world of the common people, not necessarily the leaders, but those whose ideas may not have received much publicity. The people, their ideas, their culture and religion, although a major theme of this book, are not the entire story. A number of factors have contributed to the rise of revolutionary movements. Included are conflicts of class interests and the oppressive rule of dictators. They too are given proper treatment whenever worthy of consideration. We must start with facts about a people—a people in revolution—as they actually are and not as a mere theoretician may portray them.

A point that needs to be mentioned concerns the references in this book. I have tried to provide equivalent citations that will be available to English-speaking readers. Therefore, my sources have become limited to those that are English-language documents and references to my personal notes.

In preparation, a brief clarification should be made at this time. The Iranian word for monarch is "shah." However, since people all over the world have recently learned to identify the last, deposed monarch of Iran as simply "the Shah of Iran," for convenience, we will only refer to him in this book as "the Shah." His father will be referred to by his first name, Reza Shah. Other shahs will merely be referred to as monarchs, in order to draw a clear distinction between them and the most recent rulers.

Part One

Political Features of Iranian Culture and Shiia Islam

1

The Roots of Oppression
in Iranian Society

What happened in Iran in 1978 was the combination of a number of opposition movements that, together, culminated in a revolution. Included were both secularly oriented and religiously inspired groups. Both of these included a wide range of sub-groups, each one distinct from the others in terms of ideology, objective, and style of their struggle. Both Moslem and secular groups ranged from conservative to liberal to radical.

As the struggle against autocracy and the arbitrary rule of the Shah gained momentum, its content was also deeply changed. The sum total of the demands of all these groups merged into a nationwide outcry for the elimination of monarchy and dependency. In the eyes of many Iranians, the two—monarchy and the affiliation of foreign domination—were one and the same.

1978-79 was not the first time that an absolutist monarch and foreign dependency had, together, become the target of the same protests. This has happened frequently in the current century in Iran. The new factor this time was the demand that a new social order be created that would replace the existing one. This demand was an attempt to uproot the system of monarchy.

The impulse that was the source of the political turbulence of revolution had been set into motion a long time ago. As early as the latter part of the 19th century, massive protests had taken place. They were quite limited in the number of participants and in their objectives. The late-19th and early-20th century protests were against specific arbitrary decisions. They did not go so far as to attack the very foundation of the political order. When their demands were met, most protesters were content to quit and even reestablish good relations with the monarch or his successor. In comparing the earlier phase with that of the late 1970s, it is quite obvious that an escalation of magnitude and radicalization of content in the movement had taken place. People had grown, over time, less compromising and more revolutionary in their demands and their mode of struggle.

In terms of the participating forces, a fundamental change had also clearly taken place. During the earlier stage, about a century ago, some dissentive clergy had merely united with the segment of Iran's business class that had made the major revolutionary move. They were then joined by a portion of the laity who supported the clergy simply out of religiosity. The other participants were relatively small in number, although some of them, such as the intellectuals, were quite outspoken. In comparison, the latest phase was a national uprising that included many modern forces—for example the liberals and Marxists, who were struggling through a combination of insurgency styles. Many of these groups, as a social class and as political parties, were nonexistent as early as a few decades ago.

It was the 20th century that, by means of modernization and the urbanization and commercialization of the agro-economy, had given birth to these newcomers. As they had grown in size and in professional vitality, the newly formed Iranian urban-educated middle class made a great impact by shaping the political events of the first part of this century. They had managed to shift the leadership of the opposition protests away from the traditional groups (the clergy and the business class) into the hands of those secular forces who strove for some sort of democratic order.

By mid-century, the modern political groups had even come close to setting up a full-scale parliamentary democracy in the country. Following a military coup d'etat in 1953, the country fell under the reign of a police state. Because of repression, the opposition was forced underground and, therefore, became radicalized. It found leaders mostly among secularly oriented groups, especially among young Marxists, who spoke in a revolutionary language. While the secular opposition groups were in the lead, the country was at the peak of its modernization.

The political turbulence reached a new height in the mid-1970s, because of an upsurge of religiously inspired opposition movements. The clergy-led groups brought the masses onto the scene. Their eventual victory was assured through their numbers, their lack of fear, their uncompromising attitude, and, more specifically, their unique mode of insurgency. They managed to downplay the significance of the others who had fought for years and still were involved in the uprising. They managed to lay claim to a triumph by pushing the monarchy out of Iranian history. They sealed the Iranian revolution with their own name and implanted their specific ideals and definitions upon the victory of people.

Quite clearly, with clergy domination of the ongoing struggle, they managed to detour Iran's course of social change away from a probably secular destiny towards a theocracy. They interpreted the people's struggle against the Shah's police state, and its foreign dependency, as a quest for Shiia revitalization. On this basis, the leading element of clerical groups aimed to rebuild a new Iran, in terms of the ideals derived from the experiences during the dawn of Islam. They condensed their projections into an official slogan that said: "Non-Western, Non-Eastern (non-Marxist), Islamic Republic." "Islamic Republic," according to them, is not a conception of a republican government. It is meant to express a generalized meaning that describes a totally different society, distinct from that of pre-revolutionary Iran, in which the social organizations, culture, law, and even the definitions of man and society itself are understood entirely differently. It was to be an Islamic society in which the principles of social order, social and personal life, were to be forcefully confined to the limits set in scripture, as they would be interpreted by the ruling body of Shiia clergymen. In such a society, social and personal life are highly structured, as is the pattern according to which the society is meant to grow.

The proponents of such an attempt managed to materialize one part of their historic scenario in their own way, by successfully putting into operation a mode of struggle and leadership that counteracted the Shah's well-prepared security measures, shattered the organization of the state, and uprooted it from its coercive basis. The second part of their plan is yet to be seen. It is the formation of a social organization that would be able to sustain their proposed social order in an industrial age.

The explanation of how and why the Islamic upsurge downplayed other opponents and triumphed requires an understanding of the nature of the Iranian opposition movements, their pattern of struggle, and their objectives. It is through such a historical perspective that we may be able to explain the rise of the Shiia clergy to power and the nature of their policies.

With such objectives in mind, the prerequisite is to offer an analysis of the composition of Iran's class structure with an eye on those classes that were politically active. This, in turn, requires the picturing of all changes that led to the emergence of new political groups, especially those with more radical ideals and those whose participation pushed the opposition movements toward revolutionary endings. The focal point of such an analysis could be spelled out through the following questions:

1. How deep, in the history of the country, does one need to search in order to find the initial impulse leading to the 1978 national uprising?
2. What were the main objectives voiced by the different classes and groups of people, and for what goals did the protesters strive?
3. What was the composition of the forces involved and how much weight did each one of them carry in striking at the embattled monarchy?
4. What were the effective modes of struggle that helped to spread the protests, strikes, and confrontations with the regime on a nationwide scale?
5. How did these efforts finally manage to subdue the embattled regime and cause it to lose control of the society, with its resulting organizational disintegration.

THE PRE-MODERN POWER STRUCTURE

Arid land composes the largest parts of Iran.[1] In the past, such regions were the centers of Iran's agrarian civilizations. The agrarian cells that relied on manmade water supplies were not merely a few isolated units. Indeed, they made up the bulk of pre-modern Iranian society and economy. It was in such territories that the core of the Persian culture and personality had been formed.

In addition, there were spots in the mountains around which some families had gathered to live a pastoral farming life. They were isolated points and had very little influence upon a system of power that drew its strength from the large agricultural territories of the flat lands.

There existed certain regions of the country whose agrarian condition and social organization were different from those that have so far been discussed. For example, one might note the flat lands around the Caspian Sea, which today are the most cultivatable lands in the country and have access to a plentiful water supply. Most of this region has only recently been developed and put under cultivation. In the far distant past it was covered by heavy jungles. Some other areas that are also dry, such as those in southeastern Iran and which today are important agricultural centers, came under cultivation in the last decade, when new technology became available. These areas began mostly with commercial agriculture and, because of mechanization, did not form feudal-type social organizations. There were, however, large land ownerships that gave rise to wealthy people who participated in the business sector as well as agriculture.

Combined with the pastoral territories, which were inhabited and controlled by tribal nomads, a tribal-agrarian society had developed in which urban areas, except for the last century, did not play much of a significant role.

These three main factors—the feudal societies, the tribes, and the royal system—composed the foundation of the ancient Iranian society. Being in mutual discord with one another, they had an unstable relationship that was held together mostly by force, rather than by cooperation. The exercise of force and coercion was their natural way of governance and elitism was their ideology. It was by all means a despotic order of dictators, which yielded only to the sovereignty of the strong.

Arid Lands and Despotism

An argument will be made that certain types of activities gave rise to communities centered around despotic organizations. A despotic system is one in which all power and control tends to concentrate at the top of an organized body.[2] Such communities typically depended on cultivation that utilized irrigation, because of insufficient rainfall. In such regions people must regularly irrigate their crops. If there is no access to naturally available reservoirs, such as springs, ponds, and rivers, or if what exists is insufficient, they must find ways of using underground water supplies. Given the technological capacities of pre-industrual societies, this was a difficult task, and it met with limited success. In any case, even if available resources were being used, irrigation still required the buildup of specialized networks, their maintenance, and their management. Beyond this, a certain initial capital investment was necessary. If the project was a relatively big one, it might require an organized body to perform and manage all these tasks.

Except for cases in which such labor and capital investment were collectively provided by a group of people, all of this was more than an ordinary farm family could afford. It had to be initiated and maintained by someone who had access to greater wealth and reliable manpower. In most cases, it was the rich who initiated and owned such enterprises. In these regions, agrarian communities had become a class society and one who owned and controlled an agrarian unit was a type of feudal lord. In Iran, these people were called *arbab*, or *khan*. To call them land lords is probably not the most accurate choice of words, because it was in fact the water that yielded the greatest priority over everything, and its ownership was vital. Land in such regions is typically cheap and plentiful. The owners, then, would more properly be called "water lords." One's share of a water resource was, in most places, the measure of one's ownership of the cultivatable property, reflecting the fact that water was the central concern and the prime factor in the lives of these agrarian people.

The development of this typical feudal society resulted from the source of the water supply being personally owned or controlled by those who had available wealth, eventually falling into private hands. Obviously, agriculture without land is meaningless. Therefore, to say that the land was not of much value is only to emphasize that, without water, it would totally lose its value and even be abandoned. The remains of villages that had lost their water resources were visible throughout the arid lands of Iran.

A typically constructed system of irrigation was known as a *ghanat*. Such a system was found in most agricultural units in the arid lands. In fact it was, in terms of the technology of its own time, a highly innovative construction. It made up the backbone of the agricultural activities in such regions. A *ghanat* was a network of wells connected in a row through a tunnel. The wells were drilled deep enough to reach the underground water resources. At the bottom they were connected together, so the deposited water could flow as an underground stream. At a certain point, this stream would reach the lower level regions and flow out on the surface of the land. In the same vicinity or even in far distant areas, the plots of land were irrigated through the action of this stream of water.

Agriculture, through irrigation, had a number of consequences that were more or less universal social and political features of such agrarian communities. Some of them are as follows:

1. In the case of underground water supplies, the size of the territory surrounding such a community also had to have a certain specified domain. Usually, parallel networks were not permitted because they would drain out

the reserved deposits and considerably reduce the amount of water available to each system. Therefore, the furthest well would mark the border line. Typically, these villages comprised an area of at least a few hundred square miles. Only a small percentage of this land would be used for cultivation.

2. A team of skilled workers was needed to operate this system. Quite frequently, the underground tunnel system or some of the wells would collapse. They then needed annual repair. Sometimes, if the underground level of water had dropped considerably, the whole system would become useless or damaged so seriously that it might have to be abandoned. This, too, would reinforce the position of the wealthy, especially the lord of such a community, because ordinary farmers could not afford the cost, the manpower, or the financial risk. Big land lords had access to the equipment and to the manpower with which to take care of such affairs in a professional manner.

3. The size of the community was mainly determined by the amount of the water resources available. If naturally flowing water such as mountain streams or springs were used, the amount of the water, and therefore the size of the community, would in most cases stay relatively constant. In the case of a *ghanat*, it was possible to expand the system through further investments. In most cases, especially in very dry regions, the capacity to provide water was quite limited, as was the size of the farming communities. It is no wonder that the number of Iranian villages at this time ran to about fifty thousand, with a total population of about ten million. This made an average of two hundred people per small village, assuming that the average rural village consisted of twenty to thirty large-sized families.

4. All these factors would strengthen the position of the lord. A system of feudalism emerged in most parts of Iran wherein certain lords each owned hundreds of villages. Considering the large territory that each village needed, the combined estate of such a lord amounted to thousands of square miles and included a vast number of people. Not all of those who lived in these villages were the lord's peasants, but a majority were. The big villages even had an administrative system, some defensive mechanism, and a large number of skilled men at their disposal for a variety of irrigation tasks. Some special status systems had also developed for those whose specialty was to manage the distribution of water on the numerous small plots on which the peasants or tenants worked. Such lords had a veritable country of their own and were virtually kings, even though they may not have been called by the title.

5. An important political consequence of this system was its defensive consideration. These farming communities, being mostly located in open flat lands miles apart from one another with only a handful of residents, were quite vulnerable to raids. Tribes, bandits, and even raiders sent by the rival neighboring lords were possible attackers. The fear of being raided, the possible theft of the harvest, and the abduction of their daughters were constant elements of insecurity for people in these rural areas. The older rural people

could tell hundreds of stories about such incidents, and their folk tales and songs reflect the fears and the difficulties that they had endured. For example, even as late as the mid-19th century, the Turkman tribes, whose center is now an eastern province of the U.S.S.R. (about a million Turkmans reside in Iran), had spread a reign of terror in a large part of Iran. By penetrating as deep as the central part of the country, they attacked villages, taking away property and stealing the people as slaves.

The fear of raiders was common to both lords and subjects. The groups had found a common interest in security and safety that would politically bind them together. They had no other choice but to welcome the emergence of rulers that were strong and tyrannical enough to scare everyone else into peace. The politics of the feudals was an alliance with whoever ruled. The people promoted powerful kings, even though it would cost them heavier dues.

6. Within the territory of a lord, every affair was to be relayed to him as the one who had the final word. The administrative arm of the central government did not reach inside the lord's territory. This took the burden off the shoulders of the rulers whose system was not fit to provide the various services for the entire population of the country. Some of these rulers were only the kings of the territories immediately surrounding their palaces.

7. Having this near-total power and this control over the lives of the villagers, the lord and his family could do anything they wished. However, not all lords were brutal people. If they had wanted to, they could have been. Typically, they would rule forcefully, employing merciless agents. No disobedience, disloyalty, rebellion, or resistant behavior was tolerated. They would often punish the wrongdoers (those who disobeyed them) so brutally that no one would dare to repeat the punishable acts. Torture, beating, fines, and forced labor were quite common, and in some cases, to inflict severe psychic pain, the sexual assault of one's loved ones was also included in the subjugation.

In summary, within the social system of pre-modern Iran, the rural community was the building block of a despotic system and the main source of its dictatorial ideologies.

The Tribes

Up to the turn of this century, the tribes, a good portion of them nomadic, included the second major component of the Iranian population. Economically, they were not as important as the agrarian sector. However, they played a major political role in the history of Iran. Having a pastoral economy, it was required that they maintain control over large territories, monopolizing their use and defending them; otherwise, they could not survive. Therefore, over time, they gained valuable military experience as well as the ability to be highly mobile. They basically valued autonomy and self rule, and became smaller countries within a larger one called Iran, or the Persian Empire.

Prior to the establishment of modern large-scale military forces, the defense of the country's frontiers was the responsibility of the Iranian tribes. In the Iranian mentality and culture, these tribes stood as emblems of patriotic and nationalistic ideologies.

Being highly mobile and militarily experienced, they could easily take over the residential areas and establish their rule. Being also ethnically and culturally exogeneous to the agrarian and urban communities, they had to revert to coercive measures to establish their authority. Iran's earliest and more powerful dynasties emerged out of these tribal-feudal neighborhoods. In some places, such as the south and southwest parts of the country, the agrarian civilization had developed on a large scale. These were also the seats of the ancient Persian Empire.

The Monarchy

The Iranian monarchy, which was established 3000 years ago, grew into a strong centralized power, expanding rapidly into one of the largest ancient empires. This political institution survived over time with little change. Even when foreign occupants ruled the country, they, too, assumed a despotic role, accumulating all power in the office of the monarch. Even if it was disrupted, the same pattern would soon reemerge each time an invading ruler was routed or one Iranian monarch was replaced by another. For example, when Nader, who was a shepherd's son, rose up and became a king, he grew as powerful and as despotic as those who had preceded him.

Only for a brief interlude, due to a transition period or some turmoil (chaos was the order of the day), would people have a moment of freedom from the rule of a powerful king. There were a few exceptions, though. These existed not because the equation of power had changed in favor of the people, but because some soft-hearted and gentle-mannered person had assumed the office. In such cases, however, the despotic order was not changed. What made the difference was the presence of a non-dictatorial person in the office of the despot. The Zand dynasty, for example, shows one such an exceptional case. The founder of this dynasty refused to call himself the king, but rather preferred to be called the representative of the people, or *vakil*.[3]

On a few occasions, important changes in the institution of the monarchy occurred, with fundamental political consequences. These changes affected the foundation of the justification of the monarchy. One such change was experienced in the 16th century with the Safavid dynasty. Another, which will be discussed later, followed the 1906-1908 Iranian Constitutional Revolution.

The Safavid dynasty proclaimed Shiia Islam the official religion of the country.[4] Following this, the sovereignty of the monarchs became geared to the Shiia interpretation of Islam and government. They did not completely turn the country into a theocracy, however, but only reinforced the religion as the basis for the legitimacy of their rule. The importance of this development rests in the fact that afterward, this branch of Shiiaism, called Twelfther, spread all over Iran. Twelfther Shiiaism believes in a chain of twelve Imams. According to them, the twelfth Imam, called Mehdi, went into occulation, to the realm of invisible. He is assumed to be alive and enjoying everlasting life until some time in the future, when he will reappear and assume the ruling office. It is believed that he will bring in "the universal government of Justice." Nevertheless, while he is invisible, or "absent," the sovereignty is still his, who implements the rule of God, but someone else must act as his proxy. The top Shiia clergy believe they are obliged to observe that this ruling is kept within limits and according to the principles of Islam as they have previously interpreted them.

Therefore, what the Safavid monarchs had done was to appoint themselves as proxy, in order to govern as long as the Imam Mehdi was in occulation. However, in practice, they took the position for themselves personally. They created the office called *sadr*, or chief,[5] as the highest religious figure. This *sadr* would oversee the religious aspect of the governance. The Safavid kings, therefore, while confining their rule to the limitations set by the religion, inevitably gained a political advantage by co-opting the clergy.

The Safavids helped the Shiia clerical organizations to grow, its leaders to become very powerful, and their influence in the political affairs of the country to increase. They, indeed, became the complement of the monarchical order.

OTHER BASES OF POWER

In 20th-century Iran there have been certain groups that have counteracted the despotic tendencies of the monarchs. Some of these groups were born out of new social conditions that had themselves come about as the consequence of recent social changes. Included were the modern segment of the middle class, workers of modern industries, civil servants, intellectuals, political party activists, and the better-educated youth. The better-educated youth, who made up a large stratum and were potentially anti-regime, were products of the newly built modern educational institutions. Others, such as some segments of the clergy who had evolved as an anti-regime political force, and their allied forces in the business community, were in existence even in the distant past.

Almost all of these groups had experienced expansion in size and had found a significant role in this century and especially within the last couple of decades. It was such changes that made them potential sources of threat to the regime.

The Business Class

A bourgeoisie class under the reign of oriental despotism is neither as strong nor as large as it may grow to be under other conditions. Thus was the case in Iran, where only in the last couple of centuries did the business class begin to grow. The encouragement of a monetary medium of exchange, the commercialization of agriculture, and the general growth in trade were some of the factors that helped this expansion. Yet it continued to be a rather weak group in a country where feudals, tribal *khans*, and an over-expanded royal family made up the elite.

The Iranian center of commerce, and even some smaller business activities, was located in what was called the Bazaar. The people who did business there made up a commercial community that had its own organization and cultural identity. They were called the Bazaari, which in the Iranian language means the people of the Bazaar. The Bazaar represented nearly all sectors of the Iranian economy and traditional manufacturing. Included in this stratum was a vast array of small workshops that were involved in handcrafts such as shoe-making, blacksmithing, and printing. In the old days, such shops functioned as both producer and seller. Items such as copper utensils, brass dishes, and fabrics were made in shops that were also located in the Bazaar. In the last few decades, many of these people have employed more advanced technologies for mass production. Some of them have even opened up modern factories elsewhere, making the same things in modern form. Their shops in the Bazaar have become distribution centers. In their own words, they have switched to *tou li di*, or mass production.

The Bazaari people occupy a distinct position in the Iranian social and political system, due first to their cultural identity, and second to their political actions during the last century.

Although not all the business people in Iran are religiously oriented, the Bazaaris are known to be so. Social pressure in the Bazaar community is a strong reinforcer of religiosity. Culturally, there is a distinct image that combines a luxurious lifestyle with traditionalism and religiosity. In this respect, the Bazaaris are distinct from the new stratum of large and small businessmen and women whose business centers are spreading to every street and alley in Iran. Culturally, the latter are often quite modern, and their religious faith is not known to provide them with a cultural identity.

Through their active participation for nearly a century in the opposition's protests and movements against the monarchs, Iran's Bazaaris have become recognized as the center of anti-absolutist sympathy and support. Through this identity, they have safeguarded themselves against the accusations and attacks of left-oriented groups.

The question may be raised, then, that if both despotic monarchism and businesses were such old institutions, why, in the last century, did the businessmen begin to join the ranks of the opposition groups with such commitment? The answer to this question requires some further discussion of the Iranian historical experience, especially that of 19th-century foreign intervention into the internal affairs of the country. Therefore, a more detailed answer must be delayed momentarily. It may suffice, at this time, to mention that business people may have never been very happy with a despotic regime, which was an outgrowth of feudal-tribal economies.

In general, for a business to grow and function properly, it needs to be able to influence the policies of the state. Business people need to be able to manipulate conditions in a way that will suit their requirements, and, generally, to have sufficient freedom to be able to operate as they see fit. The feudal lords, in contrast, ruled their own territory, and within their own domain of control would set their own policies. Their only concern was to be able to maintain a secure environment. But the businessmen's territory is the market, and in the absence of a democratic order, the mechanisms of rational decision making, and sound laws and regulations, they had too many unpredictable factors with which to deal. They ended up with very little influence upon the shaping of the market. Lacking, for example, were the rule of laws governing custom duties, safe roads, proper foreign policy, adequate monetary facilities, and a judiciary system that would solve their legal problems to their satisfaction. In an authoritarian regime, practically none of these needs could be influenced by them. A monarchist mentality, grown out of tribal or feudal systems, was not concerned with answering the demands of the business community. Even if some attention was finally paid to the problems of the business class (and this was actually done in the mid-19th century), it was merely a personal favor given by a single individual in the system, such as a prime minister or even the king himself. It would last only as long as that minister was in power and favored business. Besides, even if the wrong or improper decisions had been made with good intentions, there was no way for the business community to influence their reversal.

In view of such considerations, the business class had a vested interest in the prevention of a despotic regime. They may not have opposed it openly, but they had no reason to be happy with it either. The continuity of feudal and tribal order contained nothing to make the businessmen happy. Such traditional systems usually functioned as self-sustaining economic units. Within their system, the exchange of goods and services "in kind" was a common practice, and money played a very small role in the life of the peasants. Consequently, with the dominance of such an order, the circulation of money in the society and its availability to a large segment of the population were limited. So, too, were potential purchasers. This was not what businessmen would have liked.

The society, however, within the context of Iran's typical power structure, was such that these business people were so weak and small in size that an involvement in any serious attempt at opposition would have impelled a revenge by the monarchs, whose tyrannical capacities were known to all. Only when conditions were in their favor and they had found other strong opposition groups with which to ally themselves, did they begin to make opposition gestures toward the regime.

What helped to provide the business class with a major political influence in Iranian politics was their alliance with the clergy in the events of the later 19th century that led to the Constitutional Revolution of Iran. Once again in our century, a decade ago, they followed the clerical leadership. This time due to the modernization, urbanization, and commercialization of agriculture and the inflow of large sums of petrodollars into the national economy, the Bazaar had become the nerve center of Iranian politics and a vital and powerful element in the process of the national economy. During the very early days of the revolution of 1978-79, a sizable number of Bazaari sided with opposition movements. Their number was sufficient to cause a disruptive effect on the business affairs of the country. They claimed credit for playing a role in the Revolution through their financial aid and long-term strikes. Through their traditional alliances with the clergy, who finally became the new sovereign, they not only survived the revolution but may have even helped capitalism to survive in Iran. This occurred at a time when, in the post-revolutionary era, it was quite conceivable that their existence as a social and economic class might have been altogether terminated.

The Middle Class

Iran's middle class is composed of two distinct sub-strata. One is the extension of the old urban middle stratum, which was mainly composed of small businessmen, small property owners, and craftsmen who were better off than the lower classes. The other group, which is the product of the 20th century, is composed of those who owe their position to the education and skills that placed them in the ranks of the middle class. The latter, who are mostly better-educated urbanites, are referred to in this book as the "new middle class." These are the people from whose rank men of ideas, professionals, educators, intellectuals, political activists, and middle-rank administrators arise.[6]

Iran's middle class prior to the modern era was a relatively small group. There did not exist an extensive service sector nor any large-scale government bureaucracy to create numerous white-collar jobs. Cities were relatively small, and foreign trade quite limited. There was no economic basis, therefore, to support the growth of a large middle class stratum, nor was there any other major function for them to perform. The feudalism of Iran had left very little room for a large class of small property owners to emerge out of the rural areas. Therefore, what made up the Iranian bourgeoisie was mostly limited to what existed in the urban areas.

It was the expansion of the government bureaucracies and agencies, and the increase in size of the government's revenue, specifically the inflow of petrodollars, that helped to expand the stratum of the new middle class.

NOTES

1. The Persian empire emerged out of the arid regions. The remains of the ancient Persian royal city of Persapolice is located near a city called Shiraz, which is the provincial center of Farce. This region is typically arid (see Table 2 for the climatic characteristics of Shiraz).

2. K. A. Wittfogel, *Oriental Despotism: A Comparative Study of Total Power* (New York: Random House, 1981).

3. John R. Perry, *Karim Khan Zand: A History of Iran 1747-1779*, Center for Middle Eastern Studies, no. 12 (Chicago: University of Chicago, 1979).

4. The Safavid Dynasty emerged out of a cultural-religious movement headed by certain Suffii leaders, originally led by the Sheihk Safi. They rose up at the time when Iran still was under the rule of the residues of foreign invaders' rule. Their rise to power was not only a political takeover of the government, but also a triumph of the Shiia conception of Islam. Therefore, upon his seizure of power in Azarbaijan (his native state) "Shah Iss ma eel" asserted twelfther Shiiaism (Shiiaism that is now practiced in Iran) as the official religion of the state.

5. R. Savory, *Iran under the Safavids* (Cambridge: Cambridge University, 1980).

6. Theoretical works on the Iranian middle class are scattered throughout various sources. What is presented here are generalizations made from my own research, as well as readings from existing literature on Iran in the 20th century. It is assumed that professionals, highly skilled workers, better educated citizens whose income is comparable to that of the white collar employees, non-blue-collar employees of the state, and the private sector represented a socioeconomic strata that here is called the new middle class.

2

Culture and Religion:
A Different Perspective

In the history of Iran, culture has been more than a way of life. It has always provided people with a reservoir of the historical experiences of political movements, and has been a medium for political action. So, too, has been the country's religion, which is mainly Shiia Islam. Culture and religion together, as two interrelated institutions, provide a symbolism that becomes instrumental in Iranian political activities. During the 20th century, turbulence, revolutions, and uprising have been quite frequent in Iran—all with the presence of a strong religious influence. Religious activists have never just made demands, but also have provided the people with certain means of organization and mass mobilization. In view of this statement and recent revolutionary events, the relation of the people to these institutions requires a detailed explanation.

For the purpose of such an analysis, religion and culture are studied as two distinct subjects, while in reality the two are closely associated. The distinction is made because the people of Iran are religiously heterogeneous and a large number of them are more oriented toward secular rather than religious political thinking. Over one-sixth of the Iranian population is Sunni Moslem. Except for Sunnis and a small percentage of Jews, Christians, Zorastrians, and other religious groups, the rest of the populace is Shiia Moslem. In the lifestyle of all Moslem Iranians, Islamic values have similar influences, regardless of Shiia or Sunni affiliations. In contrast to such heterogeneity, contemporary Iranian culture provides a large medium of common experiences that potentially provides a broader domain for political solidarity and communication than any one particular faith. However, this cultural system is not empty of Islamic content. The Iranian cultural tradition and social structure has had some impact upon the organizational and ceremonial aspects of Iranian orientations to Islam as well. Consequently, despite the conceptual distinction, in reality, culture and religion are highly interrelated in Iran and have overlapping functions.

The rest of this and the next two chapters will be devoted to Shiiaism and an anatomy of the Iranian culture. Shiia Islam played the major role in the recent revolution, as well as in the earlier Iranian Constitutional Revolution. It has definitely been a major factor in Iranian politics.

Iranian culture provides most of the people in the country with a similar mechanism for political thought and action. It makes up for the absence of effective and widespread political parties. Even though political parties have been present in Iranian life for nearly half a century, they have never become a popularly supported instrument or one in which the masses of people have participated. They have never managed to sustain a large membership for more than a few years. The major political parties quite frequently have either been crushed, been banned, or disintegrated into a number of factions. The new factions usually had fought within themselves more severely than they fought their supposed rivals or enemies. In contrast, Iranian culture has always been a medium for the politicization of the masses. The activists, specifically those with dissentive intentions, have skillfully learned to make the best use of culture in order to reach a wider and more receptive audience. On the basis of such an understanding, a number of main features of Iranian culture can be analyzed. These features are those that facilitate political communication and thinking, include certain mechanisms for collective action, facilitate changes in people's ideological orientations. Similar features are present in Iranian religious behavior.

An observer of the Iranian culture and of Shiia Islam may wonder how far the domain of these institutions stretches and what kind of social and personal behavior falls within their boundaries. For example, an outside observer might be shocked to hear a clergymen, who holds a top political office in the Islamic regime, label as counterrevolutionary certain women who appear in public with heavy make-up on their faces—a highly serious political offence. They might be equally shocked to hear that certain music is presently forbidden in Iran by the clerical rulers, and that anyone caught in possession of such pop music tapes is treated like a criminal by the Islamic revolutionary guards. The outside observer may subsequently wonder what pop music has to do with politics and why it should be a concern to the revolutionary guards. It is quite ironic to hear Iranian radio stations play music throughout the day, a sort of music that sounds not much different than the pop music they forbid. Such observations raise the question of whether the case isn't merely that the Iranian notion of culture and religion is different from the typical Western point of view. If one is to better understand what Iranians accomplished in their uprising and why, and if one is to understand how they generated such a powerful social force by symbolic performances, then broader conceptions of religion and of culture are needed than those that we may already have. It is within such a wide open horizon that one needs to look for significant behaviors. One must also examine how deep and detailed such an observation needs to be if the crucial points are not to be missed. Any reporters covering the Iranian events should have asked themselves this question quite often.

Assuming that readers of this book are mostly non-Iranians, some remarks need to be made about the shortcomings of the cultural and religious explanation of political events. In view of the separation of church and state in the Western societies, Western readers may fail to see the full extent to which the Iranian culture and Shiiaism have influenced the Iranian political psychology and system. To alert the readers to the existence of certain limitations and biases in what they may have received from the mass media and existing literature, some shortcomings of the cultural studies will be discussed with examples from Iran.

OPPRESSIVE SYSTEMS AND PEOPLE'S POLITICS

An oppressive system of government, as has existed in the past history of Iran, has its own specific form of political behavior. The people's political awareness under such conditions becomes highly attentive to events as they relate to power and the exercise of it. Such exercises are often backed by force and violence. The oppressors pursue their own wills, and show no hesitation in using whatever means they deem appropriate to reach their own ends. Very few constraints, if any, exist to keep them in check. The tragedy is the people; they are the ones who have to pay the price demanded, be made powerless, and often be intimidated. In the people's eyes the power structure of such a society is quite visible. People see an oppressive regime as an objective reality with its center and lines connecting it to different places and groups. They can sense its presence through every aspect of their own social, and even personal life. Often they are informed of the struggles and rivalries going on between different contestants at the top. The story of such rivalries, and who is on whose side, makes up a portion of the people's own conversations. They don't talk about these subjects to kill the time. Quite realistically, they are motivated to be alert and be prepared for policies that could intensify the reign of oppression.

It is not just the political affairs at the top of the system that concern people, but more specifically what is happening in the middle and local level. These are the levels in which they are forced to participate in political activities that favor the oppressors. Their cognitive mapping of the power structure is especially articulated through such experiences. Such obligatory activities vary from forced payment for campaigns, to participation in celebrations of the ruler's birthday, to praying for the health of the ruler. In some cases, people might even be forced to spy for the regime. In pre-revolutionary Iran, those who forced people to participate included certain local managers of government agencies, or even city officials. They would outdo themselves to show their abilities in bringing people onto the stage, and thus keep their job and receive promotions and other attractive rewards. Such a regime's criteria for promotion was, in fact, not based on helping to make the economy grow or improving education, but merely on showing how well one exercises power or implements the demands of the higher authorities in order to please them. That was what the oppressors valued most. Their main criteria in judging subordinates was the ability to take orders and to show loyalty by safeguarding the ruler's interest. A very popular folk story makes a sarcastic statement that perhaps truthfully applies. It tells of how, centuries ago, a *khalife* (an Islamic ruler) appointed one of his servants governor of Egypt. When the time came to collect the dues and taxes, the people did not have much to hand in because it happened to have been a bad year for farming cotton. The governor was angered to hear the bad news and screamed, "Why, these idiots should have planted wool, not cotton!"

A few examples of the regime's political behavior in pre-revolutionary Iran may help the reader to picture causes of opposition more realistically.[1] Once a year, beginning in 1962, on the occasion of the anniversary of the Shah's reform decree, called the "White Revolution," the people had been asked to stage a procession. Some probably participated because they had actually benefitted through the reforms, while others participated simply because they were asked to do so. The group the government was most interested to involve were public employees, small businessmen, and well-educated people in general. These were the ones who were most often not on good terms with the regime, and who made up the main body of any active or potential opposition movements. The regime was determined to force them to participate in order to show that its reform had eliminated the opposition's excuses. Professors of the universities were also forced to participate. In a number of ways they were informed ahead of time, directly or indirectly, that their attendance would be monitored by certain agents and that those not attending would bear the consequences. For instance, on the day after one march, an officer of a university who was an active organizing agent complained to a professor who had attended the march unhappily, out of fear. "When I saw you on the T.V. you looked grim," the agent said. "Why did you not show a smiling face? Don't you care whether people get the wrong impression [about us], seeing that kind of unhappy face?"

Other examples concern the elections. Usually, there were elections for the house of representatives and city officials. These institutions were created by the Iranian Constitutional Revolution, but eventually became hollow concepts through the gradual restoration of power to the office of the Shah. Almost every member was assigned by the Shah and secret police. Then, in a sort of mock election, the people were asked to vote. The regime could then pretend that the election had been conducted according to the constitution. The winners would be announced, having run against prechosen losers. Most people knew the final vote tallies ahead of time. A large turnout was desired, so the agents of the regime would do their best to get as many people as possible to attend. A campaign was offered, but few people would ever see the candidates. They would only see the posters and banners hung in the squares and public places. The day before the election, in a well-organized manner, a good number of those who had reached voting age would be approached individually or in groups and reminded of the consequences of not voting, or they would, indirectly, get the message. The regime knew that everyone would tell their friends and relatives how he or she had been coerced, creating an intentional atmosphere of fear and intimidation that would impel nearly everyone to get out and vote.

At the polls, after the voting, each person's birth certificate would be stamped. The store owners feared that if their birth certificate was not stamped, their business licenses would not be renewed. The workers feared that they would not get their promotion and pension benefits. Certain public employees and schoolteachers who were unwilling to cooperate were threatened with the loss of their jobs. It is apparent that the authorities did not care whether the people viewed the whole affair as a show. The definition of an election and the notion of politics in this type of system differs from what may appear the same in democracies. For the oppressors, political participation was a test of their own ability to run a show for their own purposes, forcing the people to act by government demand, and ensuring that they actually had the organizational capacity and ability to exert such force. The regime merely wanted to maintain its grip of power, letting everyone know who was the boss.

Political development in such a regime did not have the same meaning as it typically had for social scientists. From the point of view of the oppressors, it meant the formation and articulation of a machinery that could force people to act on demand. It included the anticipation that people would eventually develop the desired habits and adjust to the point where they would show no resistance.

Parallel to the regime's political actions, another mode of political activity was practiced. This one took the people's viewpoint, who practiced it through whatever means they found at their disposal. In view of the fact that the definition and exercise of political activities and decision making had been monopolized by the autocrats, the people were left with no legal options. Their options were limited to covert and indirect actions. They learned to incorporate and hide their political activities within other forms of social actions that were legal and were commonly practiced by the populace. For example, they were embedded in religious ceremonies, works of art, or cultural activities. They usually picked up a medium of action that was very dear to the public and sacred, and whose practice was something the people would not easily abandon. Therefore, even if the regime wished to, it could not forbid the people from practicing it. Let us call this the "implicit mode" of political action. The objective of the implicit mode of political action is to neutralize the regime's propaganda, to propagate dissentive ideas, to safe-guard the people against the arbitrary actions of the rulers and their agents, to reverse the demoralization and intimidation campaign staged by the authorities, and to invite the people toward resistance and uprising.

The regime's manipulation of the people and the people's reaction, mostly embedded in their cultural activities, are a political whole. By its very nature, the implicit mode of political action undertaken by the people is dissentive, agitating, and potentially at the service of opposition movements. In Iran, it was able to create an alternative to what had been undertaken by those in power. The people themselves tried to create their own source of power, a power that ought to be exercised by the people.

SOURCES OF CULTURAL HETEROGENEITY

Centuries of life, in the context of such despotic orders, had a wide variety of cultural, religious, and political consequences. There exist two distinct categories of consequences that are of a political nature. The first category includes cultural items and orientations that are in accord with the despotic order and function as its supportive basis. Included are individuals and groups who have modeled themselves according to the style of dictators and despots, with pro-dictatorial ideologies, apologies for autocracy, and the ignorance of people's civil rights. The second category includes ideologies, personality traits, and cultural items that resist despotism and counter elitism.

The former orientation has accepted and ingested the ideologies, the mentality, and the lifestyle of the ruling groups. It teaches the people to serve the despotic king and the feudal lords, and to imitate their lifestyle. It helps to maintain and even promotes a despotic social and political regime. This orientation admires the despots, and encourages people's aspirations for a ruling class and a "lordish" lifestyle. People socialized into such a subculture would act toward their subordinates as kings, feudals, and the tribal khans would have acted toward their men. They are the creators and consumers of stories, poems, tales, and mythologies in which kings, rulers, and men of power are the main characters and chauvinistic ideas are promoted.

The latter orientation has helped to promote egalitarian ideologies, liberation mythologies, poems, and other cultural creations that sided with the weak, the ruled, and the humble people. What may stand out as the significant part of this category (and which will be discussed later) is the development and promotion of the cultural mechanisms that help these people to resist oppression to generate a power of their own, and to counteract the rule of the despots.

Another factor that contributes to the cause of cultural pluralism is the heterogeneity of the people's historical backgrounds. Iranian history has also provided certain counterexamples to the dominant cultural trends that developed in the arid regions. These are the social organization and cultural patterns of the people whose type of agrarian society was different from what was dominant in the rest of the country. The existence of such regions and the interaction of their typical cultural types with those of the rest of the country have contributed to more heterogeneity of the Iranian way of life. An example of a different agrarian system and its cultural orientations is the lifestyle of the people who live around the Caspian Sea. They are called the Northern people, because their homeland is located in the north of Iran.

In this area the agricultural conditions differ from the rest of the country, because, with the exception of the high mountainous areas, there is an abundant supply of water. Despite the fact that water is plentiful, land is rather limited. Since land is a scarce and valued commodity, the feudalism that developed in this area was based on the ownership of land. Land lords of this region had less power than those in other parts of the country, and included a large stratum of petty land owners in addition to those who lived by fishing, carpentry, and the production of charcoal. This was more of a pluralistic society in terms of its economic foundations as well as in the cultural make-up of its people. Liberal tendencies are still quite strong in this region, and the people are more open to modernity and to new political and social ideas. Their rural cultural make-up, in general, stands in distinct contrast to what has been observable in the rural regions of the rest of the country. An indication of this difference is the position in their society of women, who distinctly receive less chauvinistic treatment than those elsewhere. Many Iranians, who were brought up in a more chauvinistic environment, have developed a distorted image of these Northern women. They have resorted to making a lot of sexy jokes about the people of the North, conveying a flirtatious image of the women and a morally careless role of the male.

SHORTCOMINGS OF CULTURAL STUDIES

Reporting and explaining cultural and religious behavior is not an easy task and is often not performed successfully. The difficulties encountered are due to certain shortcomings and limitations of one's observational abilities. The causes are the structured way of looking at things and the limited ability to properly communicate what is observed. The details of these limitations follow.

Cultural behavior includes both external exposure and some subjective aspects. Only the former is observable. In other words, we see the act, not the whole action. The latter must be ascertained indirectly, often through the help of theoretical reasoning. What is included in the subjective part is the person or group's definition of their action and their objectives. To assume that what is observed is defined the same by both actor and outside observer is often misleading and results in error in judgment.

Relating the argument to our analytic task, Iranian culture is found to be highly complex. It includes sets of symbols that stand for abstract ideas, many of which have multiple meanings. A political meaning may be only one option. A reference may be made, for example, to the reemergence of Islamic dress for women in Iran in the mid-1970s. What made this a significant political and religious issue is that the cultural stratum involved was a population that had not worn Islamic dress for generations. This style of dressing calls for covering the whole body, specifically the hair. The covering looks like a large sheet, ordinarily plain black, and is called the *chadour*. Only a part of the face and the hands may be exposed, as it completely covers whatever may reveal the form of one's body. Ladies wearing the *chadour* look amorphous, with little left to show their identity, which effectively downplays their public attendance and participation. Iranian women, mostly city dwellers, wore it for generations until Reza Shah tried to stop them. He forced people to convert to the Western style of dress. Fascinated with Western society, he began a comprehensive program of Westernization in Iran that included dress standards as well. From that time, a new definition concerning the wearing of the *chadour* was layered upon the existing ones—which was really a political action. Some people's insistence upon wearing it could be interpreted as an opposition to the Shah's policies. In 1977, when hundreds of thousands of Iranian women held regular street demonstrations all over Iran, they increasingly appeared in black *chadours*. It looked rather strange in view of the fact that, for a couple of generations, a large segment of the city women had been wearing Western-style dress. Especially notable among these women who appeared in demonstrations were those who worked in the public sector and attended colleges. The same women not only had accepted and preferred the Western dress, but some even used to despise wearing the *chadour*. The subsequent popularization of its use was a significant political turnaround. In addition, by wearing the *chadour*, these women symbolized the rejection of the social policies advanced by the Shah.

Not all women, however, wore it for the same reason. Some of them, the secularly minded intellectuals, began to wear it in order to identify with the common people and reduce any social gaps, so that they could eventually lead them. Some women were associated with secular political parties who, due to some long term considerations, wore the *chadour*. The infiltration of the Islamic movement, which promised to become a major theme, might also be a substantial reason. A large majority of women wore it because they preferred it on religious and moral grounds. A few were even secret police agents in disguise, reporting on inside activities. To an outside observer all these women looked the same—merely devoted Moslem women. A cultural study, without the content of "intent" toward the action performed, is sure to lead to wrong conclusions and misinterpretations.

Another shortcoming arises not so much from observational limitations, but from communication problems. Our concepts, definitions, even sentences and paragraphs do not always have the flexibilities to reflect what is observed. Limitations may be due to a number of reasons. One important reason is that cultural elements are not constant over time. Their meaning, from the point of view of those involved, may change over time, as do their function in society. Such changes take place for various reasons. As people's social, political, and even scientific awareness alters, they develop different perceptions of their cultural and religious performances. Let us provide an example.

While Iranians were in a state of uprising, they often had to perform their prayers at a time when they happened to be in the midst of a mass protest demonstration. If it was the time for noon prayer, they would interrupt their programs to perform the prayers no matter where they were, including in the middle of the street. Long lines of thousands of people standing in prayer in the streets soon became symbolic of the Iranian Revolution. What they were doing was no longer the same action previously done in an ordinary manner. New social and political significance had been attached to it. It resembled Prophet Mohammad's mass prayers while he was on the battlefield.

Eventually many people would take this up, not so much as a religious duty, but as a political show of solidarity—for strengthening their measure of discipline. But to an outside observer, all seemed to be merely prayers; it was even called prayer, just as it had been before.

Another example of divergent cultural perceptions is the institution of the mosque, the Moslem's equivalent of a church in Christianity. A few years prior to the Revolution, signs of the alteration of the role of the mosque in Iranian society became visible. The activities and concept of the mosque were becoming increasingly attractive to politically minded youth, college students, and groups of people that ordinarily would have stayed away from it. It was actually a cover, and a sacred one, for many dissentive groups. Others found the mosque itself a revolutionary concept and a collective institution. Even today, nearly seven years after the Revolution, the mosque has still retained a political-religious status. Now it is the political headquarters for the supporters of the regime. It is still, however, called "mosque," a concept that implies merely a religious place.

Another set of problems is due to the preconceptions and theoretical anticipations of our socialization. There are pictures of "reality" already mapped in our heads, and certain meanings attached to them. These ideas are what give us our understanding of cultural and religious reality, and we may superimpose such ideas upon the situations that we intend to study. The following fictional story clearly reveals such misjudgments. An observer was watching a group of natives, of a hypothetical society, from a distance. They were kneeling and bowing down in front of some burning materials, putting their faces close to the ground. He reported that they seemed to worship the fire. In fact, they were blowing into the fire, trying to keep it from dying out so that they wouldn't be cold.

Existing theories may also bias our observations. In social studies, culture and religion are quite often viewed as static institutions, not capable of causing major changes of the social structure itself. Relying on the Iranian data, one has to be cautious not to let such static views interfere with the observations. In order to avoid pre-judgments that may close one's eyes and mind to unanticipated but quite significant events, certain options must be examined. One option is to define culture in a way that allows for more flexible boundaries. One has to have a definition that has taken into consideration some of the consequences of the shortcomings that have already been mentioned. The analysis should begin with a rather loose definition, one that allows the facts to be revealed and allows different features of the Iranian cultural system to be exposed. Gradually, as the analysis proceeds, a more comprehensive picture of this reality emerges. One such definition is that culture implies the sum total of a people's common social awareness, their ceremonies, values, intellectual products, historically accumulated experiences and wisdom, and their mechanism for solving social problems and adjusting to social conditions, which together provide them with the blueprint of their social and personal life.

It might be concluded that the people of Iran have lived under specific conditions that have had a high propensity toward repressive regimes. A consequence of this condition was the development of certain cultural mechanisms that enabled them to resist, undo, and even rebel against this political repression. In the following chapters, we will explain in more detail this cultural system.

NOTE

1. The oppressive nature of the Shah's regime is an established fact. Besides the existing documentations on the tortures and maltreatment of political prisoners, there was widespread censorship and other acts of repressive control of the masses. An example is the creation of a single party called *Rastakhiz*, which people were forced to join with no exceptions. This was a clear case of the regime's disregard of popular ideals, forcing its own ideal of an absolute monarchy upon the people, yet still considering such forced participation to be a sign of its own legitimacy and popularity. J. Green, *Revolution in Iran: The Politics of Countermobilization* (New York: Praeger, 1982) addresses itself to the political conditions of the Shah's era and views people's reaction to the regime's policies as politics of the countermobilization.

3

Political Potential of Iranian Culture

Whenever Iranians have social gatherings, their talk often includes many political arguments. They may not have intended originally to speak of politics, but it simply emerges through their interactions.

One may wonder how they would openly discuss politics under a repressive system. This is exactly one of the reasons why I have introduced the concept of implicit political action and plan to go into a detailed analysis of certain cultural and religious behaviors of Iranians. At the moment, it will suffice to mention that they discuss politics using open expressions, words with double meanings, and ambiguous statements that by implication lead the audience to the speaker's intended meaning. This is done quite skillfully because, for generations, they have learned to do so in order to avoid the reaction of the repressive regimes.

Talking politics in private under the rule of a repressive regime generates some excitement. It is also a compelling form of gossip, which contains a bit of adventurism and a show of intellectual pride. Talking politics, therefore, has developed into a widespread habit, and is practiced whether the country is in turbulence or not, as though it were a hobby or a sport. People continue to argue with each other, becoming emotional, without any conclusion or end in sight to the discussion. As a pattern, the more such talks are lengthened, the more they branch out into divergent points of view.

To have a point of view and talk about it is not specific to any special class, nor to certain politically active groups. However, members of certain strata, such as college students, tend to be more concerned and active in politics. Lay people, even less-educated or uneducated ones, also often have their ideas and insist upon them. Why they all show such concern is a question with no easy answer. A partial answer is probably to be found in their cultural background and their common experiences of living in an oppressive society.

Life in such a society produces common sources of anxieties and insecurities, and subjects them to similar threats and exploitive policies. As a consequence, they develop the shared behavior of talking politics in an implicit manner. Yet, due to certain other factors, they do not end up with shared conclusions in their political discussions. The persistence of such conditions over the centuries has caused certain fixed norms to develop in the building of their culture and behavior.

A few of the more salient features of this political behavior are lack of serious concern with empirical facts, skeptical thinking, and a dualistic view of political reality. Iranians often tend to view the political order and political occurrences as two sides of a coin; one side is "real" and the other is "false" or "pseudo." The real part is not totally, or even partially available to public. What is available, and empirically observable, is the false side. Something remains to be dug out—something that is secretive. It is referred to as "the stories behind the curtain." Such a dualistic view of political affairs applies to local, national, and international cases.

Ever since the advance of colonial powers in the region, the influence of alien powers is assumed to be present in nearly any political event in the country. Iranians often envision foreign influences running the show with the local officials acting as the puppets. In cases where the people are assured that such intervention does exist, the exaggerations they might make have no relation to the real weight of such influences. Sometimes their imaginative speculation extends these events to such extremes that they sound more like fantasy than reality. It was and still is quite common to hear people relate all major political events in the country to British foreign policy and, lately, to American policy. The British invisible hand was not only assumed in Iranian affairs, but even in that of its powerful rivals. An example is a widely circulated joke about British influence in the political affairs of Russia. It stated that when Joseph Stalin died, his rather famous mustache was shaven before his burial. Underneath the mustache was written "Made in England," implying that the Russian head of state was a British product, an agent disguised by a Russian mustache. The fact is that Iranians tend to express many of their strongest beliefs in terms of jokes, and their interpretation of political events in terms of cultural and religious outlooks. For example, let us examine the political interpretation of "Satan."[1]

Today the word "Satan" has a political connotation as well as a religious one. It has been used recently to refer to global superpowers, specifically the United States. The United States has been called the "Great Satan." This term refers to a power that is the source of corruption that influences a population to sin and penetrates the political system to make them behave according to its Satanic design. This concept has mapped on the mind of the people a picture similar to the one drawn by its religious definition. Although the application is political, it is believed that Satan was an angel purged from his rank because he refused to obey God. He had to live until the end of time as an outlaw, as the source of wrongdoing and of immoral acts, influencing human beings to sin. The mechanism of this influence is quite peculiar. Satan exerts his influence not by interaction, but by acting "inside" the person. It may seem as though the person is the wrongdoer, but in fact it is Satan, standing in the person's shoes, who is doing wrong. When this form of thought is applied to political reality, Satan stands for a similar influence and performance. A global superpower, labeled as Satanic, is seen as more than just an alien political power outside of one's country. It is imagined as the invisible evil exerting its ill intentions internally. It is something that needs to be repelled and to have its tricks neutralized. Such an analogy quite easily fits the mentality that is already trained to have a dual conception of the political order. Recently, even some Marxists, whose radio programs address Iranian and Afghan people, have frequently tended to refer to the United States as the "Great Satan." For the majority of people whom they address, this notion may communicate their political message more clearly than the notion of Imperialism, which they also often use. Of the former, the people already have a definition. In contrast, for the latter they additionally need to understand the political economy and modern history. Obviously, the two notions are not the same, but may serve the same purpose.

Life under the repressive regimes that have denied the people freedom of expression may have been one reason contributing to the lack of emphasis on objective and rational discussions. Life under an oppressive system breeds secrecy and, in turn, leads to the distortion of facts. The state of oppression that has prevailed in Iran for millennia has led to the integration of secrecy with Iranian culture and personality. Subsequently, the distortion of facts and a low presence of rational and open discussion of social and political issues has become quite common. Suspicion is built into the citizens' psychology whenever they relate to others in political matters. They show a high propensity toward suspicion, even of those political figures in whom they purport to have strong confidence. This is why they can be quite easily talked into believing that the figures they trust are indeed untrustable. How this state of mind may ever change is not known. To break through what history has created and engage in rational political thinking would probably require a long, long time.

The lack of serious concern with empirical facts is balanced by a heavy emphasis on persuasive reasoning and logical consistency. In most cases, these people prove to be experienced and clever in such manipulations. Often, when documents are cited, the arguer intends not to provide clarity, but to prove his point. These citations are not always plain facts; sometimes, their so-called "facts" are products of speculation or are concluded from previous hearsay. The reliability of such documents depends upon whether or not one agrees with the person who is providing them. Yet, if one can support a hypothesized claim, the claims are accepted as real. It is equally easy for others to challenge and disagree with them. The skeptical mentality, which is typical of Iranians, reinforces such disagreements and leads to a continuous state of argument in political matters—everyone insisting on their own point of view to no end.

While these people tend to be overtly subjective, their ideas do include some strong elements of truth. Often their conclusions prove to be quite sharp and valid. They can see their reasoning put to the test whenever the so called "behind the curtain stories" are made public. Occasionally, such publications do occur, because in a nondemocratic society, the transition of power operates by force. Those who are put out of office, therefore, must be discredited, their social image ruined, and their influence neutralized to "dry up their roots." In the process, most of their secret dealings and wrongdoings are made public. This not only provides the people a chance to see how close to reality their speculation and reasoning had come, but also reinforces their belief in the dualistic nature of the political processes.

Iranian culture provides models of social and political change that are incorporated into mystical tales, historical reports, poems, proverbs, and words of wisdom. For lay people, these are the equivalent of political and social theories. They think in terms of them and use such culturally provided mechanisms to reason and to orient themselves with respect to the social and political happenings of their society. In a number of ways, these cultural elements facilitate a sustained state of political turbulence and a reception of anti-status quo addresses, and make it difficult for the sovereigns to establish any legitimacy for their rule. Some of the main cultural elements relevant to Iranian political thinking follow.

In order to provide a detailed explanation of the implicit mode of political action, an analysis of Iranian cultural behavior is needed. The main purpose of this analysis is to show the existence of mechanisms and concepts within the culture that facilitate political thinking, political communication, and collective action. Such facilities have always been employed to resist oppressors, to generate mass movements, and even to engage in revolutionary actions. Such was the case early in this century's Constitutional Revolution and in the Revolution of 1977-79. It is in light of this understanding that some dark corners of this latest Iranian Revolution may be fully understood. Pursuing this objective, the Iranian culture is viewed in terms of its politically loaded aspects and dimensions. The dimensions chosen are the ones most available to public participation and the communication of political intentions, and which contribute to collective actions.

Poetry

Poetry plays a variety of roles in Iranian life. It is not just a branch of literature and a form of expression. It is not just a concern of some people, but a medium known and practiced by all. Even illiterate Iranians know some poems, mainly some of the works of great poets. Such poets are more than the historically popular men of art and literature, but are viewed as sources of wisdom. The subjects of Iranian poetry are any that one might conceive, including political thought, social theory, dialectical philosophy, astronomy, love affairs, romance, historical experiences, and war cries. For every occasion there are some beautiful poems. In Islamic Iran, this was probably the only form of popular artistic expression that was not subject to any restriction. Music, sculpture, and dance were not encouraged, therefore leaving poetry as a popular channel for artistic expression.

Another factor contributing to the popularity of poetry may have been the presence of a sustained state of oppression. All through the history of Iran, people were not able to exert much influence upon the course of political events, and had to recreate their desired world in their minds. In making such a hypothetical world, they themselves decided how they wanted the order of things to be. By projecting what they had internally constructed as poems, they satisfied certain inhibited thoughts and wishes of the populace. Some of what they created as poems also fit the state of mind of the oppressed masses as well. Therefore, their poetry became a common medium in which art, reality, and fantasy all met, a medium in which certain political-minded poets found some degree of freedom to exercise their thoughts in a world that was not concrete but poetic.

There exist some institutionalized social settings, centered around poetry, that can also have political consequences. One such a setting is the public gathering, where poets draw large crowds to read what they have created. In the 1960s such gatherings would have attracted thousands of people. The last college-student phase of the turbulences that escalated into the Revolution of 1979 originated from one such gathering (discussed in Chapter 9).

There are a number of other institutional settings that center around poetry and may have certain political significance. One of these, for example, is a form of story telling that has been common in certain Iranian leisure time gatherings for centuries. Mythological and actual historical incidents are expressed lyrically in these poems, which are read by professional readers called *Naghal* in a special musical tone. They may include both story telling and ordinary poetry. Most often, the poems are taken from a famous Iranian book called *Shahnameh*, which means "the book of the kings." But occasionally, very famous love poems are also read. One of the places where such readings are frequently performed is in the tea house. In the past, Iranian men, either in the evening or on weekends, used to gather in tea houses to pass the time and to socialize with their friends. In Islamic Iran, bars that allowed mixed sexes, as in the West, did not exist. They have only existed in the last few decades, and only for a very limited number of Westernized urbanites. Typically for these men, leisure time gatherings outside the residential domain meant mainly congregating at the tea houses or the *Zoorkhaneh*, where native sports were practiced. In fact, tea houses are only a little more than a century old, but the *Zoorkhaneh*, which is equivalent to a gymnasium, is a very ancient gathering place.

At the *Zoorkhaneh*, sportsmen engaged in their practices are accompanied by music and songs. The singer, called *Shir Khoda*, sings certain poems while accompanying himself with the rhythmical beating of a drum. The sportsmen move according to the rhythm of his drum. The intent of such songs is to generate excitement and images of power or bravery, and to reinforce the cultural and religious values. These values mainly encourage young men to be patriotic, altruistic, helpful toward the weak and oppressed, and resistant to aggressors. Usually, stories of the braveries of Imam Ali (the first Shiia imam) underlie the image that the poems try to promote. Imam Ali is, beyond his religious position, also a symbol of strength, bravery, and the defense of the rights of the oppressed. In the eyes of most Shiiaite Iranians, he personifies the ideals men admire and to which they aspire. Many poems are made in admiration of Ali. (He is also the idol of many Suffis, of which a sub-branch is called Darvish.) These poems are sung by a small group of professionals (usually two singers), called *Molavi* or *Maddah*. They may be invited to sing their songs for celebrations or even for the mourning for a deceased person. Where music was discouraged by Islamic teachings, such religious/cultural songs were a good substitute. Under the current Islamic rule, playing music in celebrations is once again discouraged and sometimes forcefully stopped. Instead, it has become very common to invite these religious and cultural singers to entertain the participants. In this practice, Iranian culture and Shiiaite ideals meet and merge.

The occasions on which Iranian mythology and legendary poems are read have always played some significant political role. They served as entertainment and historical education, as well as assisting the people to preserve their linguistic and cultural identity. In view of the fact that the preservation of both the Persian language and its culture was difficult under the rule of invaders, especially the Arabs, the significance of poetry readings in different forms as mass entertainment needs to receive more emphasis. This practice, coupled, for example, with the poems of *Shahnameh*, creates a mechanism that encourages national pride, motivates patriotism, reminds the people of the greatness of their past as a sovereign nation, and reaches the very masses that otherwise might have lost their link with the past through illiteracy. *Shahnameh* was, indeed, created by Ferdoussi, one of the greatest Iranian poets, under patriotic motives. It was created at a time when the Iranian language and culture was forcefully being replaced by an Islamic-Arabic alternative, and the rule of the Arabs had almost totally accomplished this goal. As the poet himself puts it, he "liberated an Arab-conformed Parsee (*farci*) language" through his book of poems—*Shahnameh*. *Shahnameh* became a great source of inspiration and national pride, a rich source of Iranian mythology and ancient history for generations of people who had nearly lost their historic identity. Reading *Shahnameh* in ceremonial gatherings, as an outlet of pure entertainment, was in fact a politicization of the people. It was an artistic, persuasive way of feeding the hopes of the masses with the ideal of a valiant resistance and establishment of national sovereignty. In this respect it was a grass roots movement reaching all people, not just the politically active. An outstanding feature of Ferdoussi's work is his complete avoidance of Arabic words. He helped to popularize the Farci language, which had become heavily mixed with Arabic. Obviously, both the creation of this book and its popularization through the practice of *Naghali* were resistant to foreign rule. But this is not the only case when poetry was used for political purposes. The political struggle of Iranians, all through their long history, has been associated with a deep and complex intellectual process. Such intellectual works are mostly expressed in the language of poetry.

Poetry plays another role in the life of Iranians that may have some political consequences. Some poems are established as logical statements or as social and psychological theories. When people reason, they may say, "As the poet says," then read a line of a famous poem. For them this suffices, as though they had cited a theory of sociology (or psychology). In a cultural system in which the wisdom of the ages is personified in certain great wise men, the poet plays a dual role. He stands in the shoes of the wise man, and also uses language that is persuasive and emotionally appealing. Therefore, his poems find widespread usage in everyday arguments and the reasoning of the masses of people. On this basis, contemporary political activists found the language of poetry a very effective channel for implicitly communicating their ideas to the masses. It was a channel often left open by the regime, who considered it a cultural and literary activity. One example of such modern works was a poem titled "Phoenix in the Rain." The poet, who was a Marxist, was trying to explain the dialectical processes of social change in the image of the mythical death of the phoenix. It is believed that the death of this bird occurs through a unique process, during which the bird generates internal heat by squeezing itself tightly. A new bird is then born out of the ashes of the one already burned.

A good number of such poets became national celebrities, political idols, and ideologues because they endured long terms as political prisoners. Their words became as influential as any social theory, even upon the best educated Iranians. Some Marxist poets were among the most influential. Golsorkhy is a contemporary example who was executed by the fallen regime for certain revolutionary attempts. Saiid Soltanpour was another who had spent long tortuous sentences under the rule of the monarchy. In the post-revolutionary era, he was finally executed by the Islamic regime. It was not necessarily the Marxist ideology that was controlled. Politically loaded poems were restricted, although enforcement of such restrictions was not an easy task, since words with dual meanings and highly symbolic language were usually used in such political poems.

Shields and Sanctuaries

A consequence of living under the reign of autocracy, the whims and wishes of autocrats, and the constant threat of foreign invasion is that the people become highly insecure. They search for buffers to protect them against the direct exertion of irrational rulings and try to find sanctuaries in which to take refuge when pursued by the threat of punishment. The state of insecurity that prevails is not, then, limited to certain individuals, but is common to all—even to those people close to the ruling circle.

Iranians have been unfortunate to live in a land that is vulnerable to invasion from all directions (except from the south, which borders the Persian Gulf). Iran was the site of the formation of one of the most highly centralized feudal systems, the epitome of "Asian despotism," and the social origin of autocracy and dictatorship. The domestic, despotic rulers, the class of feudal lords and the agents of those lords, and certain tribal chiefs were no less cruel than any foreign invader. People lived in a state of terror created by the families of the feudal lords. For the Iranian people, then, there was no place nor any ruler whose reign could provide peace of mind and a feeling of security. They could not see any permanent security in the goodwill of certain exceptional rulers or strength of protective armies, but only in the spiritual composition of people. To them only internal constraints and social taboos could provide a preventative mechanism against cruelty and inhuman actions. They had witnessed the fall of strong rulers and disturbances that could have easily cost them their lives, property, and the abuse of their women.

Some of the historic examples in which the people believe may clearly reflect the painful experiences that they have endured. To mention one case, it is believed that when the Mongol invasion of Iran was over, Genghis Khan asked his soldiers if in killing Iranians they ever felt pity. One soldier said that once, in a massacre, he had tried to kill a woman who had a baby in her arms. After killing the mother, he tried to stick his sword in the mouth of the child. The child, expecting the sword to be something to eat, smiled. The soldier said, "Then I paused for a moment, and later I killed the baby, too." Genghis Kahn executed the soldier for not being merciless. Certain Iranian feudal rulers were no less merciless. Under such conditions the value system of Islam, providing some protection for one's sex and property, allowed life and social status to be held highly as an ideal.

The presence of some moral order, of certain values and sacred elements in the society, was more protective of the people's rights than an alternative order that could be depended upon only temporarily, as a stable regime that might only possibly provide less cruel rulers. The mechanism built into the people's religious and cultural order could more properly answer their demands. An emotionally supported commitment to uphold such mechanisms would guarantee that they would operate successfully. Only such socially supported protective devices could function as a shield between them and arbitrary rule. Such shields and sanctuaries could not stop the oppression and brutalities of some domestic and foreign invaders, but they could provide some measure of protection.

One important protective device was sought in the institution of the shrines, and to a lesser degree in the sacredness of certain occasions. The shrines could provide a safe place in which to take refuge. These shrines, which are the graves of the "Innocent imams" and their offspring, are assumed to be beyond the control and the rule of secular powers, and are viewed more like foreign embassies where the authority of another sovereign rules. In this case the sovereign is assumed to be of the supernatural order. The management is carried out by a self-administering body of "servants of the Imam" who is buried there. The high level religious leaders, in or outside the country, have some role in the administration of the affairs of the shrines. In the early 20th century, during the Constitutional Revolution, the Bazaari (business class) protestors and their clerical allies often took refuge in shrines that were within a few miles of the capital city of Tehran. The more sacred places in which to take refuge were shrines in the cities of Ghom and Meshad (seats of high clergymen).[2] Such refugees could stay in the territory of these shrines for days or even months, and by then they would often be pardoned or ignored, and told to get out. Some secular equivalents of these sanctuaries (in recent times) were foreign embassies, the House of Parliament, and (prior to 1962) the campus of the University of Tehran. Usually, when pursued by the security forces, one could flee to a shrine and seek asylum. As long as the person was there, he or she would remain more or less untouched. In a country where the massacre of crowds of anti-regime demonstrators could happen so easily, such sanctuaries became the site of protest gatherings. What makes such sanctuaries so sacred is the set of beliefs and ideologies that surround them.

Certain days, such as the 21st of the month of Ramazan (the month of fasting), coincide with the martyrdom of Imam Ali, who was assassinated. The Ashura is another example of a sacred time, and will be discussed in the next chapter. During such times, the chances of brutal actions against individuals and groups of people are very unlikely. Even if the rulers do not believe in the sacredness of the sanctuaries, their manpower that enforces their rule may themselves believe, and may hesitate to carry out the superior's orders.

The Practice of Historical Comparison

History, for Iranians, is not just something that happened in the past. They see the present in the light of the past. The lesson history provides is that of analogies that quite skillfully apply to present situations. Knowing their past history, such analogies are portrayed by using a key concept, which the comparison makes specific. The rest of their knowledge about that historical experience is then taken as the interpretation of the case that has just been made specific. For example, most Iranians know that when the Mongols, headed by Genghis Khan, invaded Iran, they massacred many people, destroyed cities, and nearly destroyed every mark of the civilization in the land. The entire horrifying story can be expressed simply by the use of the name "Mongol" or "Mongolish." In 1962, the security forces of the regime invaded the University of Tehran, which had previously enjoyed political and police immunity and was in effect a sanctuary. This 1962 invasion was called a "Mongolish" invasion of the University. It was enough to enable people to picture the atrocities taking place.

Another example of the historical analogy is the image of *Zahak*, the cruel and ancient mythic ruler who killed young men in order to save his own brain, and fed their brains to two snakes that had grown out of his shoulders. The Shah was often called *Zahak* by his opponents, a name that automatically identified him as the killer of the nation's youth, i.e., its revolutionary youth. Some Iranians refer to Ayatollah Khomeini as *Zahak*. Their reference is to his regime's execution of thousands of the Iranian youths who supported the radical movements. Similar analogies are also made, as when the ruler or military force that supported him is called *Yazid*, reminding the people of the ruler whose men beheaded Imam Hosein. The use of these analogies is not limited to dictatorial figures. Those looked upon favorably are pictured in the historic image of those heroes the people admire. Often, the names of these historic figures symbolize a patriotic legend.

Some people even name their newborns after these heroes. The name of the newborn infant is often chosen on an ideological basis. By picking the name of a religious or historic figure, the people hope that the infant will grow in the image of the admired personality. Names such as Rostam, Siavash, Babak, Maziar, Afshin, Farhad, and Arsalan for men, and Roodabeh and Tahmineh for women are typical of the ones that carry a well-known story of the past. The same is true of those taken from Islamic traditions, such as Ali, Amir, Hosein, or Abbas for men and Fatemeh or Zahra for women. Hardly ever have the names of those identified as mean or cruel been picked, such as Yasid, Shemer, or Zahak. Even the new generation is often following this norm with their modern idols. Among the Iranian Marxist intellectuals, it is a common practice to name one's children after those who have lost their lives as devoted Iranian nationalists or Marxists, struggling against the regime. Names such as Roozbeh, Pooyan, and Khosro (Khosro Golsorkhi), are becoming common.[3]

Another means by which the past is kept alive, acting as a blueprint to provide insight into the present, is through proverbs, words of wisdom, and historic examples, which are frequently cited in people's discussions. The regular practice of a lifestyle that keeps history so close to everyday life eventually leads to a general vision of history that becomes personal in nature. The political consequence of such a state of mind includes reliance upon a symbolism that easily condenses and codifies the Iranian past and the communicability between Iranians. It is a system of codes that leads to a political outlook. A Persian proverb says: "You give me the first letter of the first word, and I will read through it the whole story." For such an analogy-based mentality, already programmed by the extensive knowledge of the past, it is not difficult to grasp the symbolic message and picture that the opposition groups are trying to map onto the people's minds.

THE IMAGE OF CHANGE IN IRANIAN CULTURE

Included in Iranian culture are a variety of ideologies and world views that frame the people's image of social and political order. They learn to see their whole existence, specifically the political order, as undergoing an endless process of change, and changing in a way that raises some to the position of power and later on dispatches them to the realm of powerlessness. Certain of these ideas come close to the theories of the "circulation of elite in society," proposed by V. Pareto and G. Mosca. The Iranian concept of the motion assumes a broader domain, seeing ups and downs in all areas of social and personal life.

These images of social and political order, which follow such patterns, are embedded in tales, poems, proverbs, and a wide variety of cultural items. One example is a story, most probably a real one, about an Arab khalife (head of state) and his Iranian prime minister. The minister was from the Barmaki clan, which was of Iranian origin. Because of his excellent managerial skills, he had been promoted to this very high office. Other Barmakis were also positioned in high offices. One day the khalife and his minister were taking a walk in a garden. The khalife desired that an apple be picked from a tree, but their hands could not reach it. The minister climbed up and stood on the shoulders of the khalife. Still, he could not reach the apple. Finally, he stepped on the head of the khalife to reach it. An Iranian gardener happened to be present watching them. Later on, the khalife told the gardener to make a wish and that he would fulfill it. The gardener said he had no other request except for a written and sealed certificate saying "This Iranian gardener is not one of the Barmakis." Both the khalife and the minister were surprised to hear him wish not to belong to an honorable clan. However, the certificate was given to him. After some time the minister fell into the khalife's disfavor and was purged out of office. The people were attacking Barmakis, kicking them out of office and persecuting them. They arrested the Iranian gardner also, suspecting him to be a Barmaki. He showed the certificate sealed by the khalife, and they inquired concerning the wisdom of his action. He answered that on the day the minister had stepped on the shoulders of the khalife, the minister's fortune still had more room to rise. But when he stepped on the khalife's head, he had reached the limit and his days were numbered. Sooner or later the Barmakis would be eliminated, the gardener said, and as an Iranian feared being mistaken for a Barmaki. So he had asked for the certificate. This story is typical of both the view of political change and the way lay people think in terms of such cultural elements. There are a great number of other items consistent with this view of political and social change.

An oft cited proverb says:

> Fountain descends after reaching its peak.

Prior to the fall of the Shah, Iranians resented his show of power. Quite often, when the people heard him or others talk of his power and arrogance, they would whisper this proverb and add that his days were numbered. Did they know that very soon there would be a revolution, overthrowing the Shah? Probably not, but if there was to be such an attempt they would accept it because they believed in what they had learned to believe.

Another case is a proverb that says:

> Sometimes one sits on the saddle, sometimes one is saddled.

A similar case is a line taken from the context of a poem. It refers to a historical situation, and has become a common proverb. It says:

> The idiot sons of a minister (king's aid) had to go to villages to become beggars. The knowledgeable sons of peasants were assigned to be the secretaries of the king.

Another conception of "motion" extends beyond historical events. It, too, is similar to the above examples, as it sees the whole existence moving, like a spinning ball (or a spinning wheel). Then the pattern of change of everything is an endless rotation that keeps nothing in one place. The position is not a spatial one, but refers to the state of things in the composition of all existence. Explanation of this motion is quite complicated and requires a detailed knowledge of Iranian philosophy and ideologies. The objective is not to explain the philosophical school of Iran, but to show how empirical reality is mapped in the culture and the people's minds. A good example of this outlook is a well-known poem, often read with a musical tone. It may be read to someone who is sad and in despair in order to break through the deadlock of hopelessness and sorrow. Although its implication is greater, it serves to remind the person of the changing state of things, including the unfortunate conditions in which one presently finds oneself. The poem is addressed to Jacob, the father of Joseph (the prophet). It is believed that Joseph's brothers, being jealous of him, took him on a journey with the intention of getting rid of him. They pushed him down a well, and returned to tell their father that Joseph had been eaten by a beast. Jacob lost his sight from too much crying. In reality, though, Joseph was rescued by some people who passed by the well, and was taken to Egypt where he was raised in the palace of the pharaoh. The poem, supposedly spoken by a source of wisdom that knows all facts, calls upon Jacob, who assumes that his son is dead, telling him:

> Your lost Joseph will return home (to kan aan)
> don't be sad
> the house full of sorrow turns into the garden
> of flowers

don't be sad
if the spinner, for a while, did not spin in
a way to satisfy us
it will not spin in the same way forever
don't be sad

Such poems and proverbs are more than just a few cultural items that play an insignificant role in people's lives. People think in terms of such culturally provided viewpoints. These are, in effect, their sources of wisdom, logic, social theories, and principles. They use them in their reasoning for guidance in everyday life, in understanding the events that happen in their society, and in deciding what position to take in political issues. Simply put, people, essentially lay people, think in terms of culturally provided wisdom.

These views of change suggest a transient conception of empirical reality. The political consequence of this state of mind works in both directions, against and in favor of the sovereign order. It undermines serious concern with empirical reality, impedes the formation of a durable loyalty to the regime, and makes it difficult for sovereigns to establish the legitimacy of their rule. People in this social system are inclined to be receptive to anti-regime proposals and invitations. At the same time, quite to the contrary, the culturally induced wisdom assures people that unfavorable conditions will not last forever. Such assurances may cause some of them to not consider seriously an attempt to change the conditions. This being the case, such views may function in a manner similar to the religious views that Marxists refer to as "the opium of the masses." It was with good reason that contemporary radicals put a heavy emphasis on collective action and struggle. They believed the people needed a push, or otherwise would remain confined in a state of dissent and political argument.

Another proposal could be suggested concerning the Iranian people's inclination to seek a political solution in the teachings of religion. While they could not see a fixed preferable political order in the examples of their history, Islamic teaching, especially Shiiaite preaching, did make such promises. Not finding any ultimate truth in empirical reality (as culturally suggested), those who firmly believed in the religious teachings knew that the ultimate solution to their social and political problems must be sought elsewhere. The promises of an Islamic State, in their view, had the promises of such an everlasting attraction.

Literature and Intellectual Products

In the complexity of Iranian thought, other elements are involved as well. These people receive more sophisticated intellectual and theoretical ideas from literature, from mass media, and from preaching. Preaching is a general practice that is not limited to the religious ones.

In contemporary Iran, those who have been exposed to modern education are more or less aware of modern ideas about society and politics. The content of mass media includes some theoretical materials. In schools, students take some social science courses, but the main body of modern political and social theories are communicated through personal channels or in secretive manners. Most often transfer of such ideas uses the medium of cultural activities. These include poems, plays, movies, story books written for children, and translations of foreign literature. Prior to the revolution of 1979, some theoretical books in the social sciencies and humanities were available. However, they were subject to censorship by the regime. Still, they included the main body of social theories, Iranian and non-Iranian philosophy, and other fields within the humanities.

Contemporary political activists have made good use of cultural activities for political purposes. A number of ideas were incorporated into some of the art and literary products whose consumers were mostly better-educated youth and the middle class. For example, teaching a dialectical approach to the study of social phenomenon was the objective of many such works. This is the version of the dialectic that includes Marxism. Other types of dialectical thinking have also been present in Iranian tradition. One of the greatest books of poems, known as *masnavi*, includes a form of dialectical reasoning. It is centuries old and its poems are simple to memorize. A good number of these poems are common knowledge to all Iranians, who whisper them with a musical tone.

The intellectual contribution to social and political thought was not limited to radical thinking. Nearly all sources of modern ideas were introduced, mostly through the translation of books. The readers were a large stratum of the political activists. Many Iranians do not read books to learn, they read books that fit their ideology. Therefore, the mere presence of a book in the marketplace would not attract the attention of the prospective readers. It would have had to have been suggested by some politically minded groups in order to be widely read by the hotheaded Iranians of pre-revolutionary days. Therefore, just as in the past, 20th-century Iran was also a melting pot of imported ideas. Books from nearly every country were translated to farci. They included modern philosophy (especially existentialism), Marxism, and some of the critics of Marxism. Some other widely read books were about the anti-colonial movements, as well as poems by some politically active South Americans and Africans. Typically popular works included the writings of such authors as Fanon, Gorky, Sartre, Trotski, and Herbert Marcuse, plus some non-political books such as those of Eric Fromm. One can see that in this respect people were not just interested in one specific theme, although politically they may have reached some common points of emphasis.

Collective Value Orientation

A major theme of recent intellectual works was the promotion of collective orientation. This was a political theme, highly emphasized by nearly all opposition groups. It meant giving priority to the interest of the masses of people, in contrast to pursuing one's own individualistic goals. Therefore it was both an alternative and a reaction to what we could call "individualism." Typically, in the Iranian context, an individualist is a person whose priority is marked by personal interest, lack of commitment to the common cause, nonparticipation in times when others show group solidarity, and sticking to one's own ideas when solidarity is deemed necessary. The Iranian value system does not encourage individualism. Yet, quite ironically, there is a large segment of the population who fall into the category of individualists. Collectivism versus individualism is not an issue for the contemporary generation because it offers alternative value orientations and preferences. It is an issue because of its political consequences, and is subject to a political judgment and interpretation. These people see the alternatives in terms of such issues as how they may serve or impede the revolutionary cause, the struggle against aggression, and the expansion of the bourgeoisie lifestyle. Some of these concerns may not be new; they were concerns of earlier generations, too.

Iranian culture has been heavily loaded with procollectivist items. Its ideals and idols are the devoted, committed figures who give priority to the common cause. The contemporary generation, in general, also shows no disagreement with what has been admired in the past. If there is anything that distinguishes the present generation, it is the ground on which it has based its support of collectivism. For the past generation, except for occasional practical reasons, collectivism was advocated for moral and religious reasons. Contemporaries derive their views from the theories of social change, politics of resistance, and revolution. Therefore, they advocate collectivism on theoretical grounds, trying to emphasize its theoretical and tactical advantages. They intend to show that collective action and solidarity are not merely one of the alternatives, but the only alternative to solving common problems and struggling against aggression. They try to show that working together leads to better solutions. They have successfully managed to communicate their point through cultural channels as well, in a wide variety of works of art and literature. Such works were directed even toward children.

The stories written for children by Samad Behrangi are a typical example of such efforts.[4] Behrangi was a young village schoolteacher whose mysterious death was suspected to have been a murder by the Shah's secret police. For a while he was an idol of the radical-minded Iranian intellectuals. His works have different themes, and his writing is filled with political messages. While not directly addressing the reader, some of his stories would show the disadvantages of not cooperating with others and the advantages of collective action. Today a generation of artists, cartoonists, and producers of books and entertainment materials for children have followed his example. For a large group of artists and writers, he gave direction to politically loaded works of art.

In revolutionary Iran, collectivism was the theme of political slogans too. The symbolic slogan in the student demonstrations was *solidarity, struggle, victory.* A line taken out of context of a contemporary poem was read in many of the student demonstrations. It reads: "If you sit down and I sit down everybody sits down. If you stand up and I stand up everybody stands up." In practically all of the politically intended works of art, the theme of collective action and struggle is included and encouraged.

It is quite apparent that in the decade preceding the revolution, Iran experienced a leap forward in the domain of art and literature. In one way or another the invitation to revolution, to collective action, and to being socially committed was associated with preaching against individualism.

NOTES

1. "Satan," as it is used in contemporary Iranian language, does not always imply a religious meaning. It also refers to a behavior that is not necessarily a crime, but that is disruptive and annoying. However, the concept is well developed and originates from Islamic teachings.

2. A shrine (*Ziaret gah*) is a tomb of an Imam. Some shrines are tombs of the descendants of the Imams. Most Imams are buried in Iraq; only one is buried in Iran (in the city of *Meshad*), the 8th of the 12 Imams who is called Imam Reza.

3. *Khosrow Golsorkhi* was a Marxist Iranian poet and writer who was sentenced to death in the mid 1970s. He was charged with attempted armed activities. As a rare incident, a few minutes of his trial was shown on Iranian National Television, showing him refusing to appeal the death sentence, while facing the judges, calling them criminals, and warning them that the people of Iran would sooner or later punish them. The scene of this trial shocked many Iranians and boosted the moral of the anti-regime activists. I watched this scene on Iranian National Television and my reference to that is from my personal notes.

4. Samad Behrangi, *The Little Black Fish and other Modern Persian Stories*, translated by Eric and Mary Hooglund (Washington, D.C.: Three Continent, 1976).

4

Political Potential of Shiia Islam

The Shiiaite involvement in politics has many roots. Historically, the Shiiaite branch of Islam began because of a controversy over who ought to succeed prophet Mohammed in leading Moslems and in ruling the Islamic state. The discussion of the legitimacy of the government was therefore built into Shiiaite political thinking.[1] This controversy has subsequently grown into the profound conception of Islamic government—a formula that Shiiaism idealizes as a legitimate government. Having their own ideals, Shiiaite clergymen find reasons for intervening in the political affairs of the country.[2] Shiiaite clergy, especially those in the hierarchy of religious authority, assume such intervention is their obligation. Their eyes are wide open to what is going on and they would not let themselves miss a second in letting their points of view on major issues be made known to the government. Sometimes, if government decisions are found to be in violation of Islamic principles, they react strongly, asking their followers to protest. Their preaching always includes references to the early days of Islam. They go into detail in analyzing social and economic aspects of life in the time of the prophet, a full fourteen centuries ago. They try to show how the government, after prophet Mohammed, fell into the "wrong hands." This analysis does not end with the prophet's historical era. It progresses to a more important historic moment a few decades later, known as the Karballa incident (680 A.D.).

THE KARBALLA INCIDENT

The Karballa incident came about when one of the prophet's grandsons, Hosein, rose up with his followers against the sovereign who then ruled the Islamic state—a sovereign tradition inherited from the prophet. It derives its name from the town in central Iraq where the uprising took place. It is also referred to as "the incident of Ashura," meaning the tenth of the holy month of Moharram, a month in the Arabic calendar. It means a sacred month.

Hosein is considered the Third Imam (leader/saint) in a long procession of saints following the prophet. An Imam is the leading authority who over-looks and guides the believers. Those Imams who are descendents of the prophet are innocent, according to Shiiaism. Their behavior is irreproach-able and their teaching infallible, according to Islamic principles, and they have never committed any sin. In Shiiaism, therefore, the Innocent Imams are the perfect examples of holy Moslems. The example of Hosein is even more significant than this, for Hosein's uprising is transformed into a drama-tic incident of military confrontation between two forces—right vs. wrong, religion vs. secular motives, legitimacy vs. illegitimacy. Viewed as an upris-ing, it is often referred to as "Hosein's Revolution." In Shiiaite ideology, revolution does not mean the restructuring of a new form of society, but an uprising of the believers to correct the wrong, to put things back on the right track, to reestablish the rule provided by God descended through his prophet.

The account of Karballa, therefore, is in fact a lesson in revolution. Intel-lectually, this incident is conceived as an example, the means toward a theo-logical and moral end. It is viewed as a lesson for followers that it would be better to be dead than to compromise with "injustice." For the masses of people the incident is an end in itself, providing something to mourn and an excuse to display their degree of religiosity by showing how deep their sor-row is. In the recent Iranian Revolution, highly emotional protesters who faced machine guns and became agitated when they saw their friends shot would shout the slogan "Every place is Karballa! Every day is Ashura!" (the day Imam Hosein was beheaded). They imagined themselves, in singing this slogan, in the state of holy revolution—a revolution with Imam Hosein at their side. They regarded their fight as a continuance of the Hosein's holy war against the rule of injustice and illegitimacy.

Hosein, then, is viewed as the savior of Islam and the prophet's tradition, which was believed to have fallen into the hands of pseudo-Moslem rulers. Shiiaism views his struggle against Yazid, the Moslem ruler of his time, as an effort to reinstate that which originated with the prophet himself, who followed the will of God. The government against which Hosein rebelled was the same one that ruled the Islamic Empire, calling itself the "Islamic" government. Shiiaism believes that it was a corrupt government, seduced by secular goals and motives, and that it was an oppressive government whose behavior was not Islamic, yet which hypothetically legitimized its rule in the name of Islam. This historic incident, which left Hosein and most of his fol-lowers slain in an unequal military confrontation, was considered both a revolutionary and a religious duty for him. It is dramatized in Shiiaite think-ing and in their ceremonies with the intent of arousing great emotion and to educating people to a set of values. Emotion is evoked by picturing the de-tails of the incident. The incident of Karballa pictures Hosein as the supreme martyr, a saint who set an example for resistance against injustices and the rule of illegitimates. The commemoration and dramatization of this incident is the nucleus of Shiiaite ceremonies, making these ceremonies highly political. Most Shiiaite ceremonies are mass gatherings, intending to show indignation for the cruelty inflicted upon Hosein and his followers in the incident that occurred in Karaballa. It is an occasion to release hate and anxiety and to direct it against those who killed this "innocent" Imam and his followers, especially those followers who were children.

Politically minded preachers try to convince the people that they should follow Hosein's example. They preach that the Imam knew that his forces were outnumbered and that he knew for sure that his forces would lose the battle and be killed. He engaged in the uprising, however, and rejected any compromise in order to teach his followers a lesson and set a record that there should be no compromise between wrong and right. He believed, they say, that one must defend the right, even though one's blood may be shed. Therefore, the preaching and picturing of those events is intended not only to show the drama of the incident, but also to explain what happened and what moral lesson ought to be learned from it.

The political significance of the Karbala incident is evident in numerous ways. One is that it provides the Shiiaites an excuse to hold processions, ceremonies, and mourning meetings to remind themselves and others of what happened on that historic day. These practices are repeated every year on the anniversary of the occurrence thirteen centuries ago. Then, in their preaching and interpretations of the incident, they include some of their own contemporary political experiences. They try to draw a parallel between the political and social climate of their own time and that which steered Hosein into a holy uprising. In the past, such a gathering would often become political, and in some cases would devolve toward anti-regime activities. It is often through such ceremonies that true believers are taught how to engage in extremist political acts. An analysis of one of these ceremonies may help to give the reader a better understanding of the event and of some participants' emotional involvement.

A rather rare example of this involves inflicting wounds upon oneself. In this bloody and horrifying ceremony, participants inflict wounds upon their own heads. It is held in the afternoon of the Ashura, on the anniversary of the hour Hosein was beheaded. A group of participants, wrapped in white robes that symbolize their readiness to die, perform the ceremony. They engage in a mass singing of some religious songs about the incident of Karbala. They become increasingly emotional and their singing and body movements show extreme anxiety. Their singing is gradually simplified to only screams of hysterically chanting "Hosein!" over and over. Their whole bodies tremble from excitement and emotionalism. Meanwhile, they repeatedly beat on the top of their shaven heads with the flat sides of swords. The place where they beat becomes swollen, as a large amount of coagulated blood collects under the skin. In one dramatic moment they hit the crown of their heads with the edges of the swords. The blood gushes into the air all over them, and the bystanders charge into their rank and remove the swords from their hands. Some resist, but eventually give in. They continue, however, to repeatedly beat on the wound with the palms of their hands, splashing their blood. To an outside observer, it appears to be a masochists' orgy of blood. To the faithful, it is a form of sympathy with the martyred Imam and a way to show, symbolically, that had they been with him on that historic day in Karballa, they also would have volunteered to die for his cause. The little bloodshed today is merely to show their willingness to be a martyr.

It is precisely this sort of people who, under the order of the supreme Shiia clergymen, charged into the streets, walked toward the machine guns, and sat in the streets to block the road to tanks. Later, in the war between the Islamic regime and the Iraqi forces early in 1980, the same kind of believers volunteered to walk over the mine fields. They did so in a war that had been proclaimed by the clergy as a holy war, and their intent was to neutralize the mines to make it safe for others to walk over their dead bodies toward the Iraqi bunkers. It takes an unimaginable sense of devotion, the internalization of martyrdom as a value system, and an extremely altruistic personality to engage in such an act.

A clergy system that can command such believers is not only a political nucleus in a country, but has the equivalent of the power of veto on any unapproved activity. The history of Iran has witnessed these clergy veto not only certain policies, but even challenge the sovereign. All that was required was to create the analogy of their contemporary political situation to that in which Hosein was slain. All the hatred would then be directed toward the sovereigns. Today, the ceremony just described is rarely practiced, though as recently as a few decades ago, it was practiced in every city or village of Iran where Shiiaites lived.

The masses of people usually engage in a more moderate exhibition of their sorrow by showing some symbolic form of their endurance. The exhibition of this enduring sorrow is performed according to the cultural system of their respective societies. Without exception, marching in streets is common practice of all of them. In most of these ceremonial gatherings in Iran, some of the participants, in a well-orchestrated manner, will beat their chests or their bare backs with chains while singing in unison very sad songs about Karballa. Occasionally, they will stage a mock battle, called *taa z yeh*. In this play, some people dress in 7th-century costumes and ride horses, singing songs that are actually a dialogue between the two fighting sides about why they are fighting. It is at once a fight and a debate. They portray the incident as it actually happened, while the audience watches these ceremonies, exhibiting both excitement and sadness upon seeing the mock Imam beheaded and his followers killed. It becomes both a religious ceremony and a lesson in how to stage an uprising.

Another political significance of the Karballa incident is that the ceremonies marking it require skillful management and extensive organization. Organizing mass meetings and demonstrations for such a large number of participants has resulted in the emergence and institutionalization of other large organized groups, a permanent network of organizers who resemble a political party but are actually a religious one. They are provided with large sums of money donated by the believers. These organized bodies are, in fact, the nucleus of the mass movement of Shiiaite believers that had occasionally rocked Iran. Typically, such ceremonies in large cities, which are the political nerve centers of the country, attract tens of thousands of people to meetings and street demonstrations. In these demonstrations people march in line for miles carrying banners and flags. Sometimes they include marching bands who play mourning music. It looks exactly like a political carnival, only a sad one. Marchers accompanied by a band playing a sad musical tone sing sad songs and exhibit deep sorrow. People pour into the streets to watch them, while some bystanders mourn, with tears in their eyes revealing their sorrow. It is a show of anger, anxiety, sadness, and hatred toward those who slew the martyred Hosein and his followers. Some people become hysterical with sorrow during these ceremonies, screaming and even fainting. It is in fact a protest demonstration against the government of Yazid, the head of state whose soldiers, under his command, beheaded Imam Hosein.

The Karballa ceremonies also provide the clergy with an opportunity to preach and offer long speeches. They either implicitly, or occasionally quite explicitly, criticize the regime while making their clerical viewpoint known, and exhibit a show of power as the spiritual commanders of the mass of Shiia believers.

The dramatic aspect of the Karballa incident is not the only element of Shiiaite ceremonies. A chain of Imams, many of whom were also martyred, are considered in addition to Hosein. The first is Hosein's father, Ali, who symbolizes bravery and devotion to Islam, and is a true example of an Islamic *amir*, or ruler. Imam Ali, for Shiia Iranians, is a role model of a man whose personality had accumulated all the positive traits that Islam could recommend. He was also martyred at a time when he was the head of the Islamic Empire. Most other Imams are similarly pictured as strugglers against injustices and deviations from God's will. In some cases, when an Imam had shown passivity, painful justifications are offered for why he did not act violently. Certain acts of the Imam Hassan, the second imam, are one such case. Except for the Karballa incident and martyrdom of Imam Ali, though, other cases are assumed as minor.

THE SHIIAITE CLERICAL NETWORK

The Shiiaite involvement with political affairs is not planned according to any arbitrary decision. It has been decided by the religious hierarchy, in accordance with certain principles. This hierarchy is composed of three main levels. At the very top are a few clergymen known as "grand ayatollahs," meaning "evidence of God." They are also called "references," because people refer to their religious rulings. The grand ayatollahs assume ultimate authority to make religious prescriptions, and offer a religious interpretation of whatever people encounter in their social and personal lives. Practically the whole domain of such experiences is open to their ruling. People are free to choose one of the top ayatollahs as their reference. Once they choose a reference, they are obliged to obey his rule and demands. These clerical rulings are limited to the cases of behavior that are not distinctly explained in the writings of Islam or by the prophet. They might be initiated because of new conditions not in existence in the prophet's day, such as the question of whether the faithful should use the birth control pill. It is up to the reference to provide a religious ruling on such subjects. No force is exerted upon the faithful to guarantee that they obey, except that their voluntary actions are constrained by their religious consciousness.

Ayatollah Khomeini was one of these grand ayatollahs. At the time of the Revolution, and even now, there were a few others who had achieved the same rank in Iran and Iraq, but politically, Khomeini became superior to all of them. Grand ayatollahs have a network of less prominent clergy who are considered their students and disciples. Through such disciples, who are spread all over the country heading different mosques and mastering Shiiaite ceremonies, the ayatollahs relate to the masses of their followers. There are some religious taxes that either the grand ayatollahs themselves or their representatives can collect in their names. Even though it is a religious duty to pay them, people are not forced to do so. They are more or less voluntarily paid. These religious taxes are collected to be spent on religious programs.

One of the significant effects of such rulings is to assign taboo status to a behavior which is ordinarily not taboo. In Islam, a strictly forbidden act is called *ha rum*. To engage in such an act is to commit an unforgivable sin. What the clergy may do is exert their political control to announce, under certain conditions, that a particular act is now forbidden. For example, a particular historic ruling using this mechanism ignited the Iranian Constitutional Revolution (see Chapters 5 and 6).

The second hierarchical rank is a level of ayatollahs who are still considered top clergymen. These ayatollahs also have reached a point where they have finished their religious studies. However, they are not as experienced, nor as influential, as the grand ayatollahs. They also, like the grand ayatollahs, have students whom they train to be clergymen. Below these stand a large stratum of ordinary clergymen who run the day-to-day religious affairs of the people, such as preaching, attending at ceremonies, and reading sermons at funerals and weddings. The lowest stratum contains the students of theology.

When political violence, holy struggle, or even religiously prescribed assassinations are involved, the Shiiaite people may not make decisions on their own. Decisions must be made by a top ayatollah who is well known as a "reference," or at least approved by him, just as a decision made in a court must be approved by a qualified judge. For example, a ruling might be made that states that certain individual acts, usually by significant public figures, have caused fundamental damage to Islam. It may then be proclaimed that, if such a person is killed, the killer is not a sinner. Such rulings are rarely made, but have occurred. A group called *fa da eian Islam*, or self-sacrificers for Islam, during the last half of this century, had engaged in a number of political assassinations. Their targets had been certain prime ministers and high officials in the Iranian government. They usually did not act on their own, but had to obtain permission from a top clergyman whom they considered their religious leader. An act of protest could be a ruling, for example, of prohibition against the payment of tax to a regime, or the noncooperation with its organs.

Usually, the clergy does not make such rulings even on their own authority, but in the name of the "invisible Imam." This notion is pivotal to Shiiate political thinking and its conception of the Islamic state.

The idea is based on a belief that the twelfth Innocent Imam, in the chain of Imams following the prophet, entered the invisible realm about a millennium ago. It is believed that he is alive but invisible, and that, through some representatives, he is still in contact with certain clergy and other people. He is assumed to be the religious leader and patron of the Shiiaite nation. It is believed that some day he will step out of the realm of the invisible and establish a government of justice and peace. This will be a government formed according to the principles of Islam, having global appeal. It is to be a "perfect" form of government, because it will lack the deficiencies of the social orders devised by men. Some believers insist that this event will take place when oppression, injustice, and corruption reach an unbearable level.

Although consensus differs on how such a government is to come to power and what its basic features are to be, there is, however, no disagreement between Shiiaite clergymen on the existence of an invisible Imam and on the assumption that one day, such a society, as promised to his followers, will come into existence. It is generally believed in Shiiaite folklore that in the invisible Imam's promised society, money would be of no use and everyone would have all their needs met. To belong to the promise all one must do is say a blessing to Mohammed and his people. Lately, some organizations, modeled on this idea, have been established in certain places near the Iran-Iraq war zones. They are cafeterias, auto repair shops, etc., and exist mostly in places where servicemen are present. They are called *sa la va ti* organizations. *Sa la va ti* means blessing, and implies a blessing on prophet Mohammed. They offer free services.

During the Iranian Revolution some deeply committed Shiiaites believed that Ayatollah Khomeini was leading them in place of the invisible Imam. These groups do not usually call Khomeini "Imam," as he is called by others, but refer to him as *nayeb Imam*, which means "representative of the Imam." By this they mean the representative of the invisible Imam. They envision in the Iranian Revolution a striving to prepare the proper conditions for the promised Islamic government that will eventually be headed by the invisible Imam himself.

The idea of the invisible Imam is not just a hope to keep the people looking toward the future. It is an effective political instrument in all times. People speak of him as though he were present. For example, the true believer would stand up whenever his name is mentioned. Standing up, in the Iranian culture, signifies respecting a superior while being in his presence. When they stand up, therefore, it means that they assume that the invisible Imam is present but invisible.

Every year, on the occasion of the birthday of the invisible Imam, Iran experiences a celebration that is no less than a national holiday. For three days all the streets are decorated, and the spirit of a carnival prevails. In many places, especially in commercial centers, people are treated with candies and soft drinks. The political aspect of this celebration is reflected in the slogans on the banners hung in all the streets and celebration centers. These slogans, originally religious, now have political messages. The celebration provides an opportunity to talk about an alternative society and polity. The orators, preaching and singing in mosques, private centers, and houses where the celebration occurs, picture the society as led by the invisible Imam, emphasizing that it will lack any deficiencies. This picture obviously intends to contrast the new society with what people consider the deficiencies and injustices of the society in which they now live. It therefore provides a chance to criticize the status quo and to indoctrinate people toward alternative socio-political settings. The content of the banners hung in the streets is comparable.

As late as a couple of years prior to the fall of the Shah, while large sums of money were spent by the government on propaganda to picture the regime as a progressive one, one could observe a counter attempt by the Shiiaite activists. The regime was attempting to picture itself as committed to establishing justice and equitable social welfare throughout the country. Ironically, on the occasion of the birthday of the invisible Imam, one was able to read on the banners hung in the main streets of the capital city, "O you the savior! Our era is full of injustices. We cannot wait any longer! Are you not coming to establish the government of justice?!" (Similar ideas are put into some songs that people sing in religious celebrations, especially on the occasion of the birthday of the invisible Imam.) Although these banners were an open invitation to change the regime, and an affront to the monarchy, no one would make the effort to take them down. In contrast, if they had been posted by a political group, the group could have well expected severe penalities. The political content of Shiiaism is extensive. These are merely a few key notions relevant to political action.

Shiia clergymen obtain income from a variety of sources, which is spent under their supervision for religious and humanitarian purposes. Included are taxes that devoted followers pay. The managing clergy take a small percentage of the income for their services. Large lands, water resources, and other sorts of real estate are dedicated by devoted religious people to the religious institutions. These lands are called *vaghf*, or "dedicated." They are managed by certain clergymen, with the income spent for religious and philanthropic purposes. So also is the case with the religious taxes the clergy receives. Therefore, in this author's view, despite the fact that large holdings belong to the religious institutions, one could not consider the managing clergymen as a class of feudal lords or capitalists.

Now that certain politically loaded concepts and practices of the Iranian people are familiar, it is possible to see how they were applied. In the subsequent chapters, it will be explained how a chain of revolts and uprisings took place, paving the way for the Revolution of 1979.

NOTES

1. Shiia believes that in a place called *Ghadir Khom*, on his return from a pilgrimage to Mecca, the Prophet Mohammad introduced Ali to his followers as his successor. Therefore, the rule of others who succeeded Mohammad is not recognized as legitimate as far as Shiiaites are concerned.

2. What is portrayed as Shiia Islam in this book is its contemporary conception held by the Iranian people. Shiiaism is a much broader concept for academicians and theologians. For detailed academic works on Shiiaism see the following sources:

Hamid Algar. *Religion and State In Iran 1785-1906* (Berkeley and Los Angeles: University of California, 1969).

Said Amir Arjomand. *The Shadow of God and the Hidden Immam: Religion, Political Order, and Societal Change in Shi'ite Iran from the Beginning to 1890* (Chicago: University of Chicago, 1984).

Khomeini, Imam. *Islam and Revolution*, translated and annotated by Hamid Algar (Berkeley: Mizan Press, 1981).

Nikki R. Keddie. *Religion and Rebellion in Iran: The Tobacco Protest of 1891-1892* (London: Cass, 1966.

_____. *Sayyid Jamal al-Din "al-Afghani"* (Berkeley and Los Angeles: University of California, 1972).

Part Two

Iranians Struggle for Revolution

5

The Constitutional Revolution of 1906-1909

ONE CENTURY OF UNREST

Revolutions are like the eruption of volcanoes. They are noticed and taken seriously by observers, after they have erupted. Then they are watched carefully. The crucial point, which may pass without proper notice, is the period during which the conditions of rebellion were in a state of fermentation, when the revolutionaries were getting ready to rebel.

In most cases, to people who lack the knowledge of history, the meaning of what is happening fails to be self evident. Ignorance of how the turbulence was built up may leave some people confused as to how the background issues and events create a narrative of the revolution. It can, however, be quite misleading if the focus is only on the historic days when the revolution was at its peak. In that state of emotionalism, idealistic statements are made and people shout and respond to slogans that later may fail to materialize. The true nature of ongoing movements and where they are headed may not easily surface from beneath the cover of the rhetoric that keeps them hidden.

A historical view of how the revolution is built up may overcome such observational shortcomings. Such an approach may reveal the underlying forces and motives that create such an event by answering a number of questions. These may include from what social position did the impetus to oppose the status quo originate, why did people sympathize with the opposition's desire to revolt, why they have chosen to follow certain leaders, and why was a certain mode of struggle chosen by the opposition.

The above argument relates quite closely to the happenings in Iran. In 1977-79, the world was all at once informed of the eruption of wide-scale protests in Iran. What people all over the world saw was a brief portion of an ongoing struggle. This snapshot of the events was taken out of the context of a decades-long anti-monarchical struggle. The world saw scenes of confrontations between demonstrators and enforcers of martial law, the former using symbolism and religious-cultural actions, the latter using guns and ammunition. The demonstrations were heavily integrated with mass prayers and Shiia ceremonies, an integral part of the method of struggle against and confrontation with the regime. To an observer, it looked more like the rise of a new prophet, a religious rather than a political happening. It posed some ambiguities concerning why the revolution was so religious in context, and why supposedly conservative clergymen were engaged in such a progressive action as a revolution. Obviously, ignorance of the past Iranian opposition attempts and a mere superficial exposure to the ongoing events could lead to wrong answers to the above questions. They would say something about the revolution, but not the whole story. In this case, as in the case of every story, one needs to know the entire context of the events and where they had begun. That context would give proper meaning to the acts that we observe and define the relationship that exists between the leaders and the led, and between different elements who are on the scene. Such a historical approach needs to have a beginning, which can then help to follow up the trends that, upon their escalation and transformation, have resulted in a revolution. An analogy, for example, might be entering the theater in the middle of a movie. One may very well fail to properly recognize the role that the actors play and may cheer for the characters that the other people would boo.

Unlike the example of the movie, which is made to have a beginning, a revolution may have no precise beginning. Depending on how one analyzes social events, different points in history could be marked as the beginning of the same events. Each one would then provide a different story. For example, if the beginning of the recent Iranian revolution is assumed to be in the past century, then a variety of political groups and their contributions are included. With these taken into consideration, this revolution would not look as monolithically Islamic as it became. However, if what the present clerical rulers would suggest is taken as the beginning (June of 1963), then the revolution becomes the escalation of a Khomeini-led mass protest that erupted in 1963 and triumphed fifteen years later. With this proposed beginning, the revolution would be interpreted according to the clerical story, making it solely a Shiia uprising.

According to the following analysis, initially anti-monarchical attempts occurred in the later nineteenth century. From then on, this objective was ceaselessly pursued by different groups of the opposition until 1978. This point will be made clear in the following sections.

Those Whom the Cameras Missed

During the events of 1978-79, the Iranians' overwhelming support for Ayatollah Khomeini was so heavy and the religious coloring of the confrontations so attractive that other political groups were, by comparison, invisible. These other groups were opposition secularist forces (liberals, Marxists, nationalists, etc.), non-Islamic revolutionaries, and even Islamic radicals who had their own leaders. Undoubtedly, they were all present during the events of 1978. In fact, until a couple of years earlier, they had been the ones carrying the flag of opposition to the regime. In those days, in the eyes of many Iranians, these "others" were the would-be leaders of the forthcoming revolution. Even though the cameramen and reporters may have missed them or thought them unworthy of their attention, they were indeed a significant force. Through years of experience with political turbulence and opposition movements, they had gained valuable skills and organizational capacities that they could contribute. They were especially good in helping to politicize and activate the employees of the modern organs of the society. Some of them masterminded strikes in schools, universities, factories, and industrial and service organizations. These were middle-class-manned organizations with their members mostly followers of those whom we have called the "others." Their strikes and cooperation with the Revolution helped to paralyze the functioning apparatuses of the regime and decisively speed up its downfall.

For a number of reasons, despite their active participation, these other groups were less visible. These reasons were as follows:

1. They were not large in number, but were highly effective in their capabilities, scattered as they were within the masses of demonstrators. They were, for example, in offices where apparently no violent action was taking place. It was there that they would contribute in such positions as writers for radio stations or newspapers, or as computer operators in banks.

2. Nearly all major political groups chose to rally behind Ayatollah Khomeini as the leader and speaker for the revolution. Khomeini spoke with a national voice, demanding that "the Shah must go!" This was a priority with which most political groups would agree, or which they would follow. Having such a common priority, their differences were downplayed. Although there were a lot of discussions about the revolution and where it was heading, not all of such discussions were in congruence with the clerical leadership's point of view. However, there seemed to be a tacit agreement, or better yet a political wisdom, that in such criticism they should not quarrel among themselves. Only a few factions of some parties deviated from this rule. It was a general practice not to raise the issue of differences until the Shah was out of power.

3. Some veterans of the earlier decades of opposition politics wondered whether they could go along with the objectives of a clergy-led revolution. Not seeing a pause in their sustained opposition attempts, they had no reason to see themselves and their respective movements as alien to and a non-participant in the ongoing happenings. They still could identify with the revolution, and had no reason to think that it was not their own.

4. Certain groups, mostly Marxists, would not take the people's expressed slogans as the final word. They would see the religious character of the events as a temporal

coloring that would change when the present conditions changed. Therefore, no matter what the clergymen or the demonstrators would say, what was happening was still assumed to be progressive in nature. It was viewed as a significant historic phase in the life of the nation. There was a general feeling among most opposition groups that their ideals could not and would not materialize unless the police state was removed. It was this objective, not the means of its accomplishment, that they valued so much.

All these groups involved made a wide range of opposition experiences, skills, and capacities available. The significance of their presence may be fully understood if their historic role in the Iranian opposition movements is clearly pictured.

People Against Monarchs

Revolutionary events of the later 1970s were not the first of their kind. As recently as 1906-09, Iranians had uprisen to revolution. What was new for them was to participate in such events on a nationwide level, and to demand that the institution of the monarchy be completely removed and their social system altered. With these objectives they had gone beyond what they had ever before demanded.

Nearly a century of anti-monarchical struggle could be pictured as a succession of a number of stages. Each stage has some basic distinctions that make it different from the ones preceding or succeeding it. The distinctions are not the result of the change of one feature of the movement, but of its total composition. It is the totality of the actions undertaken at a certain period that makes the difference. That is, there occurs each time a well-integrated composition of leadership, active participants, political concerns, and mode of struggle. It is this composition that makes up a stage. Viewing the build up of the Revolution from this perspective, a series of stages can be distinguished.

1891-1906. During this period, the leadership of the opposition was in alliance with the clergy and with the Bazaaris, who represented Iran's business class.[1] The mode of struggle was symbolic, relying heavily on the religious behavior of the people in order to generate popular pressure directed at the regime.

1906-1909. This was the era of Constitutional Revolution. It was Iran's attempt to establish a democracy.[2] It began with the clerical leadership, typically following their traditional approach to political opposition. Following the severe reaction of the despotic monarch and his military attempt against the newly formed parliament, the opposition spread to a wider range of social classes and groups. A popular uprising was staged by a heterogeneously formed leadership mostly from the ranks of the urban masses. Typically, they valued secular political objectives, and their mode of struggle was armed movement. Their demands were more radical, as they asked for the sovereignty of their people.

1910-53. In this period the leadership of the opposition was secularly oriented.[3] Nationalism was the single most important characteristic of this era, making it distinct from the earlier time when the political orientation of the opposition leadership was formed through their religious sentiments. The leadership was striving for the administration of the country through the institution of parliament. It was a highly turbulent era with a continuous struggle between the office of monarch and the parliament, each trying to become the center of power. It was in this era that modern Iranian political parties were created, with their center of social support and recruitment concentrating on the middle classes. The mode of struggle was the exertion of power and influence through the instrumentalization of a political party. For Iranians this was a new experience.

1953-76. This was a period that began with a military coup against the parliamentary democracy.[4] It was an era marked by the reign of the military and police control of the society, in which all opposition actions were banned. The main political feature of this era was opposition through the utilization of revolutionary organizations, ideologies, and methods. Two distinct features of political activities during this era were the heavy emphasis on theoretical formulations of ideas and the projection of objectives in terms of these formulations. Unlike the earlier stages, demands were not confined to political change. The agenda of the activists contained the complete alteration of the system.

Earlier in this era, secularists were the leading influence on the shaping of opposition events. However, Shiia revitalists who spoke in political and even revolutionary terms began to strengthen their influence within all classes.

1977-79. In this era, opposition took the form of a national uprising, mainly utilizing culture and religion for the purpose of insurgency. Once again the clergymen were in the lead.

ANTAGONIZING CONDITIONS

Both Russia and Britain had established a strong political influence in 19th-century Iran.[5] Each had its own mechanism with which to enforce its demands upon the Iranian regime. By that time, Iran's monarchy was at one of its weakest forms in the long history of the country. The country's defensive system was still archaic, dependent upon the traditional system of feudals and tribes to secure their own territory. The national military forces were small, weak, and outdated. The financial resources of the country, having been spent on a luxurious and over-expanded royal court, left very little to finance the military needs of the country. In contrast, both Russia and Britain had powerful modern military forces that they could employ to exert pressure on Iran. Russia, sharing the northern boarder with Iran, could most easily move military forces into the country. Britain had made the Persian Gulf its own private lake, through which all the coastal borders of Iran could easily be threatened. In addition, Britain had a strong eastern presence in Iran's neighboring countries of India and Afghanistan. Both Russia, and more so Britain, had established relations with rival political groups inside Iran. Each had its own allies within the Iranian political elite, and by pulling the right strings were able to manipulate them as agents of their own respective policies. Given the delicate political equilibrium that maintained Iran's territorial integrity, they were able to challenge this integrity by causing internal strife and conflicts.

As their industrial economies were developing, these alien superpowers were further inclined to seek new markets for their manufactured products and new sources for raw materials with which to feed their industries. Their other demands, the political and military, were mostly designed to facilitate their growing economic interests. For this reason, as they approached the 20th century, their demands upon Iran more and more often found an economic expression. With this economic expansionism they were stepping heavily on the toes of Iran's ancient business class.

Given the despotism of the Iranian monarchy, which had no checks and balances on the decisions made by the monarch, the ruler was the person the alien powers could address. Dominators were again finding the office of strong-handed despots the easiest entrance into Iran, given that these despots were friendly with them. Therefore, it was with the monarchs' consent that alien powers found their way into Iran.

Except for the brief period of 1892-1908, during which czarist Russia had the upper hand, it was the European powers who were the dominating alien force with respect to Iran. These rivals were not always on the side of the monarch; their rivalry would occasionally lead one of them to aid certain anti-monarchist elements as well. Such assistance would add to the confusion and complication of Iranian political behavior.

Undoubtedly, the interweaving of despotism and capitalist-military domination of the country by aliens was a new phenomenon in Iranian history, as was the popular reaction to it. Monarchical autocracy for the Iranians was no longer a domestic issue, nor was the monarchy's strength derived completely from internal sources. Citizens faced Iranian monarchs who were, at the same time, the embodiment of superpowers. The power of the monarchy, and the reason for its survival, had found roots in sources external to Iran. Therefore, in Iran of the late 19th century, a sequence of anti-monarchical movements had one common theme—they were against autocracy. Most often, they were against both autocracy and dependency; the two were seen as inseparable. The monarchs were portrayed by dissenting groups as the instruments of foreign penetration and, therefore, of the foreign domination of the society. Simply put, they were puppets. To what extent this charge had any real foundation depended on the time, the situation, and the particular monarch. Undoubtedly, there were some elements of truth in these accusations.

Alien powers were accessing Iran's economic sphere through "concessions."[6] This involved the issuance of a license by the monarch that allowed the receiver to open up business in Iran. Most often, this carried a monopoly right in that area of business for a long period of time, such as in mining certain minerals. Besides the monarch, no other source could issue such certificates, because all vital decisions rested with him. There was no other organ to question him or share with him in such a decision. In fact, during the second half of the 19th century, the feudal-minded monarch Nasser Al din Shah viewed Iran as his personal estate and acted independently with respect to granting these concessions. Some concessions, because of their nature, did not normally conflict with the interests of the local businessmen, as there might be no local activity in that sphere. One example might be the estabblishment of shipping lines in a major river. Possibly, the monarch thought some of these concessions might be beneficial to the country. However, there were always those that would inevitably put Iranian businessmen face to face with foreigners. It was these concessions that raised public concern and caused protests in the Bazaar. The first popular reaction against the union of the Iranian monarch and his foreign domineers was the Tobacco Movement.

Tobacco Movement

The Tobacco Movement was an opposition to the Tobacco Concession[7] granted to Major G. Talbot of England. According to the terms of this license, all business activities in Iran relevant to tobacco were monopolistically passed to this particular British citizen. The monarch, upon the issuance of this license, had received large sums of money. In addition, he expected to receive a share of the income of the company. The movement grew into a nationwide show of support for the dissentive businessmen and finally, in embarrassment, forced the monarch to withdraw the concession. It was the first show of power by the Iranian bourgeoisie, emerging as a major political force in the country.

The Iranian business class used to be a rather weak group.[8] The Iranian monarchy had its roots in the tribal-feudal sub-systems that were still a strong presence in the country. With these as the backbone of the despotic regime, the bourgeoisie was still too small and lacked the mechanisms with which to steer the masses in support of their own cause. They lacked the power to directly challenge monarchical decisions. The businessmen, whose businesses were damaged by these decisions, were only one segment of the Bazaaris. However, given the social structure of the Bazaar, which in addition to being an aggregate of businesses is a tight knit community, it could be anticipated that they would soon rally others to support their cause. Two mechanisms helped the Bazaaris toward victory: first, the ecological formation of the Iranian Bazaar system, and second, their access to the organization of people under the religious authority structure, through the alliance of the clergy in their cause.

The Iranian Bazaar included facilities used for religious purposes, which were being built by the richest people in town—the Bazaaris. Such mosques are quite large and well equipped. Even until quite recently, the grand mosques located in the Bazaar were places where influential clergymen would preach. As the seat of important clergymen, these mosques or their adjacent structures were theological schools, practically the only schools in the country. In cities that held a major shrine, the Bazaar was located adjacent to it, since these shrines were visited by masses of people and offered the best location for opening a new business. As a cultural norm, those who visited a shrine usually bought gifts and did their general shopping there as well, especially if the visitors came from villages or small towns where they had no access to a Bazaar that carried a variety of commodities.

Whether a shrine existed or not, every Bazaar was a very crowded place. As the shopping center, it was naturally visited by many people from all walks of life. In the noontime, when people gathered in the mosque for prayer, the Bazaaris and the shoppers would mix together, standing in long prayer lines. Often the prayer would be followed by a short preaching. It was on such an occasion that the preacher could raise dissentive issues and the audience, feeling respect for his authority and wisdom, would assume his point of view. This is how an issue, relevant only to the dissention of some Bazaaris, was able to cross group lines and become the concern of all. The audience coming from different classes, even from other towns and villages, would take home with them the message and spread these dissentive ideas and the reasoning behind them to larger and larger circles.

The Bazaaris were soon able to find a powerful strategy to support their aims, by winning over the support of the Shiia clergymen. Such an alliance materialized for two reasons. First, certain clergymen were already dissentive toward the regime's open door policy for foreigners and saw themselves as less involved in consultation on such matters. Second, these clergymen had a close relationship with the Bazaar community. Furthermore, their interrelationship was strengthened for the following reasons:

1. The religious taxes received from the rich (*khomss, Sahm e Imam*) formed the bulk of the clerical income. These taxes were voluntarily paid, therefore the clergy had to be on good terms with the Bazaaris in order to collect them.

2. The Bazaar, as a community, was deeply Islamic. Bazaari subculture was typically an Islamic way of life that believed in the clergy as its spiritual and intellectual leaders.

3. The clergymen were also in charge of the judicial affairs of the country. In Shiia schools, they had fully developed texts on business matters, making their consultation on legal matters vital to the functioning of business activities. From this point of view, they acted as the lawyers and theoreticians of the Bazaar, and were therefore informed of and concerned with the Bazaaris problems.

4. Shiia ceremonies, especially in the month of Moharram, were held in places called *tak ee yeh*. The Bazaari people, being rich, were the ones who would contribute a large portion of the expenses for the establishment and management of such places. Therefore, they were in close contact and cooperation both with the clergy and with the organizers of the ceremonies who took their orders from the clergy.

5. In the absence of any modern means of political organization and mass communication, the clergy commanded organizations that were vital to reaching the masses. With the clergy on their side, the Bazaaris could have the masses of people informed of their grievances and appeal to them for sympathy.

Given such an interrelationship between the clergy and the Bazaaris, as well as their common objectives, a potential opposition force was formed. All they needed was an excuse to trigger their dissentions into open protest. Finally, they got one in the Tobacco Concession.

It was within this context that the Bazaaris, in cooperation with the clergy, began to raise their voice against the Tobacco Concession, and therefore the monarchical autocracy. Obviously, since the clergy would complement their explanation as a case of infidels taking over the affairs of Moslems, they could add drama to the case and agitate the laity. In Islam, business with non-Moslems has certain conditions. One cannot engage in any type of business one chooses, nor do business with any kind of people one wishes. For a basic commodity, one can do business with a non-Moslem if there are no Moslem businessmen available. From this point of view, the British-owned company had no priority over the Moslem businessmen and the very idea that an alien company might have monopoly rights was actually completely void and unbinding in the eyes of Moslem theologians and in terms of Islamic law.

Following the protests against the concession in a number of cities, certain top clergymen advised the regime to withdraw the concession. Upon the refusal of the regime to positively respond to these calls, a top Shiia clergyman formed a ruling, *Fetva*, on this matter. This clergyman, who was residing in Iraq, had earlier asked the monarch to cancel the concession. He then sent a message urging the faithful to refrain from smoking. His ruling implied that doing business with the tobacco company and smoking was prohibited for Iranians. For the faithful, this meant that any disobedience of this ruling was the committment of a sin. Upon receiving his message, all over Iran and wherever they learned of it, the people quit smoking. The company was left without any customers with which they might do business. An example will show how seriously people took this top clergyman's word. It is known that the monarch had desired to smoke, despite the ruling. When he asked for his pipe, he was informed that all the water pipes (it was common to smoke tobacco with the use of water pipe) in the palace had been destroyed by the ladies in his court.

The ruling of the Shiia leader intensified the already emotional atmosphere. Now the issue had become a religious obligation with which one could resist the monarchical decision. A mechanism that helped to enforce this obligation is built into the Islamic teaching and practice. It is the religious obligation of each Moslem to prevent his fellows from doing "wrong" and to preach to them about how to do "right." Now, with this ruling in force, it was the people themselves who would see to it that no one smoked or did business with the British company.

Following these events, some violent demonstrations were staged during which a number of people lost their lives. As the situation was getting out of hand and rebellious, the monarch had no other choice but to withdraw the concession. The company was dissolved, but Iran had to pay them large sums of money. The burden of the cost was ultimately left with the people, because the government had to borrow the money.

Despite its revolutionary consequences, which were still felt a decade and a half later, the Tobacco Movement itself was not a revolution. It did not create an institution to implement the will of the people in the formation of policies. Its objectives were limited to an issue and did not challenge the monarchy as a regime. It did, however, raise a single issue that called the people's attention to the limits that a despotic monarch must observe. It therefore provided the people with an awareness that was fundamental to the emergence of the subsequent Constitutional Revolution. The legitimacy of the practice of autocracy had been invalidated in the eyes of the populace.

With the victory of the clergy-Bazaari in challenging the monarchical decision, a strong opposition force was formed in Iran. In addition, the religious-cultural system of the country had proven its significance in facilitating the politicization of the masses and the mobilization of an opposition force. Ever since the Tobacco Movement, the alliance of the clergy-Bazaari and their unique methods of protest have been an integral part of Iran's anti-monarchical struggle.

Later, a discussion will be provided concerning how, once again, the alliance of the clergy-Bazaari played a leading role in the Constitutional Revolution of Iran.

CONSTITUTIONAL REVOLUTION OF IRAN: 1906-1909

The Constitutional Revolution of Iran was a struggle that triumphed through two distinct phases. It began with opposition attempts headed by the joint forces of the clergy and Bazaaris, leading to the formation of an institution of National Assembly. Once again they employed a symbolic mode of protest. It was followed by a second phase in which the supporters of the secular polity played the leading role.

The first phase was an accomplishment that was only one step beyond what had been accomplished by the Tobacco Movement. The clergy-Bazaari leadership, who had already established themselves as a powerful opposition force in the late 19th century, managed in the 20th century (1906) to both pressure and persuade the monarch (Mozzafar Al din Shah) to accept the formation of a "house of justice." This rather vaguely defined institution was to provide them with a voice in the governance of the country. At that time, the idea of a constitutional system was not yet fully developed. Those who spoke for the opposition were themselves limited, both in their concerns and in their political capacities to fight for a full-scale democratic order and a constitutional regime. In no way could they be considered radical groups. The opposition even included some of the top members of the ruling elite whose support of this opposition was in no way influenced by an interest in democracy or the hope of an alteration of the despotic order. Their involvement may have been due to a conflict of interests and concerns within the ruling elite. Each faction, therefore, was trying to promote its own specific political objectives. The clergy, portraying themselves as the benefactors of all the people, spoke with a universal language. They assumed a commitment, politically and religiously, to speak on behalf of the nation of Islam. They typically spoke in this type of language even though, in practice, their efforts may have resulted in benefits for some specific group interests. For the Bazaaris, there were primarily more specific grievances, although injustice would be done to them and to certain clergy activists if they are not given credit for some of the nationalistic and religious concerns they held toward the wrongdoings of the regime. It was in such an atmosphere that the concept of the "house of justice" was proposed to the monarch. What he had accepted, and what was satisfactory enough for the opposition leaders to call off the strike, was indeed an elitist proposal. Supposedly, this body would include certain members of the landed and royal nobles, plus the top Bazaari and clerical representatives, with the monarch himself presiding over all.

With the monarch's promise to accept the protestors' demands, the turbulence and strikes ended in January, 1906. However, by not implementing his promises immediately, the monarch was enflaming the already sensitive conditions. These delays, intensified by the introduction of more repressive measures by the administrators, once again led to protests. This happened a few months after the termination of the first set of protests. Nevertheless, in the new round, wider classes of people were involved, especially the politically active small groups called "societies," or *Anjomans*, which were composed of highly politicized members. In most cases, they were under the influence of intellectuals and revolutionaries. With their presence, more democratic objectives were voiced. Due to the further popularization of the protest movement, the demands of the protests became more articulated and radicalized. The new round of protests finally ended when, once again, the monarch proposed terms acceptable to the leaders of the opposition. In the order issued by the monarch, the formation of a constituent assembly was proposed that would prepare the groundwork for the formation of a National Assembly. The Assembly was to lay the foundation for the reform of the structure of the Iranian government and to make decisions on issues relevant to matters of national interest. In this royal order could still be seen the elitist outlook, probably shared by the leaders of the protest. The composition of the Assembly members, as was proposed, downplayed the masses by leaving them with the most meager representation.

Finally, on August 19, 1906, the Constituent Assembly convened to draw a plan for the election of the National Assembly. The latter formally began its work on October 7, 1906.

The Constitutional Assembly convened with high hopes, but soon faced disappointing consequences. It became apparent that what had been accomplished on paper, as royal orders, and what had passed through the assembly as a constitutional blueprint, might well face difficulty in being implemented. The mere presence of the newly established constitution had not changed the minds nor the practices of the despotic rulers. Their class interests, personalities, and view of people as their subjects had not changed. These had been formed over time and were deeply ingrained in their social and personal life. It was therefore impossible to make them realize and accept overnight the realities of a democratic age. Even if they had realized it, they would have found it counter to their own interests to be yielding to the sovereignty of the people. As the tensions rose between the Assembly and the royal circles, it was quite clear that despite the presence of the Assembly, constitutional sovereignty was still some distance away. These difficulties were more ponderous because of the development of a growing opposition to constitutionalism. In the mind of certain constitutionalists the European experience was identical with what they believed a futuristic and democratic system ought to be. From this point on, the opposition of some clergymen to constitutionalism began, because Islamic conceptions of man and society, specifically within its judicial principles, did not fully agree with the secular views of European nations. This attitude was propounded by certain clerical elements who, in turn, encouraged the despots. These clergymen were not happy with the ideological content of this constitutional development. Some basic notions of the constitution were taken from that of Belgium, which these clergymen found objectionable. They found some of these notions alien to Islam.

These difficulties became even more intense upon the entrance of a new monarch to the office following the death of the one who had granted the constitutional rights to the people. The new monarch, although he had verbally taken an oath to respect the constitution, was totally opposed to it. He was a despot with tyrannical manners and was devoted to collaboration with alien interests, especially with czarist Russia. He finalized his year long resistance to the constitutionalists' pressure by staging a military coup against the National Assembly. The military units under his command were dispatched to order the surrender of the site of the Assembly. Then, under the command of Russian Colonel Liakhof and his elite *cassacs* (soldiers) unit, the Assembly was shelled by artillery and destroyed (1908). It was a bloody battle, in which the site of the Assembly and an adjacent grand mosque were totally ruined. A large number of people had already jammed the site to defend the constitutional body, some of them well armed. Some civilian defenders and certain representatives lost their lives either in the Assembly or as captives. The despotic order was reestablished and the practice of democracy was officially terminated. The scene of the incident was a classic revolutionary example of two forces facing each other—one standing for democracy and progress, and the other for despotism and the restoration of an archaic polity.

The second phase of the Constitutional Revolution now ensued. Unlike the earlier one, the mode of struggle was not symbolic and religious. The second phase included a wide range of groups and classes, and resembled what was generally understood worldwide to be a national revolutionary uprising. The bombs that had ruined the Parliament had not shattered people's will toward democracy, which they were determined to restore. Protests were staged nationwide and democratic institutions were set up locally in many major cities and in some provinces. In order to restore the constitutional regime, volunteer armies were organized in different locations mainly in the two states of Azarbijan and Gilan.

With the popularization of the movement and its militarization, some basic changes in the leadership of the opposition and its ideological content took place. The constitutional movement, once exclusively under the leadership of the clergy-Bazaari alliance, was entering a new phase. The emerging leadership belonged to a wider spectrum of social groups and classes. The main objective now was fighting for freedom, for constitutional government, and for nationalism. These were universal secular notions and were radically different from what the clergy or Bazaaris had emphasized before. Most of the struggle was radically changed. Democratic committees were the backbones of these resistance movements, intending to force their demands through an armed struggle. Occasionally, they would engage in military actions to pursue their objectives. The royal troop had confronted the constitutionalists in some major engagements in a northwestern province of Iran. There, the city of Tabriz became the military center of the struggle and symbol of popular resistance to the rule of despots.

Finally, a well-coordinated design was put into practice and the pro-constitutional armed units marched on the capital city, conquered it, and forced the military units of the regime into surrender on August 4, 1909. Having lost his military support, the monarch fled to the czarist Russian consulate to take refuge. The constitutional order was once again established by men who spoke through the barrels of their guns. Following their victory, they immediately recalled the National Assembly to a session on the site of the ruined building.

The first decision made was a vote cast to force the monarch to abdicate. His child, heir to the throne, was voted into office, although with their vote, they in fact legitimized his assumption of office through the power of the people whom the Assembly was representing. With their vote, a new era had begun that was distinctly different from the earlier time when the kings assumed office by a coercive takeover of the regime or according to the rule of tradition.

Following its reestablishment, the National Assembly was generally more inclined to speak on behalf of the masses of people then for any special class. Unlike the earlier phases of the movement, the clergy was not in the lead. There were some influential clergymen who still were playing a leading role in the Assembly, but their popularity was, to a great extent, in their democratic ideas and national concerns. Quite clearly, political modernists were in the lead. The anti-constitutional position of certain clerical elements, prior to the victory of the armed constitutionalists, had weakened them as a stratum. The way they saw it, the trends of political change had departed from what they would have projected for an Islamic society. The widening gap between proponents of constitutionalism and these clergymen was articulated in two distinct orientations. One was called constitutionalist, or *mash-ro-ti-yet*, and the other was called "legitimate," or *mash-ro-ee-yet* government. The two positions were basically different.[9] The former were in support of constitutional monarchism. The latter strived for a theocracy.

With the constitutionalists in the lead, both modernization and the secularization of polity were on the top of the list. Toward such objectives, the growing urban-educated middle class, the nationalist parties, and the intellectuals would later play a decisive role.

In the next chapters we will show how the era of political secularists was finally terminated with the resurgence of the Shiia fundamentalist movements in the 1970s. The mainstream of the latter's thought was similar to that of half a century ago, with the proponents of *mash-ro-ee-yet*. However, this time, the alliance led by clergymen included various political groups and pursued a much broader objective than that which they had striven for in the past. In the 1970s they were determined to take over the regime by replacing it with a Shiia theocracy, an alteration that would put the clerical views in total command of the society and Islamatize the economy, polity, educational structure, and culture. They were not interested in building upon the accomplishments of the Constitutional Revolution. Quite to the contrary, they were out to undo the social history of the last few decades, detour the course of the social and political development of the country, and redirect it toward a system that would seek its legitimation not from the people, but from the divinity and his representatives.

Certain aspects of the Constitutional Revolution and its consequences need to be examined, and some detailed explanation is required. In particular, Where did the divergent views on the political development of the country originate? How did the political secularists, at least for a while, rise to the leading position? How did the historical experience of the Constitutional Revolution influence contemporary events in Iran? What modes of struggle were followed under different leaderships? and What major obstacles hampered the further progress of democratic drives in the country? In Chapter 6, we will address these questions.

NOTES

1. Nikki R. Keddie. *Religion and Rebellion in Iran: The Tobacco Protest of 1891-1892* (London: Cass, 1966).

2. E. Browne. *The Persian Revolution of 1905-1909* (London: Cambridge University, 1910). This is one of the best sources on the Iranian Constitutional Revolution. It includes detailed reports on conditions that led to the revolution as well as on how it happened.

3. For general information on the decades of 1920 to 1950, see the following:

A. Banani. *The Modernization of Iran, 1921-1941* (Stanford: Stanford University, 1961).

J. Upton. *The History of Modern Iran: An Interpretation* (Cambridge: Harvard University, 1968).

Sepehr Zabih. *The Mossadegh Era: Roots of the Iranian Revolution* (Chicago: Lake View Press, 1982).

4. James A. Bill, *The Politics of Iran: Group, Classes, and Modernization* (Columbus, OH: Merill, 1972); L. Binder, *Iran: Political Development in a Changing Society* (Berkeley and Los Angeles: University of California, 1962); R. Cottam, *Nationalism in Iran* (Pittsburgh: University of Pittsburgh, 1964); M. Fischer, *Iran: From Religious Dispute to Revolution* (Cambridge: Harvard University, 1980); C. Issawi, ed, *The Economic History of Iran, 1800-1914* (Chicago: University of Chicago, 1971); A. Saikal, *The Rise and Fall of the Shah* (Princeton: Princeton University, 1980); and Donald N. Wilber, *Contemporary Iran* (New York: Praeger, 1963).

5. The existing literature on 19th century Iran is loaded with reports of the rivalry of Britain and Russia, each trying to have a greater share of the Iranian market. Their presence in Iranian politics was reinforced by occasional military pressures. Following a military defeat in the early 19th century, Iran had signed certain agreements with Russia that included some trade and economic concessions. Great Britain, being the most powerful superpower in the Persian Gulf, had military influence in the southern regions of Iran bordering the Gulf. For details of the foreign policy of Iran in this period see R. K. Ramazani, *The Foreign Policy of Iran: A Developing Nation in World Affairs 1500-1941* (Charlottesville: University of Virginia, 1966), pp. 63-80.

6. The colonial powers began their interaction with Iran as early as the 16th century. During the reign of the Safavid dynasty, Britain, which lagged behind the Portuguese in the colonization of the Persian Gulf islands, approached Iran to establish political and economic ties. For more detailed information see R. Savory, *Iran under the Safavids* (Cambridge: Cambridge University, 1980); and C. Issawi, ed, *The Economic History of Iran, 1800-1914* (Chicago: University of Chicago, 1971).

7. E. Browne, *The Persian Revolution of 1905-1909* (London: Cambridge University, 1910); and Nikki R. Keddie, *Religion and Rebellion in Iran: The Tobacco Protest of 1891-1892* (London: Cass, 1966).

8. This requires rather complicated theoretical reasoning. It could be hypothesized that under the Asiatic mode of production the bourgeoisie found no chance to develop into a powerful force capable of challenging the regime. They were relatively much smaller in size than what had been formed under the European conditions.

9. From various sources (in *farci*) about the Constitutional Revolution, it could be clearly concluded that two lines of political outlooks had emerged. One was theocratically oriented; the other was secular and had an ideology of Constitutionalism.

6

The Reign of Nationalist Modernizers

Reforms do not occur in a vacuum. Some may face obstacles that can easily be removed. Some reforms require basic political changes such as a revolution or the destruction of the power structure of a class or powerful interest groups. The class power structure of Iran, prior to the Constitutional Revolution, was a major source of resistance to any structural change and modernization of the society. Consequently, after the Constitutional Revolution removed the traditional despotism as a major political obstacle, an era of modernization began. In addition, a large number of middle-class activists were drawn into the political arena, and assumed an uncompromising commitment toward bringing about basic social changes simply to bequeath something positive to their motherland. The revolutionaries, who had just reestablished the Constitutional regime by force of arms, were ready to take measures that ordinarily were not feasible for others. By following the dangerous road of opposition to a tyrannical despot, they had proven their commitment to the national cause. Therefore, they had no difficulty in justifying their motives. In addition, as revolutionaries, they feared less than others to face the difficulties caused by those who opposed them. As a Persian proverb says, "they were not that kind of willow to weep with a gust."

However, the Constitutional Revolution was not a nationwide uprising using one political language and a set of unifying issues. Those who had led the armed victory of 1909 were tribal chiefs, radical revolutionaries, nationalists, and the laity. They were present in the revolution with a national excuse, but many of them were pursuing their group interests. With these people in the lead, the National Assembly became a microcosm of a country full of group, ethnic, and tribal rivalries and uncompromising power struggles. Whatever heterogeneity had always made Iran a politically unstable society found its way into the Assembly. The shaky coalition of the Constitutionalist

Movement disappeared shortly after with no unifying leadership being formed to keep the different groups in cooperation. This state of disunion inside the Assembly, with practically no centralized organization of state outside, encouraged tribal and ethnic anarchy. For a decade, Iran became a land of lawlessness and disorder. The country was disintegrated and national sovereignty had ceased to exist.

Out of this condition, certain leadership and ideals emerged that encouraged an ardent nationalism. This nationalism called for a national sovereignty and strength through social and economic reforms and through the emergence of a militarized state that would ensure law and order in the land. An iron-fisted leadership headed by a military strongman (Reza Khan, who later became Reza Shah) thus emerged and led the country along a path of secularist modernization—in the image of the Western societies. In the decades of the 1920s and 1930s, Iran followed a course of social change that accomplished a great deal of progress in nearly all areas of social and economic life. These developments led to the emergence of some sources of tension in the strata of the tradition-oriented population. These tensions contributed to a strengthening of the pro-clergy forces as a major opposition group a few decades later. Some of the post-Constitutional Revolution modernization efforts were among the causes of such tensions.

Modernization of Iran

Modernization is an ambiguous concept. The ambiguity is caused by criticism of the conception that has equated "modernity" with Westernization. Today, a variety of developmental projections may be called "modernization" that may not necessarily follow the example of the Western societies. Modern ideas in Iran were identified with Europeanization. It has only been in the last few decades that Westernization has been replacing Europeanization as a more general concept, and has begun to include the influence of the United States as well.

Iran had begun its "modernization" more than a century ago in imitation of European society.[1] Prior to the 20th century, Europe had fascinated certain Iranians who were mostly from the ranks of the elite. Given the conditions of those days—the general state of illiteracy, the lack of a modern mass media, and infrequent travel abroad (especially for the laity)—only the Iranian elite were informed about Europe. Some of them had been there, or had a relative or friend from whom they would access information. Such travelers obviously had fascinating stories to tell. Most of them may have even failed to see the negative aspects of modernization in Europe.

In the background of the Iranian social reality, these observations posed a progressive, admirable, and desirable image because, in their absence, they envisioned Iran being confronted and effectually ruled by foreign powers. They saw the sources of such powerlessness, and other social and economic weaknesses, as originating in the way society was organized and in the ideas valued by the people. They viewed their own country full of tribal, ethnic, and other forms of domestic and foreign rivalries. The organization of the state was too weak. It lacked the capacity to reach the far corners of the country. The masses were illiterate. Despotism was the established order in the state and in the sub-organizations of the country. Given such contrasts, it was quite natural for Iranians to evaluate the West as an advanced social form. Therefore, their conception of social progress was derived from what they assumed had made Europe so strong and prosperous. It was from this point of view that "Westernization" was an acculturation not just to another form of social life, but supposedly to a superior one, carrying with it a progressive property as well. For many such observers, then, it may have been less natural to discriminate between different trends in European events by calling some of them progressive and others nonprogressive. Under these circumstances, a tendency had developed that assigned a positive evaluation and admiration to almost everything this elite saw in the West. Most probably, those Iranians who were proposing Europeanization saw no disservice to society in its adoption. They did not view giving up their own social forms as being traitorous to their national heritage. Quite the contrary, many of them did so because they were committed to serving their own people. It is only now, looking at the situation from the ideological perspective of some of today's intellectuals that this modernization finds a negative political interpretation.

The only important source of Western intellectual influence within 19th-century Iran was an academy known as the Polytechnic. Amir Kabir, in the capacity of the prime minister in mid-19th century, had helped to establish this modern academic institution. It was there that, besides modern sciences, social and political thought was taught. In the absence of a modern mass media and with the illiteracy of the bulk of the population, there was very little chance for people to know about Europe and receive a clear picture of its modern features. Therefore, those who would normally have such information and personal contacts were a limited number of select groups such as wealthy businessmen in international trade, wealthy tribal chiefs, and mostly people associated with the royal family and foreign offices. Certain intellectuals, through the written media, had gathered enough knowledge to conceptualize a rather realistic view of Europe. Even these people were not of the laity, though, because very few educational opportunities were available to the latter.

Within the top levels of the government were some individuals who believed that the existing social organizations of Europe had a superior quality, and they were interested in duplicating them in Iran. Amir Kabir, for example, the great Iranian statesman, was one of those who made an effort in this direction. Around the turn of the century, some intellectuals who happened to be close to the court tried to further encourage judicial and administrative modernization, taking European social and political ideals as the model. Political developments in the West, especially France's achievements through their Revolution, were a source of attraction for Iranian nonclerical intellectuals. So were other radical and liberal European ideas. Against the background of Iran's archaic despotism, such ideas would stand out. Therefore, the first elements of the transmission of Western concepts and lifestyles to Iranians began with these members of the elite. Still, as a society, Iran was too rigid to admit a European social and personal lifestyle, except for some aristocratic mannerisms of the nobility that had been picked up by some Iranian elite. This was nothing to transfer to the masses of the people.

Most modernization efforts prior to the 20th century had been in the military and educational domains. That is where Iranians saw the most immediate weaknesses of their own society. It was only later, around the turn of the century, that some more controversial reforms, such as in the administrative structure of the government and the judiciary, were contemplated.

In those days, the Iranian people were less aware that they were making a choice by following the Western example, nor was such a theoretical awareness present even in early 20th-century Iran. If a few were aware, they knew of no other model to idealize. It was the only example they knew that had achieved economic prosperity and advancement, scientific and industrial progress, and social and political liberalism, and had provided its citizens with the benefits of civil and human rights.

Those critics who had reservations about such social and cultural borrowings had no alternatives to offer, but resisted mostly out of a desire to stick to the old ways of life or out of a strong sense of religious and nationalistic commitment. For example, some Moslem clergymen such as Assad Abadi,[2] who were reform minded, were well versed in the accomplishments of Western society. Knowing the positive aspects of what had taken place in the West, they were encouraging Moslems to remove any obstacles to social and economic progress and to explore their own potential for growth. However, these suggestions were mostly idealistic and fell short of the formulation of practical suggestions. There were radical-minded secularists who saw negative aspects in the European system. Their ideas and ideals were also borrowed from the West, as was their reasoning, which originated in the radical and revolutionary circles of the Western societies. In fact, such radical intellectuals were more interested than others in seeing the Iranian social organizations and culture remodeled. What they suggested again had strong roots in the revolutionary experiences of the West. In most cases, no major hostility was raised against reformation efforts that consciously and unconditionally were borrowed from the West, except for occasional concerns and opposition within the religious circles.

Even in such cases, the opposition was not universally applied to all forms of social innovation. A distinction was often made between organizational reforms and cultural ones. It was the cultural and intellectual borrowing that had the most chance of being opposed. These were distinctly seen as European influences, while organizational reforms were viewed as universal trends, even though they had been innovated in the West. Even today, the Islamic regime has preserved a variety of organizational forms and concepts that were created under the recently fallen regime of Iran, although with some minor changes. These forms and concepts are indeed Western organizational types and practices; some include the idea of having a representative national assembly, now changed to "Islamic Consultation Assembly"; the notion of a republic, now the "Islamic Republic of Iran"; and the "cabinet," which operates more or less like other cabinets in Western democracies but is guided by a theocratic membership instead. Therefore, not all of what has been formed under Western influence is under attack. Although some theoretical concerns are raised about their compatibility with Islamic teaching and social philosophy, the same attitude has prevailed from the early days when Iranians had originally begun to reconstruct their society in a new form.

Another source of modernization was derived from the formation of Parliament. The Constitutional Revolution, by making the laws of the land and the state policies, had created a new condition with which to systematically restructure Iran into a modern sovereign country, and the Iranians into one nation.

Under such circumstances, post-Constitutional Revolution Iran entered an era of major social reforms on a national scale. First, the establishment of parliamentary democracy was the single most important modernization attempt. The second political innovation was the formation of political parties. Nearly every struggle within the society, whether it be against the monarch, or against ownership classes, had found its way in through party action. In this respect, Iran's political behavior had become quite modern, resembling universal features. So too was the content of the party politics. Secular thinking and objectives were fully established and had become the basis for directional projections. Marxist and non-Marxist parties were formed, all of which were inclined toward secular ideals. The Tudeh party, with a Marxist ideology, was formed and grew into one of Iran's most powerful political forces, capable of unstabilizing the regime. Its organizational structure and management outlook was modern, its explanation of events was theoretical, and its policies were intended to be highly effective. Nationalist parties also enjoyed the presence of influential intellectuals in their leadership and among their supporters, and had modern explanations and justifications for their action. Even though the latter groups did not enjoy the organization efficiency and discipline of the Tudeh party, they came very close to the standards of a modern party in other parliamentary democracies.

What expanded the social base of the party systems and added to the depth of awarenesses of their sympathizers were numerous publications that were mostly party newspapers and magazines. Such connections were either direct and explicit, or indirect and hidden. Infiltration of the mass media and the educational system by elements of different parties added another measure to the impact of the newspapers. It was in combination with these and other forms of mass media utilization that this era generated great enthusiasm and support for party politics and the formation of formally organized ideological groupings, a tendency that even today remains strong with Iranians. The repressive regimes afterward have exploited this tendency by trying to make state-controlled mock party organizations—balloon-type large parties, empty inside only as a showpiece, with people being forced into participation.

It was not just the mode of the political action that had changed in this post-Constitutional Revolution era. The leadership and sympathizers, who were the political activists of the day, were also changed. The educated, the industrial workers, the middle- and lower-rank Bazaaris, and the urban middle classes became the center of political activism. During this era, Iranians learned how efficiently public pressure could be translated by means of formal organizations called political parties. This experience advanced their political abilities a step beyond the traditional methods of exertion of pressure and of mass mobilization. For the first time in the history of the country, this new mode of collective action was put into concrete experience. Under the despotic rule, people were denied rights to free political expression. Some, therefore, would use religious authorities and institutions to approach, indirectly, their political ends. Now they could speak their minds through the party system with no need to twist their tongue in saying what they wanted to. With the party system, they found a way to speak out directly. The party was an efficient tool to translate the will of a population explicitly. This itself would separate, from the religious leadership, those who might not have followed such authorities out of faith, but as a policy.

The third important innovation of this era was the growth of mass media. With the Constitutional Revolution, numerous newspapers and journals published within Iran emerged in major cities. They grew rapidly, and less than a year after the establishment of the Constitutional Assembly, had increased from six to over 100. Up until a decade earlier, hardly any newspapers were published in Iran.[3] With an active press, a substitute was found for another dimension of the traditional form of political action. Previously, it had been mostly clergymen who had the means of addressing the public on political issues. Now, the secularist intellectuals and political groups had gained access to a means with which to address the public. They could even reach a distant audience more easily than could the clergymen in his mosque. The monopoly of the "pulpit" had been broken. Such innovations transformed the assembly, party, press—the Iranian polity—into a basically new system.

The democratic capacities of these Iranian institutions, however, should not be exaggerated. Two major problems caused severe limitations to be set upon Iranians in further modernizing their polity. They could not have modern political systems in a society in which the foreign powers interfered with the internal affairs of the country, and feudal lords and tribal rulers undermined the civil and human rights of their subjects. The despotic elite very soon learned a new political lesson. They managed to find ways to manipulate the Constitutional regime by making the parliamentary system a good instrument with which to implement their own objectives. For example, the peasant or tribal members' vote was never freely cast. The feudal lords or chiefs of the tribe would ensure that their subjects voted. Having the largest category of population under their control, they managed to secure the election of the candidates that they favored. It is still part of the political culture of Iran to bring truckloads of rural people to fill the electoral boxes with the votes for candidates whose names they had been told by their chiefs to cast.

With the traditional elite of tribal chiefs and feudal lords at full strength, the Constitutional system proved to be very weak soon after its establishment. Shortly after revolutionaries had reestablished the parliamentary order, their differences of opinion began to emerge. What divided them was the resistance of the traditional elite to measures directed at basic social changes. The tribal leaders who had joined the revolutionaries with their armed men had not done so because they fully believed in the equal right of all people, if they had, they could not have considered themselves as the chiefs and the tribal nobility. Their constitutional tendencies were to a great extent exerted out of their struggle for autonomy and their dislike of the absolutist monarch, rather than out of negativity toward the despotic order. Representatives of the feudal lords, rich businessmen, and also most of the clergymen all had similar conservative tendencies. In contrast, the few radicals, intellectuals, and especially those who led armed groups from the north and northwestern provinces, were potentially creating progressive and radical factions. The latter represented the armed volunteers, the revolutionary democratic committees, and the uprisen people who, relative to the rest of the country, had shown a deeper political awareness and revolutionary tendency than others. Some were under the influence of the radical ideas that were present in the region, areas that had been taken over a few decades earlier by Russians.[4]

Like most other parliaments, two tendencies emerged. One strove for change, even radical change; the other strove for moderation and reforms that would not alter the traditional power structure. On this basis the conservative tendency led to the coalition of the traditional elites.

The conflicts within the Parliament were reflected outside and in a way that itself was the consequence of conflicts and tensions within the society. Iranian ethnics, and autonomous units who throughout their history had been kept together by force and coercion, had been freed. Now, along with knowing the monarch had been kicked out and a powerless child reinstated, they began to break loose in anarchism.

REZA SHAH'S "NEW" IRAN

A decade of turbulence and lawlessness was experienced in which the country disintegrated into a number of tribal and autonomous territories, provincial revolutionary republics, and sovereign feudal states. The central government, as an organized body capable of exerting its sovereignty, had ceased to exist in most parts of the country. Under these circumstances, the Russians (from the north) and the British (from the south) invaded the country.[5]

This lawlessness and foreign occupation subsequently forced the ideological prerequisite of building a nation-state to form. It was under such circumstances that an Iranian military commander managed to show his ability in maintaining law and order. Reza Khan (prior to becoming a king) was a military commander who helped to establish law and order in a chaotic post-revolutionary Iran. It is believed that Reza Khan first sought British consent to move into the capital city and authoritatively demand a number of requests from the monarch (Ahmad Shah) in order to bring the country in line with the law. He helped to end lawlessness in certain regions.[6] Serving as prime minister, he proved his capabilities in helping Iran overcome, to an extent, its social and political disorganization. He was chosen by the Parliament to begin a dynasty, thereby terminating the reign of the boyish king (Ahmad Shah) who had been earlier sent abroad. His emergence as a despot needs to be explained.

With well-contemplated political maneuvers and effective military actions, he managed to become the champion by extending the sovereignty of the central government to all parts of Iran. His instrument for this accomplishment was the military, which under his command had been modernized in both its organization and equipment and had been expanded in size. All his actions were carried out through the legitimation he received via the Parliament. Quite skillfully, he made an alliance with certain political factions in the Parliament in order to reach his objectives. Eventually, he was chosen premier, at a time when the monarch had practically no role to play in running the affairs of the state. Finally, via a well-planned parliamentary maneuver, he had his supporters vote the monarch out of office and chose himself as the founder of a new dynasty. Reza Shah, ascending the throne by the constitutional procedure, emerged as a powerful king whose source of power was in his command of the military forces, his popularity, his authoritarian personality, and his ability to win over the Parliament to whatever he wanted them to do. He gradually developed into a despotic king who worked through a parliamentary system that was democratic in form but was ultimately controlled by the king himself. Emerging out of an era when the country had been plagued by anarchy and foreign occupation, he had no difficulty in proposing and implementing policies that would make Iran strong, independent, and internally at peace. As the commanding leader of the country, he forced Iran into a course of social change that favored a secular lifestyle and way of thinking. During his reign, Iran began to transform itself into a modern country, using the West as its model.

Being a military man, Reza Shah was inclined to view a modern and strong military force as the main instrument of social change. By expanding and modernizing Iran's military, as well as the urban and rural police forces, he began to eliminate obstacles and to build up the nation-state. He did not go so far as to challenge the feudal lords, however, he effectively neutralized the power of the tribes and crushed their military presence in their territories, which had effectually divided Iran into a number of autonomous ethnic and tribal states. The other group that he tried to neutralize as a political force was the clergy. He kept the parliamentary order as it was, but managed to influence the election of representatives in such a way that he caused Parliament to be basically on his side.

His policies of modernization existed on two levels—organizational and cultural. Organizationally, he helped to make Iran's administration highly efficient by emphasizing discipline and the observance of bureaucratic standards that, as a military man, he knew by experience. He established modern educational institutions at all levels. His policy was the universalization of education, copied from the West. In the economic sphere, he laid the foundations of Iran's modern roads and transportation systems and established modern industries. These attempts at modernization may have caused no serious resistance, but his cultural reforms certainly did. Under his reign, *farci* was made the official language in a land where nearly half of the population spoke other languages or dialects that differed distinctly from *farci*. Obviously, the mere assumption of an official language does not make the people learn and speak it, which is why this objective did not fully materialize until decades later, when educational services were available to the masses. However, the mass media, using mostly the official language, could reach wider segments of the population. The prime objective was to create an image of the Persian way of life and historical experiences as the core of the national culture and identity. In fact, Persians are the largest historically identifiable ethnic group of Iran, comprising over fifty percent of the population. Students were exposed to the Persian cultural and literary materials through their educational assignments. Nationalist-minded writers who had prepared these books had incorporated in them poetry, mythology, proverbs, tales, and historical accounts of the Persian-speaking ethnics. Through the transmission of these materials to the youngsters, they were trying to lay the foundation for a Persian conformity throughout the population. However, such facilities were not at once available to all strata of the society; they were mainly centered in urban areas. Therefore, it was the upper and urban middle classes who, more than other people, had access to such services.

With the feudal order left unchanged, the rural people did not have the same opportunities to enjoy such fruits of modernization. Under Reza Shah's regime, and until a new set of reforms in 1963, Iran's rural areas were far behind the cities, leaving the people typically illiterate, poor, and in a state not much different from their great-great-ancestors. Culturally and intellectually, they were kept immobile under the rule of the feudal lords. This gap was dividing Iranians into two major classes—one rural, the other urban. Westernization, then, was a sub-culture within the urban population with little trace of it observable in the rural population. Iran's rural people lived a lifestyle that had been untouched, not only by the Western cultural theme, but even by the realities of an urban-educated population.

By reverting to the use of force, Reza Shah tried to make Iranians convert to certain aspects of the European lifestyle. This phase of his "modernization" created a deep sense of opposition to his regime and policies among religious circles and their followers. He tended to crush such opposition by force. The climax of his policies was the unveiling of women. In Islamic Iran, dress was not viewed as a fashion, but was, and still is, designed with some religious considerations. According to the interpretation of Islam, which was accepted by the clergy and the people, it was a sin for a lady to let her hair be seen by men except for those of her family. The *chadour*, then, was a special form of dress that would satisfy such religiously prescribed demands. Reza Shah made it illegal for the women to appear in public with the *chadour*. If they did, the police were ordered to pull it off their head and tear it up. Men were also ordered to appear in European dress in public, wearing a special hat that became known as the "Pahlavi" hat. (Pahlavi is the family name that Reza Shah had chosen for himself.) Since the Iranian urban women did not have much occupation outside of their houses, under the new conditions they normally refrained from public appearance. Therefore, Reza Shah ordered public employees to attend certain ceremonies accompanied by their wives. In the towns, when the city hall invited people for public ceremonies, they had to bring their wives with them in Western dress. As a consequence of this era of forceful Westernization, reinforced by the spread of modern education, a stratum was formed that even after the fall of this shah retained its new cultural identity.

As the educational system expanded to provide service to wider strata of people and modern administrative systems grew, so did the stratum of people who had been socialized to be modern oriented. These services were mainly provided to certain people who were urbanites and were most probably from the middle and upper class rank. Therefore modernity developed into a sub-culture that was close to the upper classes and the urban-educated middle classes. The intellectuals, although they resented Reza Shah's iron-fisted military dictatorship, had less objection to his modernization and the idea of building a nation-state. In fact, what Reza Shah was riding on was a wave of nationalism that had begun with the triumph of the Constitutional Revolution. Such intellectuals were not necessarily approving of him, but were of the same mind as he on many of the issues for which he was pushing.

Reza Shah managed to socialize masses of people to a notion of a centralized state. They had developed a taste for life under modern institutions and
enjoyed various civil services. Except for the masses of peasants, who were
controlled by their land lord and whose authority was the supreme abiding
force, the rest of the populace knew no supreme power beyond that of the
national government. Generally speaking, Iranians had learned to be treated
by a set of standardized codes of laws and regulations, and expected to receive
some civil services. A desire for the modern services had been implanted in
their political and social awareness. Such expected services were varied, including health, education, postal, national and local police protection, the
registration of documents and licenses, modern judiciary organs, and a mass
media. These services were provided by a well-disciplined bureaucracy.

Under the reign of Reza Shah the civil organizations of the state also resembled the military in terms of discipline. They were built to be highly re-
sponsive to the client as well as the superior authority. This severe discipline,
expected from the officials of Reza Shah, was accomplished under the reign
of a tyrannical set of punishments that had terrorized the civil servants. He
would personally see to it that these organizations functioned as both service organizations and agents of modernization and change. He was not just
a shah of the palace, but a commander on the roads, going unannounced
from one place to another in order to personally examine the functioning of
the machinery of state and the military organizations. The stories about his
visits are so numerous that they form a considerable body of folk knowledge of contemporary political events of the country. With the threat of severe punishments on the spot, he was able to correct those who may have
shown signs of negligence, although he may not have been able to personally
contact each office in every region. However, unforgettably brutal punishment of the wrongdoer was the force behind the efficiency of these bureaucracies. It was not uncommon for Reza Shah to even have a high official
severely punished on the spot if he judged the wrongdoing to be a serious one.
He would practice the same punishments for those who were in certain businesses that had to do with the public's basic needs. For example, bakers who
would raise the price of bread or not cook enough in order to force bread onto
the black market were severely punished. People seemed to like such an efficient bureaucracy of state, as long as they themselves were not the officer who
was unlucky enough to displease Reza Shah. A content analysis of what people
say about the Reza Shah era, and his personal involvement with modernization
drives, shows how (as a person) he may have helped to make modernization a
valued orientation within the social and political consciousness of the people.
Two examples, gathered from older people who were young men in the early
20th century, may show how his administration normally functioned.

Reza Shah was quite concerned with material aspects of modernization,
such as building city halls, squares, and things that would make a city look

modern. Once, on a visit to Gonbad, a town located in the heart of a tribal region in northeastern Iran, he wondered why they had still not built modern squares. He mentioned to the mayor of the town that on his return two days later, he expected to see one. The mayor, his family, and everyone under his command worked hard for two days, not sleeping at all. The mayor himself did much of the manual work in order to finish up the job on time. They even transplanted big trees to be fixed around the square by the time of the Shah's return visit. In this way, Reza Shah, with a lifetime of military training, built up the efficient machinery of the state.

Another example showing how Reza Shah would combine modern leadership with the style of folk legend is seen in the eyewitness report of ninety-five-year-old Panjeh Ali. Ali said that one day a rich man had lost four thousand *touman* (the Iranian monetary unit) in the city of Qazwin. As was common in those days, someone was hired to walk in the streets, calling out to see whether anyone had found the money and would return it for a one thousand *touman* reward. A poor man had found the money, but when he returned it to the owner, the owner went back on his word and said that he had lost five thousand *touman*; therefore, he refused to pay the one thousand *touman* reward. People gathered and watched the two quarrel. The occasion happened to coincide with one of the Shah's unannounced tours of the city. Accompanied by his guards, he attended the gathering and inquired about the story. Upon hearing about it, he addressed the poor man who had found the money and threatened him by saying that if he refused to tell the truth, he would be shot. The poor man said that no one had seen him finding the money. If he was not honest, why would he have returned it to the owner. The Shah said that this man was right. Then he addressed the businessman quite sarcastically, telling him, "Go and find your money! Yours was one thousand *touman* more. Therefore, what this man has found is not yours. It is probably someone else's." He gave one-third of the money to the poor man and the other part to the officials of the town to spend on urban renewal projects.

Whether or not these stories are true does not matter much. What is important is the fact that the notion of modernity and efficient state machinery was incorporated in a legend-type image that people held in mind in the mixture of a modern and traditional folk leader. The modernizer aspect of such an image was positively valued. It was such an awareness that would eventually provide the impetus for change and modernity at a grass roots level. Iran of 1920-30 was receptive to such changes and social reconstruction attempts.

It was not just the common people who may have positively evaluated Reza Shah's efforts. At the beginning, he enjoyed some degree of support from the radicals and intellectuals, who supported his efforts to rebuild a new Iran. However, his excessive use of force and tendency to accumulate wealth later alienated such supporters.

The parliamentary-based government was not abandoned in this era. It was exactly the practice of parliamentary rule that facilitated the era of democracy in the decade that followed the fall of Reza Shah. Later, when he had been removed as dictator, once again the Parliament emerged as the central political authority in the country, finding its true meaning in the late 1940s and early 1950s.

Some of the Reza Shah's policies generated mass resentment. While his modernization of state and service organizations, industrialization, and development projects did not cause much opposition (if little admiration), his cultural policies were controversial. These policies followed a nationalistic line. However, some Western mannerisms were incorporated into the image of national culture that was to be adapted by the entire population. His most concerted attempt was to popularize Western dress and mannerisms. What engraved the image of modernity on the Iranians' minds were these cultural features that they would associate with Westernization and with the policies of the regime.

Reza Shah's era finally came to an end in the early 1940s when the Allied forces occupied Iran. They wanted to secure their control of the oil fields, and to establish a safe road out of German reach by which to send help to the U.S.S.R., which was still resisting Germany's expansionism. However, they made a good excuse to justify their occupation. Under Reza Shah's modernization of Iran's economy, modern transportation and industry was undertaken mainly through the technical assistance of the German regime. Reza Shah's good relationship with the Germans was what the Allies had objected to. This was an excuse, however, for the Allied forces to invade Iran during World War II. The Reza Shah's reign ended when, because of the Allied occupation, he was forced to abdicate.[7]

With his fall, large segments of the population joyfully returned to their traditional dress standards, which they had been forced to alter, and gave up Western mannerisms. So too did many women change, once again wearing the *chadour.*

However, a group of people preferred to keep the new cultural styles. Among them were a new generation who had been born into the new conditions, and raised and educated according to the Westernized cultural environment. For them there was little to revert to; this was their way of life. Those who kept living the Westernized way of life were from the strata that had been, more than others, expected to follow the modernization directives of the regime. These were the educated urbanites, public employees, military families, religious minorities, and educated women. With the Western cultural type being established in the society, many others began to take it as an example. What encouraged them more was the fact that this became known as the lifestyle of the urban-educated people. From then on, this influential stratum began to influence others through the sensitive positions as teachers, journalists, holders of managerial posts, public employees, and members of the police and military upper ranks. The Westernized sub-culture grew in size under the reign of Reza Shah's son.

Westernization, especially the part that had to do with harsh treatment of the clergy, secular teaching in the schools, and the unveiling of women, left a permanent scar on the soul of the clergy and their faithful followers. They saw it as Reza Shah's major crime against the Islamic nation of Iran. In their view, this corrupted the people, and propagated immorality and sexual promiscuity. Some observations of post-revolutionary Iran may be relevant to this subject.

One of the major efforts of the Islamic regime today is to erode away the cultural influences of the West. Particular emphasis is placed on the habits of unveiled women. Officially, it has been made law that all women and men must observe Islamic moral codes, including the manner of one's appearance in public. A chain of Toyota vans, each occupied by armed revolutionary guards, constantly survey the streets looking for those who do not maintain such moral standards. Another team is composed of armed women who particularly keep an eye on the women in the streets. If someone wears heavy make-up or is seen showing her hair from under her veil, she is given a warning. If it happens that she does not correct herself, she can be arrested and prosecuted as spreading prostitution, or might actually face various counterrevolutionary charges. All over the city walls there are slogans against unveiled women who, because of the terrifying punishment, dare not appear in public places unveiled. Lately they talk about "poorly covered ladies," which refers to those with minor signs of observable sex appeal remaining. For example, there was a female university student who lost her student status just a few weeks before graduation because she was accused of being careless in the observation of "veiling standards." An observer not familiar with Iran may wonder why there are such restrictions and even anti-revolutionary charges placed on some of these women. The reason lies in the fact that the Islamic regime views Westernized social conduct as non-Islamic and a consequence of the reign of the Pahlavi dynasty—in their words, a "heritage of Reza Shah and his son" (the deposed king). This is Ayatollah Khomeini's favorite phrase—to call them "that father and the son." Therefore, it is assumed that those who are faithful to the Westernized way of life are the natural allies of the fallen regime. According to this reasoning, their acts may even be charged as anti-revolutionary.

In the Reza Shah's period, however, the tensions and conflicts caused by the modernization attempts were not limited to cultural cases. The tribal elite of Iran, and those who proposed ethnic autonomy, had held their grudges. Among these groups were those who favored a multilingual Iran.

The fall of Reza Shah was not followed by major lawlessness and disturbances. Unlike the decade of 1910, this time the occupationist troops were already in the country and a number of internal conditions favored political stability. The new Shah immediately took the office of king. He was unable to rule in the image of his strong-handed father, who had become a despot, and the country would not accept the reemergence of another dictator. The Iranians had found a chance to catch their breath politically. What eased this transition of power without the experience of major disorders and disintegrative attempts was the fact that Iran had made considerable progress in the direction of a nation-state.

From what is presented in this chapter and what will be discussed in the next two chapters, the conclusion could be made that the secularist modernizers for nearly half a century paved the road for the rise of the proclergy forces to power. They helped to lay the foundation for an Iran in which a homogenized nation was to emerge. By doing so, they put into effect policies that accomplished the following:

1. They alienated and angered certain clergymen and their supporters from the entire process of national reconstruction, therefore encouraging them to seek alternative projections of their own.

2. Western-oriented ideals of modernization first had attracted and enthused, but later disappointed the intellectuals, radicals, and even some of the liberal-oriented middle class.

3. The emerging nation-state facilitated the spread of the dissentive voices, including those of the clergy, on a national scale. Therefore, it helped them to emerge as a unifying political and religious authority, which, in turn, gained the support of the masses for their causes and grievances.

It is from this point of view that the ensuing events and actions that followed the Constitutional Revolution helped the triumph of the "Islamic Revolution" six decades later. The way changes were accomplished and the ideals that were pursued implanted the seeds of deep dissension and further conflict that the clergy-led groups later harvested.

NOTES

1. G. Nashat, *The Origin of Modern Reform in Iran, 1870-80* (Urbana: University of Illinois, 1982).

2. Nikki R. Keddie, *Sayyid Jamal al-Din "al-Afghani"* (Berkeley and Los Angeles: University of California, 1972).

3. E. Abrahamian, *Iran: Between Two Revolutions* (Princeton: Princeton University, 1982), p. 87.

4. Earlier in the 19th century, Iran had lost a heavily populated region to the Russians. Therefore, close natural ties existed between people who lived in those regions and the events of Iran. All through the early 19th century, people who lived in those regions under Russian rule would contribute to popular political movements in Iran. This included sending experienced revolutionaries, volunteer fighters, and materials to help to the struggling Iranians at home.

5. In 1907 Britain and Russia had signed an agreement on Iran. They had divided Iran into certain zones of influence. North of Iran was considered the Russian sphere of influence, southeast was the British, and a neutral region was in between. Following

ing this agreement Russian forces had some presence in Northern Iran, as did the British in the south. Following the fall of the czarist regime in Russia, the Russian forces stationed in Iran became disorganized and dispersed. The revolutionary government that took over that country was inclined to make the British-Russian agreement of 1907 void. This did not fully materialize. By early 1920s the red army was still in certain parts of the Gilan province. For more details see Donald N. Wilber, *Reza Shah Pahlavi: The Resurrection and Reconstruction of Iran* (New York: Exposition Press, 1975), pp. 52-55; and E. Abrahamian, *Iran: Between Two Revolutions* (Princeton: Princeton University, 1982), p. 112.

6. Ahmad Shah, the young king who was removed by the Reza Shah, was an exception to Iran's tradition of a stronghanded monarch. During his era, when revolutionaries were seated in the Parliament, the Parliament was the center of political power in the country. The Parliament itself, however, was weakened by internal tensions and conflicts of interest, and was unable to rule the country and neutralize the strong presence of the British and Russian influence in its internal affairs.

7. It is an established fact that Reza Shah was forced out of office under pressure of the Allied forces. He was sent to exile far from Iran. See Donald N. Wilber, *Reza Shah Pahlavi: The Resurrection and Reconstruction of Iran* (New York: Exposition Press, 1975), p. 218.

7

The Iranian Middle Class Rises to Power

AGE OF DEMOCRACY

The fall of Reza Shah was followed by an era during which Iranians learned how to work with political parties, to administer the country through Parliament, and to politicize the masses through modern ideologies and nontraditional motives. They experienced two major happenings, both of which generated anti-foreign sentiments. The first incident was a separationist attempt by a group of radicals who tried to set up an independent government in Azarbaijan, which is a province in northwestern Iran.[1] They were removed by military force and with the help of people inside the province. It was believed that the U.S.S.R. was behind this group. The second incident was a movement, originating with Dr. Mossasdegh and his nationalist-liberal coalition of parties, that pushed for the nationalization of the oil industry that was jointly owned by Iran and Britain, with the latter maintaining control of the venture.[2]

The vacuum of power created by the fall of Reza Shah could not be immediately filled by his son, the Shah, because upon the occupation the Iranian military forces were disorganized and most of their men had deserted. Therefore, the Shah could not follow the same military-backed policies even if he wanted to. Besides, it would have taken him a long time to acquire the experience needed to put together a country that had been ripped apart by the presence in the north (the Soviets) and that in the south (the British). Therefore, the vacuum of the power was to be filled locally by a variety of interest groups and political collectives. Such groups were implementing their objectives through political party organizations, which were new in Iran and had been proven to be highly suitable for the parliamentary system. Parties found themselves in a favorable situation to influence the administration of the country. It was an atmosphere in which people could do more or less what they wanted to without being forced.

Even though a strong-handed despotic monarch no longer ruled, the parties faced difficulties in immediately substituting the will of the people for that of the despots and the powerful elite, because the popular base of support for these parties was limited. Therefore, political parties were still far from assuming the leadership of the nation. Most of the population was still illiterate, especially in the rural areas. They were unfamiliar with modern concepts and reasoning, with which most political parties operated. The notion of the political equality of men, reflected through their vote, was not internalized by the bulk of the population, because chauvinism of all kinds was present in their lives and they thought and acted in relation to these stratifying conditions.

The largest segment of the population was still rural, with the feudal lords keeping them at a distance from the central government, national politics, and new ideas. The second largest group was made up of tribes and those with tribal background. These people were still bound to the traditional outlook; they did not act as individuals, but in groups. Therefore, their political consciousness was still dominated by a collective identity, as tribesmen, and by tribal solidarity. They looked to their own leaders for direction, and these leaders were mostly unwilling to support a dictator monarch. Due to Reza Shah's attempt to crush their power structure, many of them were hostile to both the Shah and the military. However, such a distance from the monarch did not mean being constitutionalists in the true meaning of the term. Some of these leaders were allied with the nationalist parties, even though this would help the pro-Parliament forces. However, such support was shaky and did not add much to the strength of a democratic order, since all those parties could count on was winning over the support of a few individuals, the tribal leaders. In this case, these leaders changed their orientation, and with them went the whole tribe.

The next more populous stratum was that of lower class urbanites. This group, most of whom were rural in origin, uneducated, and traditional minded, were not the proper candidates with which to create a modern political party, nor had they the proper framework within which to fabricate a complicated party structure. They were still looking toward religious leaders for the legitimation of social and political issues. However, they could be counted on for an occasional show of support if they were sufficiently aroused by emotion to attend mass demonstrations and to show their power in mob politics.

Nearly half of the population was left out of Iranian politics because they were female. Within the Iranian cultural setting, they were kept at a distance from public and social activities in which men were present. Reza Shah's attempt to change this situation had not reached its objectives. After his fall, much of what he had done forcefully was neutralized. A negligible number of female public employees and teachers could be counted on to participate, as well as some offspring of the modernized middle and upper classes. Still, even such a small stratum would find it difficult to participate in political activities, because men were not used to seeing women as equals.

The only group left for the modern political parties to count on as the prospective members of party organizations was the stratum that we might call the "new middle class," plus those who worked in modern industries. In Iran of the 1940s, all of these groups numbered at most a few hundred thousand out of a population of about 20,000,000 people. Not all members of this rather small stratum were potential candidates for party recruitment. Certain Bazaaris could be counted on as prospective party activists, but the Bazaaris still had tight community ties. The participation of these people was sure to be in the form of a collective body rather than as individuals acting on their own.

Under such conditions, Iran's political parties developed into a form that could generate significant power without having a large number of formal members. These were small groups of politically concerned individuals who centered around a certain few well-recognized persons. They tried to play the role of the spearhead, cutting straight through with a long tail of followers. Often, there was no well-established level of authority, nor many members or branches of party organization. By appealing to the masses, the parties would support certain candidates or introduce candidates of their own choice. Occasionally, they called people to a mass gathering in which they were addressed through highly emotional speeches. The key role was played by the leader, not the ideology or the objectives of the party.

The only Iranian party that did not fully follow this pattern was the Tudeh party. It tended to follow the universal model of a Marxist organization, which is a formally structured grouping with rank and file, divisions of labor, and a multiplicity of branches and functional organs. Even they had relatively few formal members. Being mainly interested in an organized work force, they were more selective than others in whom they would accept as members. The Tudeh party did grow into a first rank political power in Iran, but most of its activities were officially banned.

Another factor responsible for this form of Iranian party system was the fact that the masses of the people dared not get very involved with these parties. In case of a crackdown on the parties, which happened quite frequently in Iran, the leaders might flee abroad and the rank and file would have to pay the price.

Political parties, as they have just been described, had difficulty in making long-term projections and faced a number of basic insecure conditions. First, they had to compete for support within a small stratum of politically minded people. This made them heavily dependent upon changes in the attitude and

preferences of this stratum. This dependency was typical of a politically turbulent Iran. Second, working under these conditions, political parties grew
quite rapidly. Making coalitions with others was essential to the growth,
power, and influence of each party. However, such alliances were highly
shaky. If the parties had large organizations, it would take a long time to
lose a large number of their members, to push through a new policy, or to
make a new commitment. With a party composed of only a few members,
the case was different. The slightest disagreements on issues or any clash of
personalities (typical in Iran) would see the coalitions terminate and a new
pattern of coalitions, often with rivals, reemerge and transform the entire
scene. Consequently, both in terms of the content for which the parties strove
and the pattern of their intraparty networks, they could easily change direction and ally with others, breaking away from previous commitments. It was
typical of this era to see political issues reduced to the personal level, and
unimportant sources of tension grow into political turmoil, parliamentary
clashes, and factioning of the parties. However, all parties would occasionally unite on a particular highly sensitive national issue.

The issue of the nationalization of the oil industry provided a unique opportunity for political parties to unite, generate nationwide concern, expand
their social base of support, and show what they could accomplish for the
country. They managed to politicize a large segment of the urban "silent
majority." Dr. Mossadegh, a man who deeply believed in the sovereignty of
people through the Parliament, had proposed the nationalization of the oil
industry. He was strongly committed to having it passed through Parliament
and enacted. The Shah was not willing to nominate him as the prime minister
of his choice. Following the strong show of popular support in the shape of
a violent mob confronting the armed security forces, the Shah was forced to
choose Dr. Mossadegh as his choice. Nearly all political groups finally supported him. Some of them were probably not willing to do so in their hearts,
but did because the popular sentiment was with the nomination of Dr. Mossadegh. In the multiparty system of Iran, in which rivalry and political confrontation were so frequent, a unique situation developed. The parties and
the people all formed a solid collective, standing behind a man who had been
approved by Parliament to administer the country. He viewed the Parliament
as the sovereign. Approaching his ideals of democracy, Mossadegh managed to use the nationalization issue to strip the Shah of his major sources
of power and control. The next step was the transfer of control of the armed
forces from the Shah to the Parliament. The prime minister, who was a civilian, became the acting commander in chief of the armed forces. This was a
historic breakthrough because the backbone of the monarchical power was
its command of the military forces. Following such a pattern, step by step,
the Shah was reduced to a figurehead.

Even though the influence of Iranian political parties was limited on a national scale, by late 1940s the parties had managed to transfer the center of

power from the office of the monarch to the Parliament. Parliament had emerged as the real source of authority in the country, and parties were the mechanism of asserting the national will.

What had enabled them to do this was the introduction of the emotional issues that raised mass enthusiasm and involvement. However, when the parties relied on mass emotion, they entered a one-way street. They could go ahead as long as they rode on the wave of mass enthusiasm, but running the country required rational decisions, which would not always please the people or cause their enthusiastic support. In Iran of the 1940s and early 1950s, the political parties' dependence upon mass enthusiasm and emotionalism had made them captives of their own mode of generating support. They could not accomplish much without introducing emotional issues.

Mossadegh had managed to employ the issue of nationalization of the oil industry as a cause around which to rally masses of people, to create a state of national solidarity, and, therefore, to make the Parliament the most powerful institution in the country. However, the British government and nearly all of the Western powers resisted Mossadegh's efforts to run the nationalized Iranian oil industries. They refused to buy the Iranian oil that was Iran's single most important source of hard currency.

Dr. Mossadegh was eventually locked in an uncompromising position with the Western powers. He had left no room for himself to make political maneuvers, and found he had two alternatives. The first was to yield to Western demands, which meant political suicide for him and his party because the rivals who had joined him would be the first to renege and call him a traitor. But he was uncompromising and would not consider yielding to pressure from the Western powers. His other alternative was to do without oil revenues, because Iran was subjected to economic sanctions by Western companies who refused to buy her oil. However, this also had grave political consequences. The new middle class and the industrial work force, which worked mostly in government-owned industries, formed the core of the party supporters and cadres. They all were dependent upon the state budget, which in turn depended on the oil revenue. Given the time, the government could put certain policies into operation to run the country even if the oil could not be sold, but this could not be done immediately. Therefore, the prolongation of the sanction deteriorated the economy and alienated the political groups who had made a coalition with Mossadegh. Gradually, those who had jumped on the wagon of the oil nationalization movement began to depart, some even making an alliance with the Shah.

In the absence of a large rank and file, and with the people's disillusionment with the earlier political projections of the nationalization drive, Mossadegh lost some of his popular support. Therefore, the fate of his regime and that of the parliamentary democracy had become uncertain. With the resistance of the Western powers in yielding to Iranian demands, with nationalist leaders unprepared for such a foreign reaction, and with massive

pro-Mossadegh demonstrations subsiding, the whole democratic movement
had become quite weak. A royally initiated military coup struck the final
blow. The coup was carried on by the Iranian military, who were supported
by a large group of capital city "lumpans" (Lumpanstrata) who, in turn, initiated mob attacks on the government headquarters. A good portion of the
mob was paid and their leaders were thugs who were the heads of street gangs.
Their leading organizer was known as "Shaaban The Brainless." Behind
the scenes, however, a good number of conservative political groups and
those intimidated with the growing strength of the Tudeh party had made
an alliance with the Shah. It is believed that the CIA and British intelligence
services masterminded the coup.[3]

It is generally believed that Western powers helped to stage the military
coup against Mossadegh's parliamentary democracy because they feared
that the Tudeh party might topple the regime and establish a pro-Soviet rule
in Iran. Their second concern was obviously to break the deadlock of the
Iranian oil problem caused by the nationalization action. In this way, they
would be able to come to an agreement with the Shah, who would assume
full control of the government, and they would once again have access to
Iranian oil.

The Shah, who had fled the country, returned triumphantly to head a military regime in 1953. He had fled when he was faced with a violent mass demonstration following his earlier attempts to remove Mossadegh as premier.
The golden age of Iran's parliamentary democracy was over. So was the era
of party politics in the country, during which the people had openly and directly spoken their political mind. Once again, Iranians were prepared to
pursue their political objectives implicitly under the rule of dictators.

In the decades that followed, it was proven that a military coup removed
some leaders from a position of power, but it did not remove the sentiments
from the people's hearts. Iranians never forgot this golden era of party politics, the struggle for the nationalization of oil, and their short-lived reign of
democracy. Following the coup, Mossadegh was idealized as a great national
leader. Even the next generation of Iranians, who knew little more than his
name, expressed deep respect for him. It seemed that no one was concerned
with the strengths and weaknesses of the policies that had contributed to
Mossadegh's downfall and had enabled the Shah and his allies to stage a
coup. What mattered was the fact that Mossadegh stood as the symbol of
nationalism defending national interests and as the epitome of a constitutionalist. He represented the ideals for which Iranians had been struggling
for decades.

From the pre-coup experiences, the opposition elements had learned some
valuable lessons, as they also did from what had facilitated the coup. It is
generally believed that the same crowd that shouted "Down with the Shah!"
on the morning he fled the country hailed his return to power with shouts of
"Long live Shah!" From such examples, the opposition learned that politi-

cally uneducated masses, emotionalized into supportive crowds, are not a force to rely upon. The bulk of such a crowd, composed of urban "lumpans," might easily switch their loyalty and ally with other groups—even with the Shah himself. The opposition, then, was determined to undertake the rather tedious task of politically enlightening the masses.

This decision was not reached in a convention or as a party policy, because there could be no such gathering held under the new conditions. It was reached by individuals and small groups of activists, as was noticeable from their later accomplishments. Not being able to explicitly state their views and pursue their politicization objectives, they had to once again revert to "implicit modes of action" to incorporate their ideas and messages into cultural, religious, and artistic activities. Due to a long history of oppressive rule, both they and the people they intended to address were experienced enough to successfully implement such an objective.

In contrast, the Shah never recovered from the political sin of the coup. Foreign involvement with the coup and the general belief that Westerners were behind the police state distorted the public image of the Shah. From 1953 on, he was considered by the opposition to be a puppet and was identified with American policy in Iran. Following the coup, the Shah tried very hard for a quarter of a century to change this image through his reforms and policies of economic development. However, he still failed to re-portray himself convincingly. It was quite common to see slogans written on the walls of the university and public places calling him the "American Shah." Political cartoons, during the latest revolution, always pictured him in association with something that symbolized the U.S., such as the American flag or Uncle Sam.

His association with the U.S. policy was made an even bigger issue after the Revolution of 1979. In post-Revolution times, when scores of cartoons appeared in the press or were painted on the walls, there rarely appeared his cartoon without it relating him to the United States. For example, he would be pictured hiding under the robe of Uncle Sam, with some medallions hanging from his chest on which the American flag was painted, or with Uncle Sam posing as a magician and pulling the Shah, with long and bloody Dracula-like teeth, out of his magic box.

The parties that had deserted Mossadegh, especially those who had been allied with the Shah, did not survive. The religious groups who had first supported Mossadegh, but who in the end opposed him, also experienced a political setback. Two parties survived, even though their party organizations were damaged by the post-coup punishments and their activities were banned. These were the National Front (Mossadegh's party) and the Tudeh (which became outlawed). They remained as the two main streams of opposition activism in the country.

This decade of party activism had a far-reaching impact for Iran. It provided Iranians with the skills of modern political organization and modernized their conceptions of society and politics. It was also dominated by the nationalistic movement that had originated with the Constitutional Revolution. However, unlike nationalism under Reza Shah, which was directed toward the material construction of the society, this decade was mainly focused on political modernization. Reza Shah's era was concerned with making heterogeneous Iranians speak, read, write, dress and behave similarly. During this era, Iranians learned to identify with the same collective interest and to develop a sense of nationhood. It was from this perspective that Mossadegh's skillful handling of the nationalization of oil issue contributed to the political development of the country. Even though such development was a major leap forward, it fell short of politically awakening all Iranians, as the preexistence of the feudal regime had kept the bulk of rural people insulated from the events that were occurring in the urban sector.

THE POST-COUP ERA

Following the coup, the government's first action was to ban all political activities and to arrest all the insurgents. The members of the Tudeh party were at the top of the list. Some of their leaders fled the country; those who were caught, especially the infiltrators to the ranks of the military forces, received the severest punishments. Some of them were executed, while others were given long-term sentences because they were less influential. The rank and file members were purged out of the public sector. A similar treatment was given to some non-Marxists who happened to be prominent anti-Shah protesters such as some newspaper editors and National Front members. However, the National Front members did not generally face penalties as severe as those given to the Tudeh party.

The militarized regime would not tolerate any opposition expression or action, crushing all attempts by any means. For all practical purposes, Iran was once again ruled by an absolutist monarch and, in the eyes of the populace, the government policies were his dictation.

A period of political cooling off was forced upon Iranians. The enforcer was an ever-strengthening police system headed by the Shah's military. The military was the backbone of the security elements, complemented by a newly created political police called SAVAK (an Organization for Security and Calmness of the State). With such armed organs ruling, the Iranian Constitutional Monarchy was no longer in existence.

In this police state, security arrangements would guarantee political calm and the enforcement of government policies, and had a crucial role to play in the pattern of change that Iran was to undergo. It consisted of a well-orchestrated composition of different organs. In the center of this composition was the military court that would deal with any opposition political action. The pillars of the police state were SAVAK, the armed forces, some departments of the police, the military court, and an array of top managers of the public organizations who had to cooperate with SAVAK. The people were given the impression that they were all under surveillance. For example, if someone was summoned for questioning, the authorities would bring an envelope full of pictures, showing only one of them and asking "What were you doing with these people in the picture?" They would give the impression that all the pictures in the envelope had been taken secretly. Upon release, the person would automatically spread the news that one's picture was being taken and one's voice was being recorded everywhere. The horrifying torture chambers of SAVAK were known to all. In counteracting opposition activities, the security forces knew no limits. They could detain people as long as they wanted, even for minor suspicions, without any confirming reason. Those killed under torture were unlucky, because no one could charge the security system with such a murder. The reign of terror had silenced the bulk of the political activists, except for some occasional outbursts of demonstrations in certain places. These included the universities, high schools, and the religious school at the holy city of Ghom, where the top Shiia clergy of Iran taught.

Despite its outside image SAVAK, was not as big as it sounded. It existed only in places where it was assumed that there was a potential center for opposition activities. Data was collected nationwide on all suspected opposition activities. For employment in government agencies and government-supported organizations, as well as for promotion to high offices, a candidate had to be approved by SAVAK. All those who wanted to leave the country also had to obtain such permission. In the university, when a professor wanted to take the students on field trips, a copy of a letter of request would have to be submitted to the public relations office. They were in touch with SAVAK and would seek permission for the trip. All publications had to be reviewed by SAVAK; only then could they be published. This was intended to discourage people from writing on political subjects. In most cases, however, those who did write would find ways of saying what they intended in an indirect manner, so as not to sound like something forbidden. It was common to say a book or an article "smells." This meant that it seemed to have some political content. "Political," then, was a word reserved for opposition materials. In the universities, there was a little more freedom as far as what was handed out to the students in manuscripts. However, in the case of a publication, the same content would be found "smelly" by the Censor Bureau and would face denial or other difficulties.

The most horrifying department of SAVAK was its "anti-terrorist committee," which was simply called "the committee." It was this department that was in charge of severe tortures, and would engage in raids upon suspected places. The stories of resistance under these tortures circulated all over Iran, creating myths, and those who were identified with such resistances became legends. Probably the most influential of such accounts was in a book put out by some Marxists as an underground publication, about a woman named Ashraf Dehghani. The book, written in an extremely fascinating form, told about the tortures this woman had received and what she reported seeing done to others. She had managed to escape the SAVAK prison while some women had come to visit her.

The book was her autobiography, although she may have only provided the story and some skillful writers may have prepared the text. By reading the book, one received a horrifying image of SAVAK and was persuaded to resist and even fight such a system, no matter what the risk. The idealization of the resistance in the book had such a strong appeal that it overcame the fears of pain and hardship with which SAVAK was trying to discourage political opposition activism. The stories of this sort were many and they counteracted the psychological warfare that SAVAK had waged against the intended opposition actions.

Nevertheless, SAVAK was only a secret police force; it lacked the capacity to confront major turbulence or large-scale opposition demonstrations and political riots. In such cases, SAVAK would call upon the military units. For example, in the early 1960s, such military units were assigned to help break up student demonstrations at the University of Tehran. It was this kind of role that was making the military the backbone of the police state.

REFORMS

Under the security umbrella of the police state, the Shah began his major developmental project in proposing his reformist acts. With this step, he began where his father had left off in his version of modernization. His main intentions were to consolidate his position and legitimize his absolutist rule. Toward these ends the regime had put two sets of policies into operation. First, there was the policy of increasingly reinforcing the security system in order to crush any resistance toward his sovereignty or the implementation of his programs. Second, there was the policy of putting into operation a systematically developed chain of projects and reforms that were to lead Iran toward the image of an industrialized country. The regime was determined to minimize the constitutional body and to direct the political and developmental affairs of the country from the top, aided by experts rather than politicians. A sort of monarchy-directed technocracy was at the heart of these futuristic projections. The central planning organization was given an important role, and the inflow of the oil revenue was to make the plans operational. Later, this projection was officially called "The Great Civilization." The regime was counting on the success of such projects in order to justify its autocratic rule, as well as its excessive use of oppression. In accordance with these assumptions and intentions, the regime was posing a nationalist-modernist image of itself.

These efforts by the sovereign helped to provide him with some limited success and some degree of popular support, especially following the 1962 land reforms. Meanwhile, some efforts were made to develop certain plans for government participation and the management of the economic development of the country. The idea was not new. Prior to his fall, Mossadegh had been working on a similar task in order to make the Iranian economy independent of oil income. The Shah, being in control of the government, implemented the opposite approach. His was the incorporation of the petrodollars into developmental projects and the national budget. The major efforts that were undertaken in this modernization and socio-economic development of Iran were a series of reforms proposed by the Shah and approved by a national referendom in 1962, and subsequent intensive efforts to mechanize agriculture and industrialize the country. Both of these cases require detailed analysis, because they had grave consequences for the Shah's regime and were the subject of criticism by the opposition.

In February of 1962, the Shah proposed a number of reformist acts and put them to a national referendum. They included the removal of the feudal system, the extension of modern educational services to the rural areas, the nationalization of water and pastoral resources, the elimination of sexual discrimination in politics (giving women the right to vote), and the right to a twenty percent share of the net profit of each major industrial company to the workers who were employed in that industry. The outcome of the referendum was almost unanimously positive. Undoubtedly, it was not a fairly held referendum, but in any case, it received a positive response. I was present at the time in one of the biggest agricultural centers, the city of Gonbad Kavoos, and witnessed the emotional support among the agricultural workers.

The reforms generated some grass roots support for the regime. The support came from those who were benefiting materially from such acts, such as the peasants who each received a plot of land for their own. The reforms caused some opposition, and some concerns also. The opposition came mostly in two forms. Some opposed them because certain aspects of the reforms would violate the traditional value system or would run against their interests, while others opposed them on a theoretical basis. Certain opposition groups saw such an action originating from the Shah as intending to nullify any revolutionary potential of the peasantry by winning over their support and by helping further the commercialization of the rural economy. The political opposition was not generally happy with these proposals, mainly because they would temporarily help to consolidate the regime and remove some sources of grievance that were currently the subject of their criticism. Generally, whatever was done by the regime would be evaluated negatively by the opposition and the intellectuals, because it was not the nature of the action with which they were concerned but with the intention behind it and with those who were initiating it. They refused to think of the regime as a defender of the interest of the people. The leftists viewed the regime as a reactionary one, the protector of a class society and the interests of the upper class and the "Imperialists." Therefore, they refused to accept that such a regime could take any progressive step. They refused, on theoretical grounds, to believe that it ever would or even could initiate any radical changes in the society, because the regime itself occupied the highest level of the class system. They believed that it would never go against its own interests. As a Persian proverb says, "The knife does not cut its own handle." Therefore, they would assume that whatever is done, even if it appears to be progressive, is indeed done with an evil intention. At the same time, neither was the criticism of these acts easy, because it had become an official practice to label such criticism as either "reactionary" or profeudal. Quite ironically, the Shah was posing as a revolutionary. Officially, his reforms were called "White Revolution," as "white" stood for achievement without bloodshed.

To what extent these acts were effective is a critical question to address. Despite their revolutionary appearance, in practice they could not significantly change the class structure of the society. However, they held major consequences for further development of the nation-state, and for commercialization of agriculture.

There is no doubt that by 1962 there were millions of peasants in Iran who were under the oppressive rule of feudal lords. However, feudal lords were no longer the only big agricultural owners. Thanks to the mechanization of agriculture in some newly developed agricultural poles, large pieces of land were under cultivation. In such places, there existed big landowners who were no less rich than feudal lords, but their agro-economy was not a feudal type. They operated on a wage system or a sharecropper system with very few people working. Such lands, in most cases, were not distributed. However, on coastal areas of the Caspian Sea where there were similar cases, large lands with peasant workers rather than wage earners were subjected to some sort of reform. Therefore, the idea did not seem to be due to any opposition to the rich but to do away with a traditional agricultural system that included peasantry.

Feudal lords, having many villages, were free to choose only one village for their own. The status of the peasants in that village, however, would change to wage workers. In the villages where the land was distributed, every peasant would now own the plot that he used to work on.

This kind of land reform differed from what a socialist regime might undertake. In the Iranian case, the land was bought by the state and sold to the peasantry on very long-term payments. The owner was to receive payment of some sort, not according to the market value of his property but according to the book value. The book value was always only a fraction of the market value, sometimes as low as five or ten percent. Therefore, those whose lands were taken were indeed the losers.

There are a number of other points that need to be made about this kind of land reform. At the time of the reform both mechanization and commercialization of agriculture was well on its way, therefore the social basis of feudalism had already been loosened up in many villages. However, because of the cheap labor provided by the peasants, the mechanization came at a slow pace. Therefore, those who lost their peasants could easily compensate for most of the manpower they needed through further mechanization. Following the land reform, those who were not feudal lords, but who had large tracts of land, tried to reduce their dependency on large numbers of wage workers. They feared that the same thing that happened to the feudals might later happen to them. This, in turn, led to the full mechanization of many large agricultural units.

The land reform affected the tribal organization also. Iran's tribal economy was not all nomadic, but composed of mixed economies of both nomads and feudal segments. The land reform, and the nationalization of pastoral and water resources, struck the last blow to the power structure of the tribal khans. These reforms, at least in theory, removed the last obstacles to the formation of a nation-state. To bring about such an objective, though, required more effort and would take years or even decades. The wide gap between classes was just one obstacle to overcome. Iran was a highly stratified society, with wide cultural and income differences separating classes of people. In the case of the rural people, they were far behind other parts of the country both in terms of income and in terms of benefits from modern services. They were predominantly illiterate, spoke in dialects or ethnic languages, were mainly unskilled, and had almost no influential political representation in the power structure of the society. They appeared essentially to be second-class citizens. They did not identify with the modern sectors of the society, nor did they know of the modern political and social outlooks.

The feudal system was removed, but there was no plan to economically elevate these people to the level of the urban population. They could now work on their own land, but the large mechanized sectors of the agro-economy were so efficient that these new small-scale farmers could not in the long run compete with those who benefitted from efficiently mechanized equipment.

The literacy program also had some shortcomings, but it still had significant consequences. The government did not have the capacity nor manpower to build modern schools in the villages; it would have taken years to construct them. High school graduates who were drafted for their military services would receive a short training and become rural teachers. The quality of such educational services fell well below what was offered in the urban areas, where regular professional teachers served. However, even this rather limited service had major consequences. For the first time, a generation of Iranians were growing up who were all (both rural and urban) speaking *farci*, were exposed to the Persian cultural content, would identify with the historical past of Persia, and were identifying with the same nationality and its political values. What complemented this process of Persian conformity was the extension of modern mass media services (mostly television and radio) to the rural areas. Through these channels, which were quite entertaining for the rural people, cultural unification of the whole country was accelerated.

Upgrading the political and social status of women also did not have any major immediate consequences, although it might have in the long run. Iranian women in the rural areas were actively involved with economic activities, and were partners with their men in production. They were as present outside of the house as men, because the small community of villages did not have the kind of differentiation between the home and Bazaar or the residential and commercial sector. There was the land that they worked on and the houses they lived in. Men and women were present in both places. In the city, however, it was not so. Except for a small segment, women in the urban areas were infrequently present in public or economic life. Those who were involved were mostly public employees and school teachers. Some newly developed industries and modern companies would also employ them. Except for those who may have developed a professional image, most rural and urban women, through cultural training, did not possess an independent image of themselves. Even if they had the chance to vote, they would do so as a family, with the influence of men being dominant. Therefore, at least for a while, their political actions reflected the demands of the male strata. In national politics, the vote of no one male or female counted for much because the regime would mastermind rubber-stamped elections. However, on the local level, some votes may have been cast freely, as in committees of a college or school. Such cases were nonpolitical and rare, and would not benefit the masses of women. Only a few may have benefited.

These reforms had other major consequences that did not benefit the regime as much as it did those who opposed it. One such case was the commercialization of agriculture. With the removal of the feudal system, the subsistence agro-economy and barter mode of exchange also disappeared. Agriculture became commercialized even at the level of small farm families who now owned their own plots. Now farmers would sell their products and pay in cash for what they bought. They had more interaction with the market. Unlike the past, peasants, on becoming farm workers, would receive money for what they did. Money became more available in the rural areas than it had been before. With money in their pockets, rural people began to learn consumer habits. These conditions were favorable to Bazaaris, who were no loyal friends of the Shah.

The boom in business activities was paralleled by a sharp rise in the flow of petrodollars during the late 1960s and 1970s.[4] The price of oil and the demand for it on the international market rose sharply. This led to a rapid growth in the service and construction sector which, in the Iranian system, is labor intensive. Therefore, when they did not have much to do on the farm, many villagers would work in towns and could take home a sizable amount of cash. This whole event added to the dynamics of the rural economy and, consequently, to the further integration of rural people into the mainstream of Iran's economic and cultural life. The isolation of the village community had been broken and villagers were coming in more frequent contact with the realities of urban life. Consumer habits had made them look a little more like city people. The mass media and education helped them to talk and think like urbanites. All these trends were heading in the direction of a social and cultural unification of the country that had never before existed. It was through such contacts that dissensions of the urban people reached the villagers, especially those voiced by the religious-oriented groups.

Another negative consequence for the regime was its failure to fill in the vacuum of authority created by the removal of the feudals. The over-Westernized state authorities were too alien to the villagers. The rural people viewed the government figures as state authorities but not as their leaders. They held a similar view of most secular political figures, especially the Marxists intellectuals who talked in dialectical terms and used complicated theoretical language and abstractions such as Imperialism and class conflict. These terms were incomprehensible to the rural people. Also, the cultural standards of the people who used them were highly secular and did not appeal to rural tastes. Therefore, they did not make a good example to follow.

Confronted with the complexities of the society into which they were integrated, rural people had a hard time understanding it. It was even more difficult to understand its politics in order to form their own independent viewpoints and their own conceptions of the national and local political issues.

In the past, the peasantry had had two authorities in the village who provided them with these explanations and suggested social and political ideas. These were the feudals and the clergy. With the old feudals removed and others failing to fill the leading position, the clergy was left unrivaled.

EXPANSION OF THE MIDDLE CLASS

Probably the most significant change caused by the joint consequences of reforms and a booming economy was the rapid expansion of the middle class. Such growth was due to the expansion of whatever organization was financially supported by the state.

A rough estimate of the growth of the middle class shows the number of families increasing from a few hundred thousand in the early 1960s to at least 2,000,000 in the mid-1970s. Just to show one component of this growth, reference may be made to statistics of higher education. In the 1960s and 1970s, Iran's system of higher education expanded quite rapidly. In addition to a rapid growth of colleges at home, tens of thousands of Iranians were attending foreign universities. Compared to the 1960s, when those attending the Iranian universities numbered approximately 23,000, by the early 1970s they numbered close to 80,000 at home and about 20,000 more abroad.[5]

The machinery of the state and the military, which were the biggest government-run organizations, were also rapidly expanding and employing better-educated people, mostly those with a high school diploma or a more advanced degree. Ordinarily, high school graduates would receive salaries that would put them at the lower threshold of the middle class. Such employment was extended to expand the existing units or the new services that had been created. In the 1970s, such employment included hundreds of thousands of individuals, making the state machinery inflated in terms of manpower. Those hired by the industrial and service organizations, which were also growing rapidly, were adding considerably to the list of newcomers to the white-collar ranks.

Because of massive developmental projects and industrial and urban expansion, the labor market for the skilled and semiskilled work force was quite attractive. In the 1970s a shortage of these workers forced the government to hire large numbers from abroad. In a large industrial firm in which I had carried out a research project (a large modern coal mine operation in north central Iran), management's main difficulty was in keeping skilled workers with the company. Quite frequently, they would leave for jobs with better pay or they would open up their own workshops. The pay for these workers was at least equal to that of the well-educated white-collar employees, and enabled them to join the ranks of the middle class.

Obviously the rapid expansion of the middle class was accomplished by recruitment of the urban lower-class workers who had access to skills and education. Some were of rural origin, but their number was not high because the generation of rural people who had received a modern education was not yet old enough to form a significant stratum of the skilled workforce. There were some within the segment of newcomers, however, who had risen up through business, especially those in the booming construction and transportation industries.

A significant element of the middle class was its cultural composition. The offspring of both segments of the middle class—the traditional and the modernized—were equally eager to receive advanced education. They were, most probably, candidates willing to fill the positions recently opened in the white-collar sector. However, the bulk of those raised in traditionalist families still had retained a deep attachment to the traditional way of life and its value systems. It would be difficult to present detailed statistics on such a composition, because the collection and even awareness of statistics was and still is an alien concept for most Iranians, especially on topics that include cultural orientation. However, an analysis of their cultural behavior could be made from physical appearances. From their musical tastes and the dialects with which people spoke, even when on duty in their official jobs or business, one could easily notice that a modernized middle class was quite rapidly becoming less noticeable in the tide of the rural and urban laity who were now entering the middle-class ranks.

As a participant observer of the development of Iran's middle class, one could obviously notice that the cultural composition was shifting to the traditionalist side. This was a stratum in which even until a decade ago, a modernized atmosphere prevailed. For example, the music, dress, and consumer goods that appealed to the modernized segment of the population was distinctly different from what appealed to the rural segment. Even lower class urban taste was not the same as that of the modernized middle and upper classes. In the mid-1970s, music typical of the laity and rural people's taste played from the loudspeakers of the shops that in the past would strictly play records that appealed to the modernized middle class. Increasingly dominant was the presence of traditionalist-oriented people in parks, theaters, restaurants, and recreation areas. A few years earlier, these places had been middle- and upper-class centers with modernized appearances.

In the early part of the century, when the new middle-class groups had just begun to form, they were such a distinct and respected group that entrance to their ranks would eventually persuade a newcomer to conform to their standard. This standard was modernity. It included certain degrees of exhibition of Westernization, partly because the official policy would encourage it. In those days, such positions were mostly educational or in the civil services of the newly created state machinery. People used to look up to these as prestigious positions. In addition, the modernized middle class contained the individuals who were influential in creating role models for the rest of the nation, especially for the new generation of better-educated youth. The bulk of them were intellectuals, political activists, academic figures, and those who manned educational services and the middle managerial positions in organizations. In the 1940s, when political parties were active, their active members were predominantly from this category of people. It used to be the zone of political secularists, modernizers, social and cultural innovators, and a social group that would create a new standard of behavior and transfer it to the new generation.

The newcomers of 1960s and 1970s were entering the rank of middle class at a time when these jobs no longer carried such distinct identity. They were merely jobs like any other jobs. The newcomers had little reason or motive to conform to the standards of modernity that used to be typical of such professions. Their insistence on retaining their cultural identity existed for a number of reasons that will be discussed in the next chapter. At this point suffice it to say that the expansion of the middle class was so rapid that it would not even be adequate for acculturation to a modern mode of life. In addition, there were no motives, as had existed earlier, to identify with a cultural type that was becoming increasingly isolated in the society. Therefore the rapid expansion had altered the earlier composition, from a grouping that was dominated by modernized individuals to one in which modern people were outnumbered.

NEW COMPOSITION OF THE UPPER CLASS

The quarter of a century of reforms and developments that followed the military coup of 1953 worked in favor of the upper class. This class was composed of the Bazaaris, large land owners, large real estate owners, industrial owners, big financiers, former feudals, some of the former tribal chiefs, and a new stratum of business owners who were not Bazaaris. In general, Iranian upper classes received the greatest share of the economic boom and the sharp rise in the oil revenue of the 1970s. Different segments of the upper class prospered for different reasons, and through a variety of channels.

The real estate and land owners, who comprised a large portion of the upper class, prospered from the high rise in the price of land and from the demand for new housing. Because of the joint effect of the mechanization of agriculture, land reform, the booming oil economy, and the attractive wages paid in the urban areas, Iran's urban centers experienced an inflationary rate of growth. Such expansion of urban centers caused an unbelievable hike in the price of land. For example, places located in the north and northeast of the capital city were wastelands and their price, in the 1950s, were at most a few touman per square meter. A decade later, they had increased to about 1000 touman or more (seven touman equaled one U.S. dollar). That is an annual increase of over a hundred percent per year. In the smaller cities, the increase was lower, but it was still many times the rate of the salaries of wage earners and public employees. In the rural areas, some increases were also experienced, especially if the land was close to the cities or in the neighborhood of a newly built industrial center. Hoping to make good profits in the future, people were buying land as far as several miles away from the cities. They knew that the cities were expanding rapidly, and what was now a wasteland could, in the future, become residential areas. It is not known what portion of the oil revenue was eventually pumped into the real estate and land business, but it was clear that a good portion of it had found its way through.

All along the coastline of the Caspian Sea, for hundreds of miles, land had become very valuable. The price of coastal land had jumped from an average of a few dollars or less per square meter in the early 1960s, to a hundred dollars or more by the 1970s. Most of this money was collected by a small class of owners who had influenced this hike in prices. By encouraging the government to lay roads and undertake urban projects in areas nearby or passing through their real estate, they could turn a wasteland into a valuable piece of property, thus making a fortune. Most such cases, then, were associated with a powerful group who had close ties with top government officials. There were strong indications that members of the royal family were the core of the real estate lords. For example, the best coastal area of the Caspian Sea is a 130-mile stretch between Babolsar and Ramsar. In a number of places along this strip, resort towns, and modern apartment and villa complexes had been built in which the royal family held a big share. Another example is a luxurious residential area, planned to include thousands of residential units, which was called Mehr Shahr and built about forty miles west of the capital city. It belonged to a sister of the Shah. This was a large area divided into residential plots of land and some ready-made villas. In addition, on this site the Shah's sister had a multi-million dollar castle built for herself. Even though the place was still underpopulated, with a few hundred houses actually built and occupied, the ministry of roads had rushed to build a modern highway connecting this city to Tehran, while other government units had provided it with telephone lines and piped gas. Such facilities were not provided for many Iranian cities. Examples like this are numerous.

Even if other people had wanted to follow suit, without having close connections with some top-level government officials and royal family members their chances of success would be quite low. The difficulty would be in working through the state bureaucracy. The Iranian bureaucracy functioned according to a set of incongruent rules and regulations. In certain cases, proper regulations were nonexistent in terms of support for such people's investments or attempted objectives. In other cases, ambiguities in the laws and regulations would make it possible for officials to keep such entreprenuers out of the close circle of top real estate lords. Other difficulties would also limit such activities to a few powerful families. For example, main construction materials such as cement were scarce, and people had difficulty in even obtaining a few tons for the repair of their houses. At the same time, influential city developers with connections to the top could get thousands of tons at the official price, which was far below that of the black market. A good portion of the shipment received by influential urban developers would, in fact, find its way into the black market. Indeed, they themselves had been creators of a black market.

Another category of the upper class was engaged with the industrial sector. The bulk of Iran's modern industries was built in the 1960s and 1970s. The main portion of capital for industrial development had its origin in the petrodollar reservoirs. Handsome loans by the government and the banks were behind most such industrial projects. To secure loans in the millions of dollars was beyond the political and economical capacity of ordinary people, for securing such loans required approval from the hands of agencies that were most often of government origin. They required possession of industrial licenses issued by the ministry of industry. Such licenses were not easy to obtain and to get one required great political influence. Given such considerations, it is quite clear why a handful of influential families were developing into the industrial lords of Iran. It was a general belief that in order to succeed, one had to offer some shares to a powerful person, such as one of the brothers or sisters of the Shah.

The nature of such industries was assembly line production, and manufactured pre-fabricated parts. These parts were mostly imported, therefore most of the newly built factories were nothing more than a commercial unit with minor industrial work taking place. In fact, they were distributors of imported commodities, with some Iranian labor combined. Such companies often operated on a license from the producer of the parts, who was a shareholder or receiver of the royalties. Consequently, a good portion of these industries were closely associated with the multinational companies. In an author's study of Albors Industrial City, citing about 250 factories, nearly ninety percent of the industries were using prefabricated parts or materials. Such importation would make these factories, which were built in the 1970s, dependent units. There was reliable evidence to suggest that only fifty families owned most of Iranian heavy industries. Such was also the case with the large modern companies dealing in meat, dairy, and poultry products that had been built on large government loans. They also used imported materials and were more or less owned by those with strong political ties.

The owners of these modern units were associated with the regime politically and culturally, as well as economically. Most of them had a nontraditionalist social image, and people believed that they were the center of a luxurious, pleasure-seeking group, living a lifestyle that included involvement with drugs, gambling, prostitution, and a variety of other immoral acts. They were the target of popular hostility for their monopoly of public resources that caused the spread of bribery and corruption. The bulk of the traditionalist-minded people, unfamiliar with the dynamic aspects of a growing capitalist economy, would associate the economically negative features of what was going on with moral issues, and more specifically with Westernization. Those having broader political knowledge would see it mostly as the consequence of the Western dependency that these people were assumed to promote. The new middle class did not share the same economic and class interests with this new segment of the upper class. However, in two respects they were similar. One was in the associations both groups had with the machinery of the state; the other was in their dominant cultural tendency toward modernity. In the eyes of laity and the traditionalist activists, who viewed the society in cultural and moral terms, these two sub-classes were seen as belonging to the same category—the Westernized one. The hostility against the new upper class, then, which had an economic-moral nature, was projected as well onto the new middle class, a group that was only the victim of their modern tendencies. They had to pay some of the cost of what the upper class was doing. Both of these groups were seen by some antimodernity activists as the products of the Pahlavi dynasty (the Shah and his father). From a cultural perspective, they symbolized a counter example of what was called the "mass culture."

BUSINESS GROUPS

The Bazaaris, together with others who are involved in business and are scattered all over the various cities and towns, form the bulk of Iran's business class. At the moment, it is likely that this stratum is the single most powerful group in the country, with the nucleus of their power residing in the main Bazaars of the large cities. The source of the power of the Bazaar community lies in the present day composition of the Iranian economy, and in its organization, wealth, political experience, and strategic connections with influential religious groups and personalities. During the economic boom of the 1960s and 1970s, the Bazaaris had also benefited significantly from the regime's developmental projects and the petrodollar inflow. With the abundance of the petrodollars, the Bazaaris had no difficulty exchanging Iranian money for foreign currency, and had their freedom in shopping abroad. They were transformed into a channel through which consumer goods from all over the world could be fed into Iran. The expansion of the middle class, the opening up of the rural market, and the abundance of money in people's pockets were all good news for the Bazaaris. They did not have to worry about demand, because the market for consumer goods was rapidly expanding.

Even though the Bazaaris had no less income than the new segments of the middle class, nor any less expensive lifestyle, they still never became the target of much hostility. This was because the Bazaaris had a political image of being unfriendly to the regime and a social image of being faithful to the Iranian cultural-religious tradition. Their 19th- and 20th-century political activities and support of the Constitutional Revolution and their subsequent support of the National Front and religious dissentive groups in the 1940s had contributed to the formation of these images. It was generally believed that Bazaaris were puritan oriented, religious, and nationalist. This image was reinforced by what people saw in the Bazaar community, which itself observed strict Islamic moral and cultural standards. In a country where the bulk of the people look at society from moral and religious perspectives, such observations blind them to the conflicts of economic interests. The Bazaaris may have been seen as profiteers and greedy, and people may have criticized them, but they were not confronted as an enemy. Within this context, the Bazaaris were indeed Iran's version of the national bourgeoisie. Culturally, they were typified as the core of the mass culture type, in the same category with the laity. The religious leaders who were antagonizing people against both upper and middle class modernists had very little to say against the Bazaaris. For example, after the Revolution, when the religious leadership took over, committees were set up in the public sector and in universities and schools to weed out those who were assumed to be supporters of the fallen regime. These committees were called "cleaning-up committees." Rarely was any such committee set up in the Bazaar.

After the Revolution, many of the businessmen who had previously imported consumer goods were encouraged to become manufacturers of these very goods. Big profits also reinforced this encouragement. Some of them received sizable bank loans and favorable licensing, which helped them manage to establish brand-new factories to manufacture the items they used to import and distribute. In such cases, the Ministry of Industry would give these distributors priority. Now, their same old business center had become the center for the distribution of their own products. With the expansion of such industrial involvement, the role of Iran's Bazaar is changing—from a commerce center to an industrial center. The Bazaaris, then, are on their way to becoming Iran's industrial capitalists.

The economic boom of the 1960s and 1970s had increased national prosperity for all classes. However, with the expansion of the middle class and the increase of their buying power, scarce resources were being farther and farther removed from the lower classes. The only exceptions were what the government would import in sufficient quantities, such as rice and cooking oil. For example, the increase in the price of land and medical services were no match for what the lower classes may have gained from the economic boom. Because of the government policy of the importation of the basic needs of the people in large quantities, people were not severely feeling the pressure of inflation. They were merely seeing the widening of the class gap. The relative economic situation was seen as detrimental to the lower classes. For example, the average government employee, who was uneducated or had less than a high school degree, would receive at most about 1000-2000 touman per month, while the white-collar employees, who had high school diplomas or advanced degrees, would receive about three times that salary. In the 1970s, there was a sizable increase in everyone's salary scale. For the white-collar employees, the increase was quite attractive, with bonuses amounting to more than a blue-collar employee's total salary. The same low-salary scale applied in industries, except for highly skilled or semiskilled workers whose skill was in high demand.

Similar arguments could be made for the rural people. The introduction of modern services and land reform had boosted their level of income and improved their living conditions. However, despite these positive aspects, the gap between rural and urban people was widening. Due to the excessive importation of agricultural products, especially grain, the price of farm products did not rise as fast as the cost of living. One of the main farm products was wheat. For a few years, the price of wheat was kept constant at one touman per kilo by the importation of millions of tons of it. This was at the time when the rural buying power was reduced by about twenty percent annually, because of inflation. It should be noted that because of the material modernization, the lifestyle of the rural people had changed and they now had new demands. Their overall expectations and living costs were much more than what they had been in the past. Not many members of the urban and rural lower classes actually tried to compare themselves to the middle or upper classes, however, to see if they were relatively better off or not. They compared themselves with their own past and many of them were happy to see some improvements. Not seeing the differential benefits that they were receiving from the booming petrodollars era, they may have felt satisfied with the economic situation.

INTELLECTUALS

Another by-product of the reforms was further expansion of the stratum known as "intellectuals." In this book we have often referred to intellectuals.

Intellectuals are a force that play a significant role in the politicization of people, at least within this century, and more so in the second half of it. The category of people who were considered to be intellectuals were the idea makers and the idols of the politically active youth, and they were respectable figures in the eyes of better-educated Iranians. Their supporters would look up to them to become enlightened on the processes that were changing their society and for insights into the directions that these changes should or would take. Not every person who held an advanced academic degree was considered to be an intellectual. Even college students would look up to a person who might not have earned a degree in social studies as the source of theoretical thinking, while at the same time totally ignore the whole faculty of a department of social sciences. The answer to why they would do this lies in what is meant by intellectuals.

To understand "intellectuals," one needs to consider certain political features of the country and its recent historical events. Iran has always been ruled by conservative political elites. The despotic kings, the feudals, the tribal khans, the religious leadership, even the influential core of the Bazaaris were all conservative forces making up the pillars of Iranian political power. Those who would seek radical change rarely had access to the instruments with which to implement their objectives, except in times of bitter quarrels between the elite and during times of breakdown of the political order. These occasions would come to an end quite soon, and once again, the system would maintain its conservative political order, with the seekers of radical social change finding themselves confined only to subjective actions. Being left out of the administrative system, they lacked the means to put their ideas into practice. What we have called the golden era of party politics in the 1940s and the early 1950s was a unique historic period during which seekers of the democratic and the radical change had a chance, despite their small size, to play a significant role in the country. Following the CIA-royal military coup of 1953 and the crackdown on radicals, such people were once again deprived of the opportunity to help bring about their desired social changes. If they were journalists, for example, their licenses were voided; if professors, they were kicked out of the university; if the head of a factory, they were removed to a less vital position. Those who could not be identified still held their jobs, though they could not act freely, fearing the reaction of the regime.

With minor exceptions, then, the only choice left for the change seekers and idealists in this society was to engage in theoretical work and subjective actions; that is, to load their work—whether artistic, social criticism, or religious preaching—with political intentions and political content. These figures were known to the people as dissentive and as having a commitment. In the case where they had experiences such as some jail sentence and torture because of their political activities, their supporters believed them even more, seeing them as being sincere in what they were saying. Quite often, the leading figures of this stratum knew one another personally, through the political prison terms that they had served, or via the works of one another that they had read. They therefore had a sense of belonging to a community—the community of intellectuals. This would make the intellectuals not just a number of individuals, but a collective and a political grouping—a dissentive social force.

This was not a closed community, but was open to those who could qualify to climb into it. Quite often, influential figures within this community would make up a pole around which other intellectuals who were their followers would congregate. In addition, this composition was a pluralistic one. For example, there were distinguished intellectuals belonging to a wide spectrum of ideologies, people such as Beh Azin (Tudeh party activist), Hadj Saiied Djavadi (liberal), Ayatollah Talghani and Ali Tehrani (distinguished clergymen), Soltanpoor (a leftist poet), and Seemin Daneshvar (an academician). For intellectuals the growth of mass media and the expansion of the better-educated stratum had positive consequences. With that the consumers of their cultural and theoretical works had increased.

It is reasonable to claim that Iranian intellectuals were the source of the impetus to ideological change, the ones who helped radicalize the people, especially the better-educated youth, and those who helped to expand the social and political awarenesses of the population in general. Through them, Iran's cultural, social theoretical, artistic, and literary creations were enriched.

NOTES

1. The anniversary of the reassertion of the rule of the central government in Azarbaijan was celebrated every year by the Shah's regime. Its purpose was to credit both the Shah and the military forces.

2. The struggle with the British company that controlled the Iranian oil industry had begun during the reign of the Reza Shah. Dr. Mossadegh later formulated a nationalization plan that he eventually managed to put into practice.

3. K. Roosevelt, "How the CIA Brought the Shah to Power," *The Washington Post*, May 6, 1979.

4. M. N. Pesaran, "Economic development and Revolutionary Upheavals In Iran," in *Iran: A Revolution in Turmoil*, edited by H. Afshar (London: Macmillan, 1985), p. 24.

5. *Iran Almanac, 1972* (Tehran, Iran: Echo of Iran, 1972), p. 555.

8

Intellectual Preparation for Revolution

THE PREPARATION FOR THE REVOLUTION

Iranians who revolted in the later 1970s had already been ideologically and psychologically prepared. With this open confrontation with the regime, a revolution had taken place in their social and cultural perspectives. This development had made some of the more politically active citizens determined to go beyond their tradition of protests against autocracy by demanding the alteration of the whole system. Their subjective preparation was made through a number of emerging tendencies that resembled a return to a traditional life and outlook. Some of the more important tendencies were the following:

1. The cultural and religious revitalization movements
2. The formation of an image of the existing Iranian society as one in which a struggle was ongoing. With such a conception, they would make specific political judgments about themselves and others. These judgments were based on what position a person, a group, or even a political force would take in relation to this presumably ongoing struggle.
3. A tendency had become generalized, so larger categories of people began to look for a new explanation of social and political reality, especially those with some theoretical content.
4. More and more frequently, people were attracted to the explanations that discredited the existing regime, its policies, and its projections of a futuristic Iran.

Such beliefs and experiences together contributed toward orienting millions of Iranians, mainly the educated youth and the middle class, toward a struggle for a new social order, radically different from the current status quo.

It looked more like an age of enlightenment, of the involvement of large groups of people with issues that are ordinarily of academic concern. Discussions about social existence, the role of religion in society, and the causes of dependency reflected in the people's new orientation toward culture, religion, and art appreciation. A new round of efforts was made by writers and political and religious ideologues to express their anti-regime ideas, mostly indirectly, through the media available to the public. Such occurrences were quite frequent, and were developing into popularly supported movements.

The intellectually charged movements were mainly concentrated on college campuses, in high schools, among the employees of the mass media, and among the better-educated middle class who were immersed in the public and private sectors. Indeed, these were the hot spots of Iran, where opposition to the regime had never stopped. In the 1970s, such strata were large enough to include millions of people. However, most of their members were not on the side of the opposition, let alone politically minded. The number who were was still large enough to make the whole stratum a fertile ground for the opposition movements. It is quite reasonable to claim that the better-educated urbanites and modern-minded strata in general had intensive political knowledge and concerns.

Two consequences of such movements were that they made the status quo look illegitimate, hollow, immoral, ephemeral, and alienating, and that they showed the people the alternative social settings toward which they could strive.

This accomplishment went beyond making the rule of an absolutist Shah appear illegitimate to making the whole social system of the country seem improper. Such a general outlook would naturally include the sovereign order as well. Increasingly, the opposition managed to make the Shah's apparently fascinating empire look ugly in the eyes of many Iranians. It even looked ugly in the eyes of many of those who were indeed benefiting from it and who had previously seen it as attractive.

In the pages that follow, the major trends of these events will be discussed. The objective will be to show how they contributed to the revolution.

THE ONGOING STRUGGLE

In the decade preceding the Revolution, the generally held view was that a "struggle," or *mo-ba-re-zeh*, was concurrent in the society. The two sides of this struggle were not clearly defined. It was more or less viewed as "the people vs. the regime." The "regime" meant the composition of the monarchy and its supportive police state, plus foreign dominators. The U.S. was considered the main dominating power. The direction of the struggle, then, was toward the alteration of the status quo.

Coupled with the notion of a struggle was another concept called "commitment," or *ta-ah-hod*. It had been started by Marxists, to whom the offering of a Marxian mode of explanation was an essential requirement of being considered an intellectual. The criterion for such recognition was the conscious attempt to contribute to the ongoing "struggle." In other words, one needed to be a social theory-minded individual who would side with the oppressed people. Later on, "commitment" became a standard cliche applied by non-Marxists as well, those whose opposition to the regime was well known, to distinguish them from others who were politically indifferent. It was a prestigious and popular identity that carried some charisma. Calling a person a "committed" author, filmmaker, or social scientist, was equal to making him or her an idol for certain groups. It should be noted that such a commitment was more than altruism. It had to be reflected in one's works which in turn would contribute to the "ongoing struggle." It therefore required having both a theoretical perspective and a political intention of opposition.

Gradually, the number of people identified as being "committed" began to increase considerably. The term began to be used in a more or less relaxed way to apply to all those who showed some sign of opposition to the regime. At this stage, commitment was no longer a word reserved for intellectuals. A wide range of professionals and large categories of people were referred to as being "committed." A "committed" filmmaker, for example, was one who would show the exploitation and oppression of the poor and weak in the society. Being known as "committed" had evolved, for a large number of intellectually oriented individuals and groups, into a sort of political fad that reflected the growth of the opposition movements.

CULTURAL POLARIZATION

As already noted, in the decades before the Revolution the expansion of the Iranian middle class resulted in the outnumbering of the modernized segment of the society. This rather rapid expansion altered the cultural composition of this stratum. Newcomers into the ranks of the middle class, however, seemed to insist on preserving their cultural identity, which was a deviation from a historical norm set down during the early part of this century. Such an insistence existed for a variety of reasons, and for many was a deliberate attempt. They would merely do so because they were raised as traditionalists and there was no reason to alter their lifestyle. For others it was deliberate because they had developed a "commitment" toward it. What had induced this commitment was due to certain ideological developments in the society that idealized traditional orientations.

During the last few decades, modernity had become a controversial issue for the general populace as well as for politically minded intellectuals. Unlike the early 20th century, in the latter part modernity was no longer viewed by better-educated Iranians as a superior way of life.

Criticism of the modernity was not new in the 1960s and 1970s. Indirect criticism had been in the air for decades, especially following Reza Shah's forceful Westernization attempts. For example, a fictional stereotype of a young man who had been overtly Westernized and called *"foo fool khan,"* was the laughing stock of the laity for decades. But it was more than a comic case. Another example was the lesser-known novel entitled *Small in New York*. Small was a sarcastic nickname for a rather common Iranian name, *Iss-ma-eel*. The character of the story, Small, was a tattooed thug, deeply immersed in the Iranian lay culture. This book put into a satiric perspective his entrance into New York and the problems that he faced because of his cultural differences. The book was read mostly in a comic manner. At the same time, however, it functioned to release a certain amount of anxiety generated by these drives toward modernization.

A more theoretical book was written by a leftist Iranian, Djalal Al e Ahmad, who was a highly respected writer.[1] The title of the book is translated as "Westomaniac." It is a critical writing on the consequences of Westernization. It includes a criticism of certain categories of people who were conditioned to see everything in the West as superior and more advanced than what they had. Therefore, they would blindly follow and advocate Westernization. From the 1960s on, this book had become the Bible of those whose ideal of a way of life was that of the traditionalist Iranians.

It was mainly in 1970s that Westernization became a major controversial issue on all social levels. It found widespread support in the middle class and the intellectual community. This was in contrast with the tendencies, in the earlier part of the century, of members of these same strata who had helped to popularize Western orientations.

Apparently, all those who had developed a criticism of modernity did not have the same reasons for their disapproval. Modernity, in the cultural sense, was identified with the regime and its projections of a futuristic Iran. For religious people, it was mostly the secular and non-Puritan exhibitions to which they objected. The radical views focused mostly on political and economic explanations. From what one would hear such critics say, one could make the following generalized explanation. They seemed to argue that Iranian modernization, in both cultural and noncultural aspects, was a specific policy, consciously directed from above by the regime. Its operators were a segment of the upper and middle class. Assuming that the regime was dependent on the West, they saw the modernization effort as a part of the Western hegemony. Culturally, modernity was therefore paving the road for a further absorption of Iran into the Western sphere of influence and dominance. Westernization would force the people to think and act like Westerners. This, in turn, would socialize the people toward Western consumption, habits, and tastes. By losing their cultural independence, they would lose their originality, and intellectual creativity. They would merely become consumers of the West, not only of the goods, but of ideas and cultural productions as well. Thus, criticism of Western influence was not due to these groups' fanatic attachment to a traditional way of life. They instead had a political reason for their actions.

Eventually, all these tendencies found one general reference called "mass culture" (*Farhang e tudeh*). This was a concept that would put the laity at the focus, in contrast to the elite-centralism that was emphasized by the regime and its supportive stratum. For the Iranians, "mass culture" was a concept that differed from its general meaning in Western social science. A mass culture orientation was a counter example to the modernized way of life. In the Iranian context, mass culture was a political-cultural term. For the laity, it was their way of life, to which they may have attached no significant political meaning. For modern-minded intellectuals, who had idealized it, it was the way of life for the laity who were still untouched by Western influence. In addition, it showed their sympathy and devotion to the lower class that was the center of the Iranian laity. They would rather see a people's lifestyle remain in isolation from Western influence and have a chance to develop in terms of its own internal potential. "Mass culture," then, was the medium through which this hypothetical, independent growth could emerge. In view of the important political consequences of the "mass culture" movement, this concept needs to be elaborated on.

In Iran, the common man had never been idealized. The monarchs and the princes had always been idealized and, for the religious people, the saints (imams) were held up as heroes and models. The cultural policy of the regime, as it was reflected in programs offered by the state-controlled media, were elitist. Although the bulk of the Iranian population was of the lower class, their problems and cultural potential, their lifestyles and potential for cultural creativity, were undermined by the media. In contrast, the movie actors, sports champions, international playboys, and luxurious-minded rich were typical of what the mass media would display. This applied more to the content of magazines and the television programs. It seemed to be the official policy of the regime. This author had a personal experience that shows that the regime was pursuing a policy of ignoring mass culture. In a textbook I had prepared for sociology students, a few paragraphs were devoted to the discussion of such elitist tendencies in the media. When I tried to reprint the book, the Censor Bureau, which was in charge of the issuance of the permission for publications, denied me this permission. They forced me to cross out that whole page from the book.

One reason why mass culture was emerging as the center of intellectual interest was the efforts of the opposition groups to counteract the regime's cultural policies. It was in contrast to the elitist orientation, promoted by the regime, that radical-minded intellectuals were trying to counteract its cultural efforts. An exmaple is the leftist writers who followed the lead of Russian revolutionary writers such as Gorky or other European playwrights and social critics in idealizing the masses. With the shift of focus from the elite to the laity, a revolution was taking place in the domain of Iranian literature, theater, the composition of popular songs, movies, and poetry. For example, the works of writers such as the playwright Dr. Sa e di held great attraction. Typically, his works concentrated on a description of the cultural and psychic behavior of the masses. He presented critiques of Iranian society in an artistic fashion. He was forceful in showing the miseries caused by the exploitation of the masses in a society that was not moving in a direction that would respond to the needs and interests of the common man. At the same time his ability to shed light on the dark corners of Iranian society was amazingly successful. His efforts were reinforced by the further help that he received from radical moviemakers. Some brilliant filmmakers made a number of movies on his writings. Such movies were both nationally and internationally well received, and generated new incentives for certain Iranians to rediscover the masses and their lifestyle.

The expansion of the educated urban stratum was also an encouragement for these writers, artists, and filmmakers because the internal market for sophisticated productions was rapidly expanding. These movies were not limited to the writings of Dr. Sa e di. A variety of intellectually oriented Iranian playwrights and filmmakers were involved with similar works. All of them focused on the life of laity, and often involved a radical political message implicit in their stories. What was happening in the realm of literature and popular art was no longer the creation of an incidental masterpiece in the life of the common man, but was a movement that had its objective in revitalizing the laity and the oppressed.

Such cultural and artistic productions were finding their most enthusiastic audience among the better-educated stratum, middle-class youths, and even some of the upper class. They were distracting these people from imported productions and counteracting "Westomaniac" tendencies. A new sense of pride was generated among these citizens, who not only saw the Iranian abilities as admirable, but who also considered some of the domestic productions far superior to the imported ones. Simply put, a shift was taking place away from the earlier elitism and Western-oriented lifestyle toward a domestic centralism. This shift was not limited to the domain of art, but was beginning to expand to political and ideological items as well. This turning away from Westernization was reflected in a wide range of the people's behavior.

For example, even up to the early 1960s, one could hardly find a first-class Iranian theater play or an Iranian movie. All the high class theaters showed Western works, particularly American movies. In parties and social gatherings of the modernized upper class and even of the modernized segment of the middle class, one could rarely hear an Iranian record being played. In the later 1960s, trends began to change. Gradually, one saw even in certain upper class youths a pride in identifying with the intellectual and artistic resources of Iran. These were the same people that earlier had despised domestic culture and ideologies. The trend was even stronger among the middle class. With such intellectual reinforcements, middle-class youths began to orient themselves inwardly in order to identify with Iranian sources. It was a political fad of the day to look and act "khaky" or "Khalghi," meaning "down to the earth," and "lay-oriented," respectively. It must be mentioned that this conversion was not a new cultural innovation, but only a shift in value reorientation within the existing Iranian cultural system. Behavioral styles and value systems, which supported such reorientation, were already in existence within the system. However, what was innovative was that they incorporated a political meaning into their reorientation and provided it with radical interpretations. It appeared that a cultural revitalization movement had been generated. In fact, what was happening, at least for these intellectually oriented groups, was not precisely a cultural revitalization but a political movement that expressed the negation of the regime's social and cultural policies. In addition, it was radical in the sense that it was promoting the causes of the laity in a system that was strongly elitist.

SHIIA REVITALIZATION

The tendency to idealize the laity received another reinforcement with the increasing demands for a theoretical explanation of their problems and potential. These concerns were not limited to secular works. Islamic activists were also providing their supporters with certain explanations that utilized concepts and approaches of an academic style. Iranian culture, being heavily interfused with Islamic values and thoughts, was making little distinction between the lifestyle of the laity and that of the Moslem people. Therefore, the new intellectually inspired interest in religion overlapped with those that had secularly motivated concerns for mass culture.

Islamic-minded intellectuals were also showing interest in addressing religious issues in terms of contemporary social scientific concepts. Their ideas were even less alien to educated minds than they were the secular minds because they used concepts that referred to Islamic values, thoughts, and practices that most people knew well through socialization. For example, in the early 1960s, Mehdi Bazargan, who was later to be chosen as first prime minister of the Islamic regime, wrote on "love and worship" using key concepts that came from his field of specialty, the science of thermodynamics. He had been a professor of thermodynamics at the University of Tehran. The Ayatollah Mottahari was touring campuses, addressing students on religious issues using academically acceptable language and interpretations. Ali Shariati was another whose works will be discussed in some detail. In the holy city of Ghom, the centers for Islamic propaganda were releasing some materials in an attempt to attract better educated groups. For example, the journal of the "Islamic school of thought," *Maktab Islam*, was trying to make such an appeal.

Dr. Ali Shariati, in the late 1960s, was emerging as the central figure of the new wave of theoretical teaching in Islam.[2] His ideas were rapidly finding receptive ears in all classes of the society. He became known as "the Doctor." It was common to hear people say, "the Doctor said . . . ," and one always knew that they were quoting Dr. Shariati. He was a man committed to Islam, specifically to Shiiaism. He was familiar with modern social and philosophical reasoning, holding a doctorate degree from France. In Iran he was teaching Sociology of Religion and had his own theories on religion and society. In his view, religion was not something for ancient generations but fit quite well into the modern era. From Islamic thought, he had derived his theories of society, politics, and even of revolution. In the post-revolutionary era, he was referred to by millions of his devoted supporters, most of them radical Moslem youths, as "the theoretician of the Islamic Revolution," or "the teacher of the Revolution." Some of his radical supporters considered his conception of Shiiaism as "Red Shiiaism," standing for martyrdom and revolution. It was to distinguish the Shiia orientations of Imam Hosein and Imam Ali from the Shiia orientation of the pacifist clergies who were sometimes called "Safavid Shiiaism." It was common to call Red Shiiaism *Alavi* Shiiaism, or the Shiiaism of Imam Ali who was the father of Imam Hosein. He symbolizes a fighting personality who fought for the promotion of Islam. Therefore, the Red and *Alavi* Shiiaism and Imam Hosein's Shiia orientation are one and the same. They all mean that Shiia Islam is the religion of martyrdom, of revolution, and of a resistance to oppression. Followers of this Shiiaism are known for their unwillingness to compromise with the political elite and their struggle against whom they view as illegitimate rulers.

Dr. Shariati's lectures, held in large Islamic centers, attracted thousands of enthusiastic youths, while copies of his lecture notes reached thousands more. His call for "de-alienation" was intended to assist his followers in returning to what he termed their own social and religious identity. One of his messages urged the "re-discovery" of one's own true being, by ridding one's self and the society of alien influences. In this case, he was referring to a return to what he would term "true" Islam.

Shariati's ideas may not be considered universal because they were confined to the domain of those socialized and committed to Shiia Islam. However, within that domain, his ideas had proven to have a strong magnetic force that attracted the better-educated youths. With him as the theoretician, the movement was generating in a nationwide form a religious revitalization that now bears his name. Nearly every concept of the movement has Dr. Shariati's name stamped upon it. It even generated an underground armed organization, which resulted in his arrest and detainment by SAVAK. Shariati later left the country and died mysteriously. His supporters believed that his death, which was announced as a heart attack, was really caused by SAVAK. Regardless, his supporters consider him a martyr and paint his face red in the posters they make of him. As previously noted, red has a dual meaning in this case; it signifies both Red Shiiaism and martyrdom.

Shariati was not offering a limited criticism of the Westernization of Iranian culture, but a general view of the de-alienation that, as one of its consequences, would include stripping the people of Western influence. His works were merely a broad discussion of the society, history, and religion. What he was suggesting was an alteration of the system in order to rebuild

it around an Islamic world view and its practices. At the same time, his work
was a criticism of Shiiaism as it was practiced under the influence of the clergy.
In his view Shiiaism was a process that, by becoming institutionalized into
the role of the hierarchical clergy and integrated into the political system of
Safavids, had lost its revolutionary potential and become a hollow concept.

For example, a glimpse of his view of history may shed some light on how
he thought. Shariati's view paralleled the Marxian conception of historical
change, although with a different form of explanation. The resemblance
was in the fact that both views assume a moving force. For the Marxian explanation, it is the conflict of class interests that is the source of change, while
for Shariati, it was human beings who were fighting for their ideals. Noting
that a martyr plays this kind of a history-making role, he said, "A martyr is
the heart of history." He also said that by offering one's blood, the martyr
"pumps life into the veins of history," and keeps it moving. He was suggesting a practical solution to changing an oppressive system. In his view, if people were ready to act, even if their blood was to be spilled, they would win.
This was why the martyr would play a central role in his conception of history. Similar to Marx, who began speaking about primitive communes, Shariati, like other Shiia thinkers having a Koranic view of history, would begin
with "Adam's" time. This is a common practice in Shiia teaching. It is a
way of keeping track of the injustices that have shed innocent blood. From
this, a historical chain of struggles and sacrifices is derived. However, unlike
the Marxists, Shariati was an idealist in that he gave priority to one's ideals.
It was ideals, specifically religious ideals, that motivate an individual to sacrifice his life and therefore become a martyr.

Martyrdom, then, is the ultimate action taken by a person who volunteers
to fulfill his religious commitments to his fellow men and is against the ty-
rants. This view of historical change is reminiscent of the Ayatollah Khomeini's message to the Iranians, issued from his headquarters in Paris during
the peak of their revolution, that "Blood wins over the sword."

In Shariati many Iranians found their own social and political theorist
who derived his ideas from the intellectual resources of Islam and who spoke
in a language familiar to them. Such a theoretical treatment of Islamic teaching was "blowing the minds" of many of the Iranian youths, encouraging
them toward radical action. Given the condition of Iran in the 1970s, the
slightest opposition to the regime cost one one's life. What challenged these
radical youths was the idea of how far they were ready to go in their anti-
regime actions. If they were going to generate a serious threat, they had to
have an outlook and logic to justify the cost that they were going to pay.
The theory of martyrdom was providing them with these justifications. This
state of mind of the radical youth can only be understood if we imagine the
powerlessness of a nation that had struggled for decades, bearing heavy losses,
and yet had not been able to do away with a dictatorial regime and police
state. Under those conditions, Shariati seemed to be offering a solution that

was reinforced by a theory of history and by the people's religious value system, and most importantly, was offering it during a time when the question, "How?" was on many people's lips. Then, Shariati's views quite convincingly suggested to many hotheaded youths that through fearlessness and preparing to sacrifice their lives, they could accomplish their revolutionary dreams. He was suggesting that if they were committed enough to offer their lives for a cause, they were guaranteed to win.

As the general trend toward religion and cultural revitalization was proceeding, the religious groups were attracting more people than any other. Their success was not without reason. For those better-educated Iranians, who had still maintained some degree of religious commitment, the acceptance of a materialistic explanation of society was rather annoying. They may have hesitated to listen to the clerical view, considering the clergy to be dogmatic and out of tune with a contemporary social scientific explanation.

The rapid spread of the influence of Dr. Shariati and other Islamic intellectuals may have also had a social-psychological explanation. For millions of Iranian youths brought up under an Islamic tradition, secular thought had a certain attraction. Being educated in the institutes offering secular content, they received a logical-empirical explanation of nature and social phenomena. In addition, they had been exposed to radical political explanations. For example, they had learned the class conflict interpretations of the social phenomenon, which was quite common to the Iranian intellectual community. Such students developed a strong sense of theoretical reasoning. This is why the supernatural explanation and reasoning of the clergy was, quite often, not convincing to most of them. However, they were still under such a strong religious influence that even if they could not logically and rationally justify their beliefs, they were not ready to give them up. Such beliefs were a pillar of their psychic structure as well as being deeply molded in their social relationships. This was specifically true for newcomers to the stratum of the better-educated urban middle class, especially those with rural and lower-class backgrounds. It was also true with the offspring of the Bazaari people and the traditionalist middle class who had raised their children with strong Islamic commitments. Such youths saw a contradiction between their educational training, which had taught them to accept only what was explained empirically and rationally, and their own religious reasoning. They were finding themselves in a state of "cognitive dissonance."

The emergence of people like Dr. Shariati was exactly what these people had been looking for. His views helped them to dissolve this state of dissonance, because he reassured them of their religious beliefs while still providing them with a similar, political reassurance through an academic style of reasoning and an interpretation of Islam that was radical and revolutionary. His reasoning and conclusions were in tune with the political atmosphere that was anti-status quo, and oriented toward altering the system. His egalitarian views had satisfied the class hostility that most of his supporters, having lower-class origins, held against the regime and the cultural chauvinism of the modernized sub-classes, which they considered the regime's supportive base.

Those who were attracted to Shariati had close ties with the masses of the middle and lower classes and very soon spread his messages all over the country. So did the nature of his teaching, which interpreted Shiia Islam as a revolutionary struggle. The two went together quite logically—social class and the mental condition of the bulk of the educated youth, along with the theoretical reasoning of Dr. Shariati. People could identify with his theoretical position and his revolutionary Shiia doctrine. These were no longer Shariati's ideas, but belonged to a movement that Shariati merely symbolized. Dr. Shariati's movement crossed the boundary of the educated youth and found a stronghold beyond. One stronghold was among the middle and lower levels of the Bazaaris, who were the central core of the Bazaar's politically minded activists. In my estimate, based on personal observations of Iranian youths in the 1970s, the young men who were Dr. Shariati's committed disciples outnumbered supporters of all other political groups who were committed to oppose the system.

Masses of people, especially from the lower class and the rural population, were concerned with intellectual occurrences on the opposition's side. Some of them were in touch with these ideas through their youngsters. In Iran, young people stay with their parents until they get married. Therefore, even uneducated parents have the opportunity to interact with a generation that is tuned in to the political events of the day. One of the most entertaining events of family life in many Iranian homes is the scene of parents arguing with their youngsters on political issues. The former, lacking the educational background of their offspring, often try to talk at their intellectual level using academically defined concepts that they have heard their youngsters use. Not properly knowing the meaning of such concepts as "Imperialism" and "bourgeoisie," they sometimes end up saying things that transform the family debate into a comedy.

However, within the stratum of less-educated people, some noticeable developments were also taking place. Following the Khomeini-led mass protests of 1963, a new sense of activism was emerging in the religious circles of the laity. Preachers, more often the young ones who had been the Ayatollah's students in Ghom, were preaching with political intentions. One major topic of which they preached concerned Imam Hosein and his uprising. In such talks, they would intentionally refer to the oppressive condition of his contemporaneous government, against which Imam Hosein had revolted and against which the whole incident of his martyrdom occurred. Some clergymen would lead their discussions in order to help the listeners come to their own conclusions about the present state of affairs, showing how the regime of the Shah resembled that of the hated Yazid, against whom Imam Hosein fought and died. Yazid's rule had no legitimacy according to Shiia believers.

Quite often SAVAK would arrest these preachers upon their departure from the mosque. This would generate concern among those who attended such preaching and would reassure them that the present regime was indeed anti-Islamic as these preachers had just been implying.

The clergy also had their own concept of an alternative to the existing system, which had some appeal to the laity. They had long ago formulated their version of the Islamic government, and were even teaching it in the clerical schools. It was a theocracy in which the clergy would implement and safeguard Islamic practices and rules. In fact, they had a full text of an Islamic economy, which was presented to their audiences.

With further fermentation of the opposition views, both religious and nonreligious, the core of the intellectual issues was shifting away from selective criticism of the regime's policies toward picturing an alternative model of society held up against the existing one. This alteration was suggested in accordance with philosophical concepts that people knew through socialization to the Iranian way of life. It was no longer just the West that was to be rejected, but Marxian regimes were also criticized. The controversy was no longer either West or East (the Soviet model), but something more ideal than both of them. Such discussions were typical of Islamic intellectuals, although they were not the only ones concerned. Moslem theoreticians were proposing an Islamic system of society as an alternative to either West or East. For example, in addition to Dr. Shariati's works, the clerical scholar Mottahari had published a number of books in this direction. Another example was the translation and publication of books written by an Egyptian author, Saiid Ghotb, on the Islamic economy. Among secularist radicals, the search for a more appropriate model of society was also a major concern. The notion of the "Three Worlds" of development was circulating through the Marxist groups who were looking at the Chinese experience as another possible alternative. "Three Worlds" referred to the alternative historical courses of change. Some were also fascinated by the ideas of Anvar Xohsa, who headed the People's Republic of Albania. His notion of a "people's republic" had fascinated certain Iranian leftists, mostly those educated in Europe. This conception was contrasted with the Soviet model of the dictatorship of the working class. Most such views were expressed in private circles and could not be found explicitly stated in published form. However, in abstract terms, they were available in academic-type publications. One heard of them and saw the leftists passionately debate them in private. Outside Iran, such debates were quite open and widespread among Iranians.

Even the theoreticians of the regime jumped on the bandwagon by putting on national television a program attended by certain famous Iranian social theorists. They also criticized both the West and the East, and were looking for something original. However, the intention behind this state-sponsored intellectual show was to prepare people for the justification of the regime's main line of propaganda in favor of "The Great Civilization." This was a model of society that the Shah was promising to the Iranians. It was an industrialized Iran centered around the axis of a military monarchy. Another theoretical justification given by the regime was to show that Iran's monarchy was a progressive one, and that the Shah was a popular political figure. His rule claimed to be vital to the survival of the territorial integrity of the country and for Iran to remain a sovereign nation.

REVOLUTIONARY VIOLENCE

The politicization of the masses was not limited to ideological socialization. It was complemented by some acts of open confrontation with the security elements of the regime. Such actions were undertaken by different groups and in a variety of forms. The major ones were the large-scale demonstrations by the followers of the Ayatollah Khomeini, in June of 1963, the assassination of Prime Minister Mansour by an Islamic group, and a chain of underground armed actions by radical Marxist and Islamic organizations. The impact of such acts under the rule of a police state was of no proportion to the size of physical force that caused their occurrence, nor to the size of the group that operated them, but was measured in terms of their psychological impact and the political awareness that they apprehended.

Ordinarily, in nonturbulent political situations and under conditions of the freedom of expression, the impact of a protest march is proportional to the number of those who attend it. However, under the repressive reign of a police state, even though the number of those who attend is important, what is truly significant is the degree of commitment they hold toward their objectives. It is the latter that determines how far people will go in taking risks, because such a regime typically responds by sending a security force to violently break up the demonstration. When the security force arrives with the order to disperse the demonstrators, a large number of participants immediately flee the scene. What matters is how many people stay to fight. If even a few stay, the situation is changed from a demonstration to a revolt or uprising. The significance of such an act is in the fact that the oppressive systems of the police state operate in a rather complicated way. They use excessive violence against people to intimidate them sufficiently to force them to internalize the external threats into a mechanism of self-regulation. When this is achieved, each individual restrains himself and will not act against the system. Therefore, the reign of state-sponsored terror becomes institutionalized and there is no further need for the excessive presence of the security force. Finally, the regime will pose as a legitimate government, as though the people themselves had accepted its rule and intended to act according to its will.

Acts of revolutionary violence, revolt, even open protest, change this state of peaceful coexistence. They nullify the regime's accomplishments by decreasing the people's self restraint. The nullification is mainly due to the fact that both the regime and the people know that the political silence, which seems to prevail, is artificial. Such incidents of disobedience signal the failure of the attempt to fully institutionalize state terror as a mechanism of self restraint, and the fear of spreading such defiance beyond control.

When large categories of people are dissentive, they are like a room filled with explosive gas. All that is needed is a slight spark to make it explode. What prevents others from taking the bold steps, which a few may have taken, is their fearfulness. The fear might fade away easily when people act collectively. In the case where violence passes a threshold by becoming generalized to others, it easily spreads to other areas as well. Those who do not participate in the demonstration or revolt have their share of participation by spreading the word in an exaggerated measure and by talking about those who performed as heroes. No matter what happens to the ones who resisted and confronted the state, the mere fact that the incident occurred is a major boost of morale for the opposition and a loss of face for the regime. The more costly consequence is in the fact that the regime has to act repressively in order to show its power and to neutralize the opposition's acts. In this case, it must once again put on its boots and reveal its true nature. It is exactly this part that expands the political awareness of the people, insulating them from further propaganda over a change of policy toward a reduction in the intensity of the repressive order. This is exactly what the revolutionaries tended to accomplish by agitating the regime and causing it to react violently and repressively.

It is apparent that the consequences of acts of violence that were sporadic in Iran in the 1960s and 1970s complemented the ideological and political movements that were then occurring. For example, Shariati's preaching on martyrdom neutralized the security measures of a system, a good part of whose control of the population was maintained by intimidation through the threat of SAVAK's retaliation. Other examples of the psychological consequences of violence are what one generally experiences during the revolution. In the days when Tehran was under martial law after nine o'clock, the whole city would become completely silent, because no automobiles were running and the people were obliged to endure the curfew hours. Then, one bullet shot would cause much excitement in every house. At once, everyone would set their imaginations to work trying to guess what was the latest sound. Had someone dared to shoot a security element? Was it a defiant of the martial law who had been shot? It was one single bullet, but it would keep the minds of millions of people, in a city of seven million inhabitants, very busy. It would remind them that there were agents of a regime out there who had denied them their freedom by making them prisoners in their own homes. It would tell them that if they merely walked out of their doors, they would be shot. The hostility generated and the political awareness developed were in no proportion to the rather simple act of a bullet being shot. The excitement grew even greater when, every once in a while out in the dark, someone hiding on the roof would scream out an anti-regime slogan. It signified that the resistance was still alive.

It is from perspectives like this that one is able to evaluate and understand the contribution of the underground movements that revolutionized Iranians in the 1970s. These underground groups would now and again surface as commando bands and engage with the security forces. The size of these groups and the physical damage they caused was not the real tool in threatening the regime. It was their psychological impact that was out of all proportion to their size.

NOTES

1. J. Al e Ahmad, *Plagued by the West*, translated by Paul Sprachman (New York: Caravan Books, 1982).

2. Ali Shariati, *Collected Works (farci)* (Tehran: Hoseini yeh Ershad, 1970-1980), *Islamic View of Man*, translated by A. A. Rusti (Houston: Islamic Free Press, 1974), and *On the Society of Islam*, translated by H. Algar (Berkeley: Mizan Press, 1979).

9

The Revolution of 1978-1979

INSURGENCY BY SYMBOLIC MEANS

In a little over a year, from 1977 to 1979, the Iranian people began a variety
of protest attempts that eventually escalated into a nationwide uprising. The
details of such events and how they occurred would make voluminous reports
that would extend beyond the scope of this book. What is intended here is to
show the pattern of the escalation, and specifically, how and why it favored
the dominance of religious parties. The issue is how people finally managed
to develop a successful strategy leading to a national uprising and why this
strategy relied heavily on religious and symbolic means.

A close study of the history of the Iranian struggle against the regime,
and the limitations of their earlier style of resistance and insurgency, may
reveal some facts about why Iranians rose up under the banner of religion.
There is a logical connection between the conditions of struggle against the
regime of the Shah and the people's choice in their strategies of revolt. It
seems reasonable to claim that insurgency through religion was not simply
their only choice, but the only effective option left to them. For several reasons, which will be explored later, pre-revolutionary Iran was a politically
tense country. Occasionally, the tension would break into turbulence.

Already, we have discussed that ever since the beginning of the 20th century Iranians had attempted to alter the rule of their dictators. After the
Constitutional Revolution of 1906-1909, they had fought continuously against
the reemergence of a dictatorial rule. Radical groups occasionally attempted
to even uproot the monarchy. One such attempt was the uprising known as
Jasmgglies, in the 1920s, headed by Kuchick Kan, which managed to establish
the Republic of *Gilan* in Gilan province. Also included in this category are
the events that lead to the royal-CIA coup of 1953. In their struggles, as recently as the last couple of decades, opposition group had put into operation

almost every strategy known to modern radicals. The attempt to assassinate the Shah, mass demonstrations, a sustained state of unrest, Cuban-style armed efforts, and urban underground armed movements were just a few. Their attempts were counterbalanced through the boosting of the security forces and the subsequent evolution of the regime into one of the most oppressive police states in the region.

Also, in the 1970s, despite the economic development and improvement of living conditions for certain classes of people, a state of unrest prevailed within nearly all classes of society. Obviously, this unrest was something that had the potential to be manifested in action. Sporadic small-scale acts of opposition were frequent, but they were not strong enough to alter the political system. The source of tension, therefore, remained unchanged.

It was not necessary to politicize the masses of people further in order to make them dissentive. They were already quite prepared for an uprising. The question one would hear in private circles was how was it to happen. Political groups were also deeply concerned with the question of strategy. Their underground documents reflect how much they were involved in discussing this issue. No one expected a simple answer. They had learned by experience that the system was quite alert and was well prepared to crush any opposition movement.

As early as the mid-1960s, some political activist groups who were convinced that nothing could be accomplished without an armed movement established armed underground movements. Such armed movements had different origins and objectives. Some Marxist youths, disappointed with the past strategies and the experiences of the Iranian leftists, became pioneers in this new phase of the struggle. They formed small groups of highly dedicated, well-trained fighters who occasionally engaged the security forces of the regime in bloody battles. Some of them tried a guerrilla movement, similar to the Cuban experience. A group using underground tactics but Islamic in its rationale and objectives emerged to prove itself also quite effective. There was even the assassination operation of Prime Minister Mansour (1965), executed by *Fa da eian* Islam, a group of fundamentalist Shiia elements that had been active for decades. But none of these attempts seriously challenged the regime.[1] They merely maintained the state of tension. Likewise, severe manpower limitations prevented the armed groups from becoming a major revolutionary armed force. In order to grow, they eventually needed a fixed base where they could set up their headquarters and supplies. Iran's military forces, specially trained and equipped for local warfare and anti-insurgency operations, were both large enough and strong enough to easily crush any such attempts. It was well known that the regime's anti-insurgency strategy was designed to kill the armed opposition's action in "embryo."

The armed groups, both religious and secular, were mostly small bands who constantly had to change their hideouts. For security reasons, they dared not invest all their potential in one large unit. Quite often they would be discovered by the security forces and their members would either be killed or taken as prisoners. Therefore, their growth was severely hampered. Another limitation was related to their training requirements. In order to maintain a deep sense of loyalty in their members and to ensure that they would not break under torture if arrested, a strong revolutionary morale and ideological commitment was necessary. Such a commitment was built up through an ideological education so deep that members would even be capable of sacrificing their lives in its cause. The training of every new member was tedious and time consuming. Therefore, even in a few years they could not grow to more than a hundred members.

Under these conditions in Iran, anyone who dared to openly act against the regime was lauded as a hero. Whether this then meant that the people could be counted on to support them as the alternative was still questionable. During this period in Moslem Iran, it was not known how much support radicals, especially the Marxist revolutionaries, could expect. In this early stage they only had to face the regime. Later, they also had to face the fundamentalist Moslems themselves. Therefore, their initial phase was built on one set of conditions that later would, if they were to grow into a viable alternative, necessarily be different.

Alternative Modes of Struggle

When the struggle finally entered the stage of armed movements, the security forces intensified their punishments of active opposition groups. Underground fighters came to expect no less than the death sentence. Stories of torture and beatings in the political prisons had intimidated citizens to the point that many dared not get involved. They muttered against the regime in their own private circles, but such minimal dissent was not considered enough to require action. Any organized activity was sure to be crushed immediately. Consequently, the people were divided into two groups. A few had risked their lives and were active against the regime, and a larger number were against the regime but would not take any action. If there was to be a successful strategy, it was imperative that those who were active find some way of activating the masses of people. A significant number of the active members needed to be willing to risk their lives in order to inspire the masses toward commitment. They hoped that this would prove to the masses that the regime was not made of steel, that it was vulnerable, and that united, the people could themselves alter their political situation. The underground groups, however, even though they were quite small did manage to achieve some change. For these basically psychological conquests, they had to pay a heavy price. Some members carried cyanide pills. If they were arrested, they might bite the pill and within a few minutes be dead. This type of suicide prevented the regime from extracting information from them by torture. For large numbers of militant youths, these sacrificial soldiers became idols, ideological references, symbols of the resistance, and inevitably, examples to be followed. Although such psychological gains were crucial in boosting the people's morale, there was still no guarantee that such a movement would grow to form a large-scale revolutionary army able to alter the regime. There had to be a simultaneous engagement occurring throughout the country in order to loosen the security forces' grip on the people's minds and lives. At that time, these forces were focused merely on a small group of active elements. The strategy was to force the regime to spread its forces across a wide front, thereby weakening its potential strength.

Such a massive engagement would require a specially organized team to further train large numbers of revolutionaries. These trained revolutionary forerunners of the campaign would take their stand on the front line, risk their lives, and send out the rallying cry to their comrades. Such soldiers required an ideological training that would instill a deep level of commitment to the cause. Mere dissatisfaction with the regime was not sufficient to inspire people to want to risk their lives. A strong commitment was essential to downplay any attachment to fear that had ordinarily prevented people from joining the movement.

It is only in the light of the above facts that the significance of transforming millions of devoted Moslems, almost overnight, into political activists can be understood. An army of well-disciplined protesters came into existence, many of them volunteering for the most dangerous acts. Some of the clerical leaders made the protest a religious obligation by subjecting the political situation to religious definitions and interpretations. The security forces quickly found that they were no longer dealing with the same undisciplined demonstrations with which they were familiar. Throughout the country, a giant was awakening. The features that distinguished this new insurgent wave of Shiia-dominated followers was that they enjoyed a number of advantages that other groups had not. This foretold the formation of a significant power. The advantages were as follows:

1. The Islamic groups had thousands, even hundreds of thousands, of fully devoted individuals under their command. These were the type of individuals who could be directed to undertake the most dangerous tasks. Some of their members were equal in Islamic ideological commitment to the underground fighters. They dared to face the armed forces of the regime in a struggle that was, to them, the equivalent of a holy war. To them, death meant martyrdom, a concept that had become an internalized ideal. Their leading organization could function more openly now because of the invested commitment of these followers. It was a religious training that had created these activities, and religious training was the one thing not forbidden in the country.

2. They did not have to create an underground organization because they already had a highly disciplined one through the line of religious authority.

3. Their members were stationed in every corner of the society. The security forces knew only the hierarchical religious leaders. These leaders were untouchable, unless the government was prepared to face large and immediate riots. The followers were mostly from the business class and lower class, and rural people who were unknown

as political opponents to the security forces. They came from the ranks of the apolitical faceless masses on whom no detailed files had been created in the data banks of the political police. The security forces had focused mainly on the college community, civil and military servants, the large industrial organizations, and other middle-class people who were politically concerned. These new activists were not only unknown to the authorities, but there was additionally no way to cut their line of communication. Their organization was, therefore, uncrushable.

4. They had their fixed bases—the mosque and other religious centers. The city of Qhom, the seat of the high clergy, was the main headquarters of the new phase of opposition. It was a large city, and a sacred one, housing one of the holiest shrines in Iran. Sacred also was the city of Meshad. A number of places where less important shrines were located were also seats of powerful clergy leaders. Each day thousands of pilgrims would travel to Qhom or Meshad, and return with the new messages. It was impossible to arrest the spread of turbulence from these centers to the rest of the country.

5. The clergy numbered in the tens of thousands and had close relations with the lay people. They had close and informal ties with a variety of people from nearly all classes, so when each chose to support the movement, he would become a central figure for the opposition.

6. Moslem groups had had valuable experiences in mass demonstrations. These experiences originated in Islamic teaching and the history of the rise of Islam.

ESCALATION OF PROTESTS

Prior to the autumn of 1977, sporadic protests were typical on college campuses, and occasionally would break out elsewhere, too. These protests would primarily begin under the cover of a nonpolitical grievance. However, once it had transformed itself into emotionalized actions, the security forces would intervene. Then, the protest would take a more political overtone and could even become violent. From the autumn of 1977 onward, however, the nature of these protests began to change. The change was mainly in the form of the extension of the protest from its center of origin (from a college campus into the streets) and the outbreak of protests from different sources, as though all those who opposed the system had begun a round of well-orchestrated open activism.

All of the reasons for such expanding protests from a wide range of groups are not clearly known. However, in early 1977, there were rumors that Americans, fearing the further growth of leftist movements, were pressuring the Shah to relax his strong-handed rule and to let other alternatives to the leftist extremism have a chance to emerge. To what extent such a rumor was founded on truth is not clearly known either. Undoubtedly, the growth in size and the frequency of underground armed actions was a serious concern of the regime and its American patrons. So also was the relaxation of repressive actions. In fact, the elevation of the level of opposition from verbal attacks and small protest gatherings to modern-style urban guerrilla warfare had made the former look insignificant. Therefore, its toleration was reasonable, because the regime had to utilize its security capacities and manpower to counter the underground armed units of the militant groups, and let less challenging actions pass unguarded. In practice, this meant that the regime intended to tolerate some degree of opposition.

The first major sign of change of policy was an unexpected permission granted for a reading by dissentive poets.[2] They were permitted to read their poems to the public at the Cultural Center of the German Consulate in the north of Tehran. This writer also attended that gathering as part of the audience. A number of poets, who were Marxists, Islamics, or independents, read their political poetry to an audience that numbered in the tens of thousands. It was an outdoor gathering of people, most of whom were college students. Among the poets were those who had served long-term prison sentences for political actions. It was an extraordinary event because even up until a few months earlier, not even a single line of these poems could have been made available to the public. The audience was amazed and could not believe what their ears were hearing or their eyes were seeing. The news of the gathering spread all over the country. The next night, the number of those who attended was multiplied so greatly that the crowd filled all the streets and alleys surrounding the German Cultural Compound.

Why this compound was chosen was never officially explained. Only some hypothetical answers were ever provided. Possibly, it was because the place had been named after Goethe, the great German poet. It could also be that no Iranian organization was ready to take the risk. In contrast, the German Institute carried some degree of political immunity. Obviously, it was still held with the permission of the Iranian security agencies, because outside the compound the police were present in a capacity similar to the guides of a convention, mostly helping with the traffic. Unlike the usual scene, there was no sign of any riot police on combat units or anti-protest police. Those who were there that night were very polite and acted as though they had been given orders not to agitate anyone and not to interfere with what was going on. For the Iranian youths, who were mostly in their teens and early twenties, it was a unique experience because they had never had a chance to attend a gathering in which the regime was criticized but the security forces did not attack the gatherers. After the first night, when the people had made sure that there seemed to be some degree of freedom in the air, their numbers increased. The next few nights witnessed tens of thousands of attendants, some even coming from faraway provinces.

The center of this new round of dissensions resided in the organs and places frequented by the better-educated people. Included were long-time activists who had had the earlier experience of two decades of party politics. Once again, some of the former political parties were returning to the scene. Not all such activities were completely tolerated. The regime might still react violently, but probably not as severely as it had in the past. For example, the

National Front held a social gathering of its leading elements in a suburb of Tehran. SAVAK had organized a group of plain-clothed agents to break up their gatherings and to beat them. The association of Iranian lawyers, dominated by radicals and democratic-oriented elements, was trying to freely choose its officials.[3] In the past, all the syndicate officers would be picked up through SAVAK influence and approved in rubber-stamped elections. Previously, anyone arrested in the demonstrations was dealt with by special courts under the charges of revolting against the security of the state. These were, directly or indirectly, military courts. Now, there was a change of policy allowing civilian lawyers to defend these demonstrators as civil disobedients. This changed the whole definition of dissension and, therefore, the regime's reaction to it.

Up to this point, the winter of 1978, secular-oriented opposition activists were still in the lead in initiating the opposition action, and would be the most visible people in the demonstrations. This situation was changing rapidly, however, and with dissensions being voiced in the holy city of Qhom, attentions were diverted toward clergy-led opposition actions.

Reactivation of Shiia Politics

This new round of dissentive activities was also building up in other religious centers. The protests of the clergy-led groups, however, were originated and masterminded in Iran's most influential Shiia clerical school, *Fay-z-yeh*, located at the holy city of Qhom.[4] Meanwhile, Ayatollah Khomeini, who had earlier led a violent demonstration against the Shah's "White Revolution" reforms, was spending a term of exile in Iraq. From there he was organizing and overlooking the secret activities of his supporters in Iran. These activities were various forms of dissension as well as the formation of secret religion-based organizations with political-religious intents. Finally, in the winter of 1978, the clerical hierarchy who opposed the regime began to unleash their followers into the streets to protest. The strategy of the religious groups was not too complicated. They would utilize the cultural and religious institutions to organize, politicize, and then lead the people to uprising. Their objectives were to stage a rather peaceful demonstration in order to win over the manpower that the regime had employed to run its military and bureaucratic machine. These people worked in the country's industries, especially in the oil industry, which provided the main funds for the government's budget. They intended to isolate the autocrats, to prevent any confrontation within the populace, to unite everyone in a national uprising against the Shah, and to force him out of office. Other objectives gradually emerged as their influence expanded. The factor that increased the size of the demonstrations was the push the people received from the Shiia clerical leaders. Gradually, the mosques became centers of opposition that sometimes attracted thousands to preaching services or other special ceremonies. In line with tradition, politically minded clergymen would preach emotionally and fearlessly, delving into issues that people would otherwise not have dared to discuss in public. Some such congregations turned into demonstrations. Other convenient events were the burials of those killed in the above demonstrations or the ceremonies normally performed on the fortieth day after death—an Islamic tradition held with much enthusiasm. These demonstrations would, in turn, breed further demonstrations seven or forty days later. One riot would conceive even larger riots.

The ice of political passivity was melting. People could now gather more easily. In their homes, they could hold small political gatherings. In demonstrations, they could sing slogans that even a few months earlier they would not have dared to whisper in the privacy of their homes. It was obvious that a revolution was finally erupting. Demonstrations and rebellion were growing like avalanches. They drew from not only one group of people, but from nearly all classes. This was the tip of the iceberg beginning to show as the early phase of the national uprising began.

Within two months, in the summer of 1978, the regime found itself facing an increasingly hostile crowd in all its cities. By September of 1978, tanks were stationed in the streets of most cities and martial law was in effect in nearly every major metropolis. The demonstrations escalated to a final revolutionary stage after the early September massacre, thereafter referred to as Black Friday.[5] The event began as a peaceful demonstration and was broken up by soldiers. No one has ever been able to determine how many people were killed, but it is generally believed that the deaths were in the hundreds or even thousands. Eyewitnesses reported that many truckloads of dead or wounded were taken from the streets. Until this point, college students, secular political forces, and long-term political activists still had some influence upon the trends of the uprising. Afterward, there occurred a noticeable shift toward the clerical leadership, as masses of lower-class and rural people began to join the movement.

As the movement escalated into daily disturbances, a general strike, and mass defiances of martial law, the people themselves began to innovate new and effective tactics of resistance. For example, in order to sing slogans at night, starting usually at 9 p.m. when curfew hours began they would go up on the roofs of their homes. They could not be either seen or shot at by the security forces because Iranian buildings have flat roofs. In this manner the demonstrations could continue utilizing the advantage of the dark and the protected roof. The security forces could not stop them. The people would increasingly express their opposition in religious language—in terms of beliefs that would emotionalize them. Details of these events follow.

The main strategy was to isolate the autocrats who ruled the country and to prevent civil war. They would, for example, give flowers to the soldiers who had been ordered to shoot the people. They would tell them, "You are our brothers. We will give secure hiding, food, and money to any who will flee from the barracks." They asked the people to preach to their relatives who served in the military, especially those in the security forces, asking the soldiers to quit their positions. Simply put, these were revolutionary people utilizing whatever means they saw as necessary in order to alter an oppressive regime. They did this mainly through symbolic methods.

Both lines of opposition action—from the secularist side and the religious side—were expanding their domain of activities independently. However, the spread of these actions to the masses would bring them into inevitable contact and cooperation. The first phase of this culmination was the uprising in the historic city of Tabriz. It took the form of a large-scale political riot, forcing the regime to put the city under a state of martial law.

The events of Tabriz had rocked the entire political and security structure of the regime. Tabriz, during the last century, had been the capital of Iranian opposition politics. It is the center of one of the most important provinces of the country, and one in which Iran's second largest ethnic group, the Turks, resided. It is on the border of the U.S.S.R., making it an even more vital region in terms of security. It was in Tabriz that the anti-dictatorial movement of 1908 had managed to survive. Because of its survival, the nationalist leaders were able to stage the armed uprising that year that finally reinstated the Iranian constitutional order and reconvened the National Assembly, subsequent to the takeover of the capital city of Tehran.

The 1978 uprising of Tabriz was the beginning of a sustained, large-scale popular involvement. It was a mass movement, including nearly all strata of the society, and differed from the earlier actions that occurred in certain organizations or on college campuses. With the uprising of Tabriz, the opposition actions escalated to a new phase. The demonstrators could no longer be accused as a single small, political or ideological group, nor as agents of foreign influence. They were the people of the nation itself, from all walks of life and ideological affiliations. The demonstrators had attacked and damaged certain key organizations of the regime. They had destroyed official cars, and in effect the city had been given the appearance of a war zone. As a consequence of this successful riot, the security forces were proven ineffective in preventing mass protests. People began to see them as paper tigers capable only of dealing with small-scale group actions.

From then on, a more important development was the specific structuring of the protests that would guarantee the continuation and periodic occurrence of these events. The protest attempts were therefore no longer random occurrences, but occurred quite precisely on schedule. The protestors were organizing themselves to fit the shaping of a new chain of the events. With each of these events, the timing of the next one would automatically be set. Such linkage and timing had originated in Islamic practices and beliefs which were, to an extent, masterminded by the Moslem organizers. They had promised that protest attempts would grow into a nationwide mass movement against the regime. The mechanism of such systematization centered around the burial ceremonies. With Iranian Shiia Moslems, as previously mentioned, it is a common practice to observe some ceremonies on the first, third, seventh and fortieth days after a family member's death. A large and highly emotional gathering takes place at the graveyard when the deceased person is buried. An even larger gathering takes place afterward. The later ceremonies are in the home of the deceased, in the home of close relatives, or in the mosque of the community where the person used to live. People attend in order to give tribute to the deceased and the close relatives. A clergyman preaches and sings a sad sermon that makes the attendants highly emotional. If the person has been a public or top religious figure, there may be some official ceremonies arranged by the state. In cases of notable figures, these ceremonies may take place in a number of cities where the person had had economic, political, ethnic, or some other form of great influence.

The best political use was made of these ceremonial practices in order to structure the ongoing protests of 1977-78. It was becoming a common practice to hold large gatherings to commemorate those who had been killed in the demonstrations. This was taken even more seriously if they had lost their lives in demonstrations led by Islamic groups, for then the clergy, having influence upon the laity and Bazaaris, would invite the public to attend and ask the shops to close down in protest. As a practice, the seventh and fortieth commemoration of those killed in one city was organized to be held in another city. They were to be held quite elegantly, with thousands attending.

In such a gathering, people would typically be made aware of the reason why these persons had lost their lives, and the preaching would become quite political. Then the demonstration would again turn into an open protest against the regime and would break into confrontation with the security elements. More people would get hurt and killed, providing the ammunition for the next round of gatherings in the next few days and weeks.

The uprising of Tabriz was an occasion of one such commemoration ceremony for those who had earlier lost their lives elsewhere. The organizers would intentionally hold these commemorations for those killed in one place at some other location. Therefore, they would spread the dissentive actions nationwide and eventually arouse the masses all over the country.

After Tabriz, Isfahan, the second largest metropolis of Iran was put under martial law. Yazd, another provincial capital, was the scene of a bloody demonstration. With such events repeated in a chain, escalating in magnitude and spreading all over the country, it was quite clear to everyone that these demonstrations were not the work of a few "traitors," as the regime would have liked to call it. Moreover, it was also clear that the escalating movements were not going to cease and vanish unless some major changes took place in the country. In other words, it was quite clear that a revolution was on its way, and it was not something that could be stopped by the police or a detachment of a few units of the military forces.

To confront a nation of demonstrators, the utilization of large-scale military forces were required. It was toward the end of the spring of 1978 that regular combat troops were brought in and stationed all over the capital city and in some other cities that were hot spots. The presence of these forces was a horrifying scene, with soldiers sitting on the top of tanks and armored vehicles, manning the guns that were pointed at the crowded streets and squares. It made the entire place look like a war zone. The presence of combat-ready troops facing empty-handed citizens was then undermining the claims of the Shah who hoped to pose as a popular modernizer. Instead of intimidating the people, the presence of these troops gave them further reason to think that the opposition must be extremely powerful. Otherwise, there would be no need for such elaborate preparation in order to confront them.

As the religiously sacred month of Ramadan (the month of fasting) was approaching, the regime was getting more nervous. In Shiia Iran there exist two months of the year in which intensive ceremonial practices and mass gatherings normally occur. Ramadan is one of those months, especially during its 19th to 21st days, which coincide with the anniversary of the martyrdom of the first Shiia Imam, Ali. It is in these months that the clergy finds a chance to address millions of Iranians with their fiery preaching. Mosques, and other religious centers, become jammed with attendants who more than anything else are there to hear the clergy address them in hours-long sermons. During these gatherings, the audiences are emotionally prepared to follow the clergy's suggestions. In the turbulent year of 1978, the month of Ramadan made the clerical leadership the center of attention. The organizers of the ceremonies had also taken a role similar to that of the party officials, who had planned and managed a party campaign gathering, for more than anything else the content and intention of the ceremonies had become political.

All these conditions favored the religious groups in assuming the leadership of the ongoing mass protests. During this month, people gathered in mosques in large and unprecedented numbers. The preachers were excited to see the young educated crowd, who in the past had been influenced away from the mosques, among their audience. In certain mosques, the preaching became so highly political that open attacks upon the regime were on the verge of being made. Some of the mosques were so crowded that there was no room left inside their compound to accept a larger audience. Large numbers of people had to stand on the sidewalks of the surrounding streets, listening to the preachings that were broadcast through loudspeakers. With mosques formed into gathering centers, the Islamic leadership had a chance to integrate the opposition's potential into a united, citywide, and (to an extent) nationwide effort. The two opposition groups—the secularists and the religious—were furthermore merging into one. It needs to be mentioned that in Iran many of those who may have aspired to a secular polity were themselves religious people. Therefore, no matter what their political ideals were, their attendance at these ceremonies would iron out some of their differences of view on the immediate issue of fighting the Shah's regime.

The first manifestation of this merger happened in the last days of the month of Ramadan and the following Friday, which later became known as "Black Friday." It is an Islamic tradition that on the last day of the month of fasting, people celebrate. It is a celebration all over the Moslem world. In Iran on this day, early in the morning all the people in the town or city gather in one large congregation to perform a special prayer. Ordinarily, this prayer takes place in the open fields or on the outskirts of the city. One reason for gathering outside of town is because the crowd is usually very large, and could therefore not be accommodated in one mosque. In this particular year, it was announced that this prayer would take place in a large, wide-open piece of land in the center of Tehran. The site was close to the upper-middle-class and upper-class residential areas.

Following the prayer, which had attracted well over 100,000 people, the participants formed long lines to march into the city shouting political slogans. Some police officers who had cooperated with them were raised and held above the people's heads as an Iranian way of showing their gratitude to someone special. People had hugged some armed soldiers, kissing them, installing flowers on the tips of their guns and telling them, "We are brothers." It was, apparently, the first time that the Shah was openly referred to by name and cursed by the demonstrators. It was apparent that the revolution was advanced enough to create an atmosphere of open expression of dissent. The march ended with a rendezvous set for the next Friday, when everyone would meet again in a square. That square was located right on the border of the lower-middle-class and lower-class residential areas of Tehran.

On Friday, beginning in the early morning, people gathered in the square in large numbers. By nine A.M., one could not even get within a half mile of the square. People from all walks of life were jammed in the surrounding streets. They were not from a single ideological grouping, but had come no matter what their feelings or associations. They all had one thing in common—opposition to the regime for whatever reason. Earlier in the morning, it had been announced on the radio that Tehran was now under martial law, but it did not seem to matter to the people. Later on in the day, trying to disperse the demonstrators, the security forces opened fire, killing and wounding an unknown number of them. It is believed that those killed numbered in the thousands. The official count was less than 100. Some of the wounded were carried by people into the nearby residential areas to try to give them first aid. No one dared to take the wounded to hospitals for fear that the secret police would detain them along with the wounded person. In a large neighborhood region, people were going house to house gathering sheets to use for taking care of the wounded comrades. People seeing the brutality used against the unarmed demonstrators began to call relatives and friends all over the city and the country. In a matter of hours, people all over the country had learned about the details of the massacre. There was nothing that the regime could do to stop the spread of the news and its exaggerated versions. That night, when the curfew began at nine P.M., international radio stations such as the BBC broadcasted the details of the massacre. It was quite clear to everyone that the confrontation the regime had been preparing for had begun.

Apparently, it was a massacre that turned the page of contemporary Iranian history. A new phase of the uprising had begun, a phase that was to bring masses of people onto the scene, escalating the protests from simple political opposition by certain groups to a revolutionary uprising by the whole nation. From the following day onward, people all over the city were displaying open anger and talking against the regime quite explicitly. The general theme of their arguments was that with what had happened on Black Friday, they no longer intended to compromise with the regime. In their view, it was no longer a political but a criminal matter when the regime could shoot down thousands of people who carried no arms and were simply peacefully showing their political viewpoints.

On Saturday, I was on the campus of the National University. It was the summer break, and for the last couple of months no classes had met. Those who came to the campus did so only for other reasons. I saw scores of angry students and staff members who had participated in that bloody demonstration. They included some of the secretaries that in the past would never have shown any sign of political activity, and were indeed quite modern oriented. Some of them openly talked against the Shah. Their participation indicated how wide a spectrum of people had gathered in that square. Some of my ex-students had been there, and still had blood stains on their clothes from carrying the wounded. Because of the state of curfew, they had been unable to go home the night before to change. The way they behaved and talked was in no way comparable to their earlier style of expressing dissent. For the first time in my memory of Iranian scenes, they were openly cursing the Shah with no fear. Some would say, "Our blood is no more red than that of those who were killed yesterday." In Persian this means, "We are no better than them to stay alive. Therefore, why should we shy away from similar confrontations? At most, they might kill us also." For the first time in all the years that I have been a witness of the Iranian dissentive actions, I saw a group of students marching angrily and shouting, "Death to this monarchy of the Pahlavis!"

Similarly, in the bank near the university, I heard people loudly cursing the Shah. One of them was saying, "We have to stop all of our work until this damned Shah is kicked out," while many others shook their heads in approval. This bank and the National University are located in the neighborhood of well-to-do people. Most of those who were now saying these things would have not even dared call the Shah by name without saying "His Majesty" a couple of months earlier. In those days, one could not see any group rivaling or opposing one another on ideological grounds. Such controversies were of no one's concern. Now, all one could hear was the cursing of the Shah and his police state. Moslem radicals, liberals, Marxists, National

Fronters, modernists, and traditionalists, were all fighting side by side. Such was also the case with those who belonged to different classes. There was no doubt that a revolution was going on and it was an "all people's revolution," an uprising of all people against one man who, as a despot, masterminded and personified a regime.

The incident of Black Friday set the people's uprising in a new direction and gave another perspective to the opposition actions. It reinforced and contributed to the unification of a pluralistic opposition force. However, following the events of the sacred month of Ramadan, the religious leadership had found a more active role. It was more or less a matter of fact that even secularly oriented groups had inclined to yield to this leadership, not because they necessarily saw them as the authority, but because in them they could more properly see the capacities necessary to move the masses. The objective of removing the police state was so important that the ends seemed to justify the means. The clergymen were able to call on the masses, they held the mosques, and they were entitled to the privileges of preachers. Why should the opposition have hesitated to support them, since they intended to remove the Shah? This was the general outlook of those who sincerely cooperated with the clergy, even though they themselves were secular minded. It probably never occurred to them that a theocratic totalitarian regime might replace the Shah's police state. Such a strong sense of solidarity was developed that it severely undermined any stratifying factor.

At the end of the summer, Ayatollah Khomeini, whose supporters were becoming a major opposition group, was asked to leave Iraq where he was spending a term of exile. He went to Paris where he was to establish his headquarters of command of his loyal forces in Iran.[6] In Paris, he was easy to reach through the international mass media and he could not be arrested by the Shah's security elements. Therefore, the city was for him a sanctuary and a place from which he could openly address the Iranian people through radio broadcasting or tapes sent home. Quite rapidly, he emerged as the leading element of the opposition movement and the spokesman of the revolution. Such a leadership was further reaffirmed when the National Front representatives met with him in Paris and accepted his terms to ally with him. With that move, he not only commanded the religiously committed followers, but he also commanded a good segment of the secularly oriented political modernists.

The situation, in the minds of the people, was being set up as a dichotomy of the people versus the armed soldiers. At least during this stage, it was not in the form of a class struggle with the poor against the rich and workers against managers. The military forces came to symbolize the backbone of the regime. As more people joined the movement, including government employees, the military people were the only ones that remained on the Shah's side. This, however, did not reflect the will and wishes of the individual soldiers and officers, but was due only to the way that the military organizations were commanded and functioned.

The strategy of the opposition was to talk the manpower of the regime's organization into neutrality and possibly desertion, to transform its organizational machinery, and to turn it into an empty shell. They would accommodate soldiers (if they deserted), would demoralize the public employees in order to stop their work, and would prevent any action that might persuade individuals or groups to side with the Shah. It was like an expanding spiral; as the movement advanced, its social base of support was expanded more and more. It was at this stage that the revolution entered the phase of general strikes, especially in the vital organs of the state.

The era of crippling the system began with the postal employees going on strike, which would gradually spread to all other organs. The Iranian administrative and service sectors were quite advanced in terms of their division of labor, but with strikes crippling certain key sectors the whole system would become dysfunctional. The consequences of the crippling of the public sector were reinforced by that of the several-months-old strike of the Bazaar and the industrial sector. A strike of the oil industry was the most vital, because it would stop the flow of dollars. This not only would make the Shah a useless ally of the West, unable to sell them oil or to buy from them, but would also make the regime incapable of paying the manpower that manned its machinery of state.

As strikes were slowing down the economy and stopping the service sectors from functioning, daily confrontations were being reported. These confrontations took the form of sharply unequal contests between empty-handed citizens and heavily armed soldiers. They left scores dead or wounded, further antagonizing and emotionalizing the people. In the autumn of 1978, the regime was in a defensive position. The organizers of the demonstrations had the initiative, could plan for demonstrations, had full command of millions of supporters, and could more properly control these demonstrations. Part of this management involved designing slogans and suggesting to the participants which slogans should be shouted, as well as when and where it should be done. To the earlier slogan of "Freedom and independence" they added the "Islamic Republic."

When the machinery of the state was almost at a standstill due to the large-scale strikes, the opposition began to form volunteer units to take care of their abandoned tasks. A network of organized groups were emerging that were on the side of the revolution and functioned as a special service organization. For example, because of the strike in the oil industry, people had difficulty in receiving fuel. Lines at fuel stations were over a mile long. Volunteers would oversee the distribution in such a way as to ensure that no one was left without a minimum of their necessities and no profiteer was able to exploit the situation for his own greedy objectives. Such management of public affairs was initiating community-based volunteer groups, which had begun to emerge as a more permanent administrative organ. Being in a revolutionary state, such groups would be quite sincerely devoted to their tasks and would attract popular support. They were the groups who, later on when the regime had eventually broken down, emerged as the occupants of the revolutionary organs. Their headquarters were mostly in the mosques, and they were therefore in close cooperation with the clergy. The formation of such groups, as well as the organization of the mass demonstrations, was providing the leadership of the Revolution with its own system of control and administration. With their enthusiastic presence on the scene, the country was not headed for uncontrollable chaos. As the authority and administrative capacities of the regime began to fade away, the opposition's system was set to replace it. In the new order, command was more or less in the hands of certain clergymen, most of whom were strong supporters of Ayatollah Khomeini.

Not all the revolutionary organizations in charge of administrative tasks were emerging from the scrapple. The bulk of the government organs that were on strike had sided with the revolution. Therefore, in certain cases, they had begun to take their orders from the opposition leadership. However, this realignment of loyalty was not making them mere followers. In most such cases, they had formed their own democratic committees, elected their own representatives, and operated according to the conscience of the employees. In this respect, they had broken off the historic tradition of management from above. Now they were running their respective organization as self-governing bodies.

It was under such conditions that by the end of the autumn 1978, the regime was also reaching the end of its rope. With Moharram, the first of the sacred months of the Shiia calendar, the clergy once again had a chance to consolidate its leadership, expand the movement to larger segments of the population, and put into operation the Shiia instruments of mass politicization.

It was during this month that the Islamic group managed to bring onto the scene millions of the so-called silent majority. During Moharram, eleven days in a row are marked by unusually intensive ceremonies with mass participation. In each community, a number of halls are temporarily decorated and used for mass assemblies to mourn the martyrdom of the Imam Hosein and his associates who died at Karballa in 7th century A.D. The organizations responsible for these ceremonies are temporary ones, although each year essentially the same people are involved with the administration of the events.

In cities, such organizers are mostly petty businessmen, the elderly in the community, faithful notables, and a large number of young people who took their orders to serve the participants. One reason why these temporary units are formed is because the existing system of mosques is unable to accommodate all the participants and handle all the ceremonies of this occasion. Larger spaces are needed for the preparation and organization of the street marches of the faithful and for serving dinner to large numbers of people. Another reason is because all of the marches are planned to go on for hours, and they pass through each mosque or assembly site created for the ceremonies. In each of these locations, marchers are to be served tea or some kind of sweet soft drinks. Therefore, even if a mosque had been chosen as the center, there would still be the need for some supplementary locations to complement it. To serve tea to approximately ten thousand visiting marchers in a matter of a few minutes requires a large, well-organized manpower unit, as well as well-prepared facilities. This type of visitation would go on for hours, with different marching groups arriving one after another. Therefore, these temporary locations would involve a good number of the residences of the community in the program. These ceremonies would strengthen community members' sense of solidarity, put them in a cooperative network, and undermine the differences in personal interest and ideology that otherwise would have separated the people. In Shiia villages, the whole population is invited and will participate. In cities, the Shiia population also participates in large numbers. In the capital city, where a traditional middle class, lower class, and upper class (Bazaaris) live, the bulk of the residents get involved in one way or another. The central figures of these ceremonies are the clergy, who in the late 1970s found a chance to speak out more freely than before.

Given the condition of the revolution and the regime's defensive position, the Moharram of 1978 was a time of freedom of speech, a freedom that people had forced upon the regime. The organizers of the ceremonies managed to attract millions of people to participate, especially for the street marches, which were taking a complete political form. Under the rule of martial law, they had a difficult time staging street demonstrations as freely as they would have liked. However, on the tenth of this month, when the street marches were ordinarily held during the day, all the marchers gathered in a few big spots to observe the final ceremonies. The revolutionary issues obviously overrode all other matters, and assembling for the ceremonies of Moharram was once again an excuse to get millions of people into a few spots in the cities to cast their oral vote against the regime.

It was on the tenth of this month that millions of people gathered in the *Azady* (freedom) square of Tehran, shouting their approval for the readings of the clergymen who had led the marches.[7] The statements that were read included a call for the establishment of the Islamic republic, which was followed by the then-popular slogan of "Death to the Shah." In Paris, Ayatollah Khomeini took the occasion to alert all governments that from now on, they should not deal with the Iranian regime because it had been voted out of office by the people themselves. From this moment on, it was quite clear that the clergy-led groups were the leading commanders of the demonstrations, and that they had established themselves as the political authority of the faithful, who otherwise would have been reluctant to take to the streets. The content of the slogans that they instructed the marchers to sing were quite religious, such as the highly emotional slogans that drew parallels between the events of the day and those of Imam Hosein's uprising. By shouting "Every day is Ashura and every place is Karballa!" they fed religious content into the political movement of the Revolution. The authority of Ayatollah Khomeini as the leader of the Revolution was already established. With a further intensification of the Revolution and an increase in the amount of its religious content, the Ayatollah was becoming elevated beyond the traditional rank of merely top clergyman, to the personality of *Imam*, or saint.

Following the religious-political street referendum of Moharram, the Shah was no longer in control. The organization of military forces was shaken by dissension, desertions, and demoralization. The government and industrial sectors were further crippled by the continuation of strikes. A civilian government was set up that was supposed to function in the absence of the Shah. Meanwhile, the Shah had no other choice but to get out of Iran for an undetermined length of time. It was a well-known fact that the civilian cabinet would only be a transitionary one for the post-Shah era. It was headed by Shahpour Bakhtyar, one of the Shah's long-time opponents from the secularist wing of the National Front.[8] This man was one of the National Front leaders who had refused to ally with the Ayatollah. He tried to put into operation a program that guaranteed freedom of expression and abolsihed the interference of SAVAK in the social and political life of the populace, as well as a wide variety of other democratic measures. If such a government had been formed much earlier, the Revolution probably would have never become so radicalized. It was too late now, however, for a secular government. The clergy-led groups were already in control of the country. In places where the functioning of the state agencies were crippled, they had established their command of the masses. They had the business sector fully allied with them, leaving little for this democratic-oriented government to administer. Very soon, in the capacity of the leader of the Revolution and on behalf of the "invisible Imam"—whose rule was an extension of the divine rule—the Ayatollah nominated Mehdi Bazargan as his own prime minister.[9]

There were now two prime ministers in the country. People were asked to demonstrate their support of the one chosen by the Ayatollah. Once again, masses of people were in streets chanting slogans in support of the Ayatollah's choice, while humiliatingly cursing the other. In most government offices, the employees began to announce their loyalty to the man chosen by the Ayatollah. During this stage, the only resistance remained on the side of certain military commanders. Certain officers were still loyal to the monarchical regime. The martial law officers in Tehran made a decision to prolong curfew hours. This was interpreted by the Ayatollah as a sign of preparation for a military coup against the Revolution. He asked the people to stay in the streets in defiance of such a regulation. Up to this point, the integrity of the command of the military forces had not yet been shattered.

The final stage of the Revolution was terminated in an attempt made by a loyal unit of the Royal Guards to discipline the dissident elements of an air force unit. This attempt led to a military clash in which masses of people intervened.[10]

Films later shown on Iranian television and a general account by observers indicated that organized units of underground armed groups (both Marxist and Islamic) had played a significant role in the incident. They had helped to defeat the disciplinary attempt made by the guardsmen. The people managed to break into the depot of a barracks and take away arms and ammunition. With people armed all over the capital city, the military and police headquarters came under attack. The same pattern was duplicated elsewhere, with people surrounding the barracks and asking the military forces to surrender. By taking over the radio stations, the revolutionaries announced the fall of the regime and the victory of the Revolution on February 2, 1979.

Armed people were wandering the streets, sacking and burning the government headquarters, arresting prominent members of the regime who were still in the country, taking over SAVAK headquarters, and breaking through the jails (especially the political wards) and freeing the prisoners. It is believed that hundreds of thousands of military weapons (mostly rifles) had fallen into the hands of the people.

It was especially interesting to listen to the radio services on the first day that they were in revolutionary hands. An overjoyed announcer's very first statement was, "Blessings to the happy souls of those free-spirited men and women who handed us freedom by sacrificing their lives!" Then some prominent revolutionary figures addressed the people. Rezaii was one of them. He had lost three of his children, the founders of an anti-Shah underground armed group, to the executioners of SAVAK. Radio Tehran was instructing people where to go for practical training on the use of military rifles. Another message was instructing the people to attack the horrifying "Evin" prison, the place where political prisoners were kept and tortured. It was the most important headquarters of SAVAK, with the most sophisticated torture chamber. The radio had been transformed into the commanding post of an ongoing armed struggle.

While giving such instructions and some advice on how to use weapons, the announcers would play revolutionary songs and march music. The announcer, every once in a while, would also read poems. One was a part of a beautiful Persian poem that said, "Open the window! Look outside! Breath the freedom . . ."

In cities all over Iran, people had attacked SAVAK headquarters and sacked some of the military barracks. According to witnesses, for example, in the city of Rasht people had attacked SAVAK, finding a few officers still in their headquarters. They had killed them on the spot, hanging their mutilated bodies from the trees in front of the compound. The same was done in some other cities with certain police officers who had been rough with people in the last few months. It took the people only a couple of days to shatter the most important backbone of the Shah's police state and arrest thousands of its key members. The whole country was headed for a state of chaos, with armed men everywhere. It would take a few days to restore security in some parts of the cities. At night, bullet shots rang continuously. In every community, mostly with their headquarters in the mosque, people appointed themselves local guards. In the Persian language they were called *"Pass dar."* These guards were the first groups that later emerged as the revolutionary guards. From the rank of the present force of "revolutionary guards," though, which has been made into a modern army of a few hundred thousand, those who were thought to be disloyal to the clerical rule have been purged.

In public offices and industrial units, revolutionary committees took charge. These committees were elected by the employees. The Islamic activists had a strong presence in all such elections, mainly because the lower rank employees, especially office servants who were often uneducated and did the janitorial and maintenance work, were numerous. These groups of lower echelon employees, mostly of rural and lower class origin, were posing as pro-clergy. Such political orientation did not necessarily reflect their true intentions, however. Under the Shah's regime the lower level employees were always pressured to show support of the regime in order to preserve their jobs. Therefore, it had become a normative behavior for many such employees to pose as supporters of the sovereign. In most of the Iranian government, and even in private organizations, one might expect to see the lower rank employees siding with the pro-clergy groups.

But in general, on the day of the triumph and immediately after the victory of the Revolution, the pro-clergy groups were dominant in nearly all organizations. For example, in the university, which was expected to have more secular elements, the Islamic groups had the majority of votes. The Marxists were rather small, but highly active. A good number of radical secularists would vote for moderate Moslem candidates. They could not in those circumstances identify with the typical modernist-minded liberals, because such an image was under attack as a Western orientation. In the committee elected in the College of Literature and Human Sciences of the National University, for example, those who had cast their votes for candidates having Islamic orientations were the dominant majority. However, out of twelve members of the elected body, three were Marxists and leftists who did not openly reveal their political preferences.

From the beginning, people had a tendency toward not revealing their true political identity. Support for the Islamic groups came not only from devoted Moslems, but from many others who would vote for them for a variety of personal or group reasons. It was generally believed that Islamic groups had played a significant role in the uprising of the masses and other brave acts, without which the regime of the Shah would never have fallen. Therefore, the Islamic orientations of the movements and their participants did not in all cases imply religiosity. To an extent, it reflected political concerns.

As soon as the military forces of the regime surrendered and the Shah's era was formally over, committees began to grow quickly. In a matter of only a few days, the whole country was covered with a wide range of committees. The most important committees were the ones set up in every community to take care of security matters, because the police had been disarmed and were not to be trusted. Armed citizens were guarding their own communities and taking care of prisoners, which included SAVAK agents and other influential elements of the fallen regime. The committees in the public and large private organs had two main functions on their list of priorities. One was to kick out those who had been proven to be supporters of the fallen regime. The other was to safeguard all documents, books, and papers in the offices, so that they could be reviewed later in order to place charges against ex-officials who had been involved in corruption or active supporters of the ex-regime.

Ayatollah Khomeini and the prime minister of the revolutionary cabinet began to assign their men to head the radio station and major institutions such as the military forces. The takeover of the state by the Islamic regime was not an easy task. The transitional revolutionary government set up by the Ayatollah was supported by the people. Those appointees who were given the assignment to head the organs, however, were not always welcomed. The democratically set up committees would not fully cooperate with the appointees and even rejected them. The difficulty resided in the fact that the Ayatollah's view of how the country should be run actually resembled that of the Shah, because he also believed that every assignment ought to be made from above, or at least have higher-level approval. Delegation of authority from the top was what both the leftists and the liberal-oriented groups, whose presence was strong in these organs, would never favor. Those employees that during the Revolution had taken the risks and endured strikes and other revolutionary acts believed they had the right to command their own affairs. The conflict was building between the forces of a new autocracy—this time justified on a theocratic basis—and that of democracy. The post-revolutionary era began with strong signs of such a conflict brewing and its consequences impending.

NOTES

1. Statistics provided by E. Abrahamian, "The Guerilla Movement in Iran, 1963-77," in *Iran: A Revolution in Turmoil*, edited by H. Afshar (London: Macmillan, 1985) indicate that most members of these armed groups were captured or killed by the Shah's security forces.

2. Detailed reports of the events from August 1977 until the fall of the Shah's regime can be found in major U.S. newspapers, especially the *New York Times* and the *Washington Post* during January and February 1979. J. Green, *Revolution in Iran: The Politics of Countermobilization* (New York: Praeger, 1982) also includes a number of precise reports on these events and provides a table in which the events that led to the fall of the Shah's regime are listed chronologically. In addition, Green mentions different groups and political parties that began to actively oppose the regime in early 1978 when the Revolution had begun to escalate. In my view, his reports are quite informative and precise.

3. J. Green, *Revolution in Iran*, provides an analysis of the events of 1978-79 that includes the actions undertaken by Iranian lawyers.

4. An article was published in an Iranian newspaper on January 7, 1978, insulting Ayatollah Khomeini. J. Green, *Revolution in Iran*, p. 154. In the city of Qhom the people, led by theological students, staged a demonstration protesting publication of this article. It set into motion a sequence of demonstrations that spread to other cities.

5. Black Friday stands for a Friday in which the massacre occurred. Black signifies death in Iranian culture. Due to the importance of this historic event it is included in many of the existing sources on the Iranian revolution. See Ali Reza Nobari, ed., *Iran Erupts* (Stanford: Iran-American Documentation Group, 1978) and J. Green, *Revolution in Iran*.

6. J. Green, *Revolution in Iran*, p. 159.

7. Military forces who opposed the religious processions eventually gave in to the demands of the people and let them have their mass gatherings for the anniversary of *Ashura*. See the *New York Times*, December 12, 1978.

8. Shahpour Bakhtiar had earlier taken a separate stand within the leadership of the National Front and was not in favor of Ayatollah Khomeini's theocratic objectives.

9. *New York Times*, February 6, 1979.

10. In Iran, large volumes of documents are gathered in relation to this incident. Movies shot by Iranian National Television photographers quite clearly show how masses of people from all walks of life had participated in this uprising. This was indeed typical of a revolutionary action through which people managed to subdue the royalist-commanded military forces.

10

Post-Revolution Power Struggles

CONSOLIDATION OF THEOCRACY

Once again, in the post-revolutionary era, Iran fell under despotic rule. This time it was a totalitarian rule that denied the people both political and cultural freedom. One may question why such a unified uprising, which had begun with the cries of freedom and triumphed with religious men respected by millions of Iranian as its leaders, turned into an oppressive regime in which thousands of people lost their lives merely because their lifestyle and thinking was different from those of the new sovereign. A partial answer to this question could be provided by considering the role of the better-educated middle class during the Revolution and afterward. The segment of this stratum that manned Iran's machinery of state, the service organizations and modern industries, had never totally yielded to the clerical leadership and did not intend to do so. Their earlier support of the clerical commanders was only a tactical one. They had tried to exert their force upon the course of social change by a number of tactics. Included were resistance to lay down arms taken away from the military barracks, insistence on pursuing their respective political party activities, and insistence on pursuing democratic objectives.

As was mentioned earlier, close upon the fall of the Shah, all groups tended to suspend their differences and unite. This union concerned the common issue of fighting to overthrow the monarchy, but did not concern what should replace it. It was after the triumph of the Revolution that major differences of opinions began to show up. By differences, specifically, are meant those which were irreconcilable. Such a differentiation did not occur all at once; it proceeded in steps. The proponents of theocracy intended to set other political groups aside and monopolize the sovereignty. First they needed to take over the agencies of the state and the major state-owned industrial and service organizations. The better-educated middle class was still in control of most such organizations. Therefore, the pro-clergy groups had to find some way to make them obedient to its own authority and to alienate them from their source of power. This task was even more urgent, because these groups were the core of the modernist political and even cultural strata that made up the main body of the secularist political forces.

The first major differences surfaced a couple of days after the fall of the old regime. It was caused by a fundamental difference in the outlook and expectations held by the clergy-led groups when compared to the rest of the population. When the Ayatollah began to send his men to head the sensitive organs of society, when he called upon the nation to go back to work and attend to their businesses, when he called upon the people to hand in arms that they had taken away from the military barracks—it all sounded as though he was saying that all would be "business as usual." It was becoming quite clear that revolution, from the clerical point of view, was basically different from that which a large segment of long-time anti-Shah activists had been imagining.[1] Many such groups and individuals thought the Revolution had only just begun and that it was too early to be decelerating. They were alerted that they should question what the revolution ought to be about. Was it intended to alter the social order or merely to bring in the Ayatollah and kick out the Shah?

Orders issued from above were not welcomed by the non-Islamic parties, nor by the radical Islamic groups. They had striven for decades to do away with autocracy, no matter what the basis of its legitimation. Earlier, when people were fighting the Shah, the unification of leadership had been a necessity that may have justified the issuance of such orders from the Ayatollah's office. However, in the post-revolutionary era, the continuation of such a practice was controversial.

Those who were faithful Shiias and who looked up to the Ayatollah as their religious reference, as well as the leading commander of the revolution, believed that obeying his orders was a quite natural thing to do. These people who follow the "reference" as their leader are called *Ommat* in the Islamic language. It simply means that they are followers of the Imam (leading figure). However, there were millions of Iranians who did not properly fit the domain of Ommat, but who were Iranian nationals. For them, the clerical leadership was merely a political authority whose authority was not yet fully established as sovereign. These people included the secularly oriented individuals, the bulk of the Sunni population (another branch of Islam). The Sunnis did not share with the Shiia their clergy nor their religious-political outlook.[2] The major sources of political unrest were developing in exactly the places where these non-Ommat groups had an intensive presence. Such places included the Sunni regions of Gonbad and the Kurdish provinces, the industrial and state organizations, and the universities and high schools. The clergy had very little difficulty with the segment of the population that was their sincere followers. This included most of the lower class, the rural, and the Bazaari people. The tension in the former areas was due to fundamental differences, both in reference to the definition of the revolution and the role of the clerical leadership.

The clergy-led groups were also not completely united in their views. For example, there were some people whose reference was other grand Ayatollahs, such as Shariat Madar.[3] Such great ayatollahs, despite their common points of view on the fundamental Islamic issues, had contrasting opinions on social, economic, and political matters.

Their conception of revolution was not that it should create a new form of society, but that it should create an "Islamic" one. From the clerical point of view, "revolution" was intended to create a theocracy that would fundamentally differ from the definition of democratically oriented groups as well as from that of the Marxists. As faithful Moslems, the clerical rulers could not compromise the principles of Islam. Such principles were not even open to interpretations. Therefore, in their view, a revolution was an uprising of the faithful to correct a system that had deviated from the Islamic principle. Revolution, then, meant a demand for further Islamitization of the society. The final projections of the society and its destiny were to be extracted from the script interpreted by the clergy, if necessary. So, also, was the conception of the Islamic government. Its basic framework was derived from the Shiia point of view and was more or less developed in theological schools as early as the 16th and 17th centuries.

For the secularists who were not bound to such principles or outlooks, this stage of the Revolution generally meant the removal of the police state of the Shah, which in turn would allow the people to rule themselves and to shape their own destiny. Even though politically secularist individuals and groups were providing a wide spectrum of ideas, they all shared some notions of a democracy. They looked up to people as the source of collective wisdom and for decisions that needed to be made. There were also religious people who had secularist orientations woven into their political views.

For most of those who did not share the clerical conception of revolution, the Shah's fall was just the beginning of the main task of making a revolution, the task of shattering the old social structure and creating a new one. In their view, it was not just the Shah or the heads of the regime that were making the society unacceptable to such groups, but a specific fabric that had permitted the Shah and his associates to do what they had done. They believed that the class system, the social setting of the organizations, the cultural patterns that had developed under the old regime, and the content of the educational materials needed to be altered in a revolutionary way. Therefore, they did not want the Revolution to stop. Therefore, also, if people were to go back to their normal life, such settings would get a chance to survive. They wanted to use the revolutionary sentiments and forces that were at their peak in order to alter these archaic structures. As a Persian proverb says, "Put the dough in the oven when it is still hot."

Within the politically nonreligious camp, there were also acute differences of opinion and even hostilities.[4] A number of Marxist and socialist groups had their own points of view and organizations, each competing to attract more dissentive individuals to their own side. Such was also the case with a number of radical Moslem groups, liberals, and a variety of socialist groups.

With all these activities going on, with guns in the hands of a variety of political forces and individuals, with the security forces of the country disorganized and not trusted by the proper authorities to fulfill their duties, a state of anarchy prevailed that resembled a free society. It differed from a truly free society in the sense that what it had provided was merely some small degree of freedom that was not due to the dominance of a liberal value system, but only to the balance of hostile and rival forces. If this balance was altered in either direction, even a small percentage, a dictatorship would once again reign.

The Invasion of the Public Sector

Immediately after the triumph of the Revolution, two sensitive regions of the country erupted into rebellion. The Kurdish province, which includes Iran's third most populated ethnic region, rose up for internal autonomy. With the help of the leftists, the agriculturally rich region of Gonbad experienced a bloodbath and fell under leftist-Turkman control. All over the country a variety of local and national newspapers began to publish, each presenting a specific political outlook. The walls of buildings and the inside walls of the government organization buildings were covered with posters, handwritten newsletters, and commentaries stating opinions on nearly any subject the people could imagine. Slogans that individuals and groups were putting up against the regime run by the clergymen were numerous, especially on the walls of the universities and public places. Most such attacks were due to the attempts of the clerical regime to put down the Kurdish and the leftist-Turkman revolts. The differences of opinion were so deep that whereever people gathered, they argued political issues with whomever they could. This occurred especially in places such as those around the University of Tehran. The secularists and the radical Moslems, having superior theoretical capacities for persuasion, had found a unique chance to expand their popular base of support. Enjoying a freedom that they had been denied for close to a quarter of century was an opportunity they would not want to miss. Political cartoons, fascinating writings, persuasive arguments, and, more than anything else, publications were their main instrument of accomplishing their objectives. It was quite clear that all through the years of the police state, many of the activists had been busy translating, writing, and preparing for just such an opportunity. In a matter of only a few months, bookstores were stacked with new titles. People were rushing to buy books and newspapers as though they were going shopping at a fifty percent off sale. Nearly every political and ideological group was putting out their own publications. Most these materials were underpriced. For example, one could buy the whole translation of all of Mao's writings, which was over 1000 pages, for less than one U.S. dollar. Even the price of the paper alone should have been more than that. The quality of all these books, and especially some of the major newspapers, were relatively high. Some, such as *Ayande gun*, even matched the level of *Le Monde Diplomatic*, the *Christian Science Monitor*, and the *London Times*.

One could quite easily consider some of their articles, especially the more analytic ones, to be at the level of junior and senior courses in the social science discipline. In the afternoon, the time at which most Iranian newspapers reach the store counters, long lines could be seen waiting for some of the more popular ones. Even though half a million copies was a record for the Iranian market, certain papers would sell a million copies. In most cases, these papers followed up a specific ideological line. However, they would present their materials in a way intended to appeal to the public taste. For example, a political-comic magazine put out by some leftists and called *Ahangar* (smith man), was a masterpiece in artistic and political respects. Its cartoons would say more than a long article. In general, the impact of such efforts by the modern-minded political groups had created an atmosphere that radically differed from the times immediately preceding the fall of the Shah, when the political climate was increasingly dominated by Shiia ideologies and sentiments, and allowed the intellectual and analytic capacities of the better-educated stratum to once again help them climb upward as the leaders of political opinion. The utilization of educational and mass media means was extending their capacities. Freedom of expression was helping them to make the best use of their abilities and to maintain their hold upon key positions in the technocratic and organizational apparatuses that were working in their favor to expand their domain of power and influence in the society. Once again, at least for about a year, the better-educated strata of the society had another golden age with which to expand their domain of political influence and intellectual leadership.

Another mode of politicization was face-to-face interaction with people, which was accomplished in a number of ways. Quite frequently, there were a number of mass gatherings sponsored by certain political groups, mostly the left-oriented youth. Tens of thousands of people would typically gather to listen to the speakers who were revolutionary heroes and idols to many of those attending. People would be addressed by leading figures who had been pre-revolutionary activists. Some of these speakers had served long and torturous terms in SAVAK prisons. Such gatherings would generate an atmosphere in which the attendants would stay around for hours afterward and talk with one another on the relevant issues of the day.

Such an exchange of ideas was not limited to these gatherings. It had become common for people to frequent the universities and other academic circles in order to obtain the opportunity to talk politics with other intellectual people, to gather pamphlets, and to read them. The distribution of the pamphlets was quite common, because in nearly all the institutions one could find paper and machines with which to reproduce or photocopy materials. With the breakdown of discipline and the reign of anarchy in these organizations, it was not difficult to find the opportunity to make large numbers of copies of whatever pamphlets one needed. Nearly every political group had taken over some such place, where the necessary facilities were available to them. On the streets, as soon as a car would stop at a red light, young high school students would rush to throw into the car a few pamphlets or pictures of the revolutionary idols, or other propaganda leaflets.

On and around the campus of Tehran University, one could see thousands of people at every hour of the day and even at night. They gathered in small groups of two or more, arguing on revolutionary and ideological issues. Probably none of them actually knew one another or cared to know each other's names. They did not even match their debate partners on an educational level. The only objective was to expand one's respective political standing and to convince more people to support one's own political orientation or group.

For the better-educated people, this was a unique chance to win over the curious laity, who had just become interested in higher-level political and intellectual discussions. The environs of University of Tehran, since it was in one of the most crowded squares of the capital city, would bring thousands of people into contact with such debaters every day. The curious people would stop for a few minutes just to see what was going on. Some of them would get involved and stay for hours. It was becoming fun to watch such randomly chosen prospective debaters, who would stay around for hours talking to anyone who was ready to exchange political ideas with them. For thousands of people, it was a way of killing time. They would argue about all kinds of issues, occasionally getting into very heated debates. No matter what subject they would begin to debate, they would always end up on the basic dialogues of the purpose of a revolution and what kind of society they envisioned. As soon as one bystander would say a word, another would respond, and after a while, those who had only just entered the discussion would drift to the side and make another small group, arguing amongst themselves. It was not difficult to find such partners with which to argue. In such a manner, the chain of these small groups would generate more and more small groups spreading all over the streets.

An interesting observation may show an example of how enthusiastically people would become involved in such small group discussions. One night, around eleven P.M., this author was driving home from the National University. I had to take a highway that passes by the Evin Prison and its surrounding areas, linking the northern part to central Tehran. I noticed hundreds of cars parked on either side of the highway, while their would-be occupants had gathered outside in the agricultural fields, making a large crowd. It looked unusual for such a crowd to be there so late at night. I stopped to see what was going on.

Surprisingly, I found out that hundreds of people had made small rings and, quite enthusiastically, were engaged in hot political arguments. What was more surprising was to find out how, in the middle of the highway, they had decided to stop, get out, and talk politics. I supposed that it had started with a couple of them being out for some purpose, and that the others had gradually joined them out of curiosity, just as I had, and had got involved thereafter in their arguments. Then they had generated into small rings and were eager to continue what they were doing. I supposed they had been there for hours and would stay for a few more hours.

The pro-clergy groups were also actively involved with their own practices of mass politicization. They had taken over the radio and television stations and had all the nation under the cover of their programs. In addition, they had devised ways of addressing millions of people on a regular basis and keeping them up to date on their own version of the political issues. The Ayatollah Talghani, a radical Ayatollah with nationwide influence, would conduct the Friday prayer on the campus of the University of Tehran. The attendants, who would fill the streets for miles, would number in the hundreds of thousands. A part of this prayer was composed of two political addresses.

Similar gatherings were held in different cities. Every night, the Ayatollah Khomeini himself would appear on television, during prime time, and talk for about half an hour. He would address the nation on the national networks and would present his political and religious views. The prime minister (Mehdi Bazargan) would also face the nation regularly and report to the people what the cabinet was doing.

The protheocracy people were not as persuasive with the white-collar employees and better-educated masses as they were with their loyal traditional supporters. Most of their supporters were the newly politicized laity who were politically no match for the better-educated middle class and the radical youth. Therefore, the clergy frequently had to call upon their supporters as street marchers for different exhibitions of mass activism, as they themselves claimed, "to keep them on the scene." In contrast, their rivals had no need to make such an attempt, because political activism and involvement had developed almost as a personality trait for the educated youth and many of the new middle class. They had grown up as political individuals.

As early as a few months after the triumph of the Revolution, it was quite clear that a differentiation was taking place, in which the bulk of the modern-oriented middle class and the rest of the better-educated people were standing at a distance from the clerical projection of a theocratic state. The clerical leadership, whose victory was to an extent due to the support that they had received from this influential segment of the middle class, was losing them.

Once again, the clerical influence was shifting back to their traditional domain, which was centered in the lower class, the Bazaaris, and the rural people. Such a tendency was reflected in a variety of ways. There were certain hostilities and criticisms in the air that they directed against the intellectuals and modern-minded middle class. The Ayatollah himself had begun to openly attack intellectuals, the nationalist political groups, and the radical-minded groups. Well-organized, fanatical, uneducated street gangs, under the name of the revolutionaries' ally, would attack the headquarters of the radical youths, tear up their posters, and write slogans against almost any group except those who were pro-clergy.[5] They would engage in fist fights, heckling, and the disruption of the gatherings of those who were not followers of the ruling clergymen, forcing them to disperse. This was becoming a common scene.

Manifestations of intolerance of different political groups were easy to notice in the public addresses of the ruling clergy. The attack was generalized to the sub-culture of modernity, which they used as a stigma in order to discredit the new middle class, intellectuals, and other secular political parties. Their instrument of confrontation was to typically call upon their supporters to march on the headquarters and the strongholds of their opponent groups or, indirectly, by dispatching organized gangs to quiet the opponents forcefully. The opposition papers began to refer to these gangs as "stick-holders," or *Cho magh dar*. These confrontations escalated into more violent incidents, and gradually, were institutionalized as the security policy of the new regime. The opposition would make cartoons of these gangs holding sticks in their hands, attacking other groups, and compare them to the black-shirted gangs sent out by the Nazi's during Hitler's reign in Germany.

Universities had become the center of opposition activities against the new sovereigns. The political secularists had almost grown to obtain full control of many college communities. In my university, for example, on the eve of the Revolution candidates supported by the Shiia fundamentalist groups had the majority vote. Once a few months had passed, though, they had hardly any chance of getting elected in a free election. A similar trend was occurring in many of the public organizations as well. The industrial sector had fallen heavily under radical pressure, with the leftist organizers finding a strong footing among certain workers' committees. It was quite obvious that the atmosphere of political freedom was working in favor of the secularists and those whose political views and reasoning had a modern theoretical background.

On the Islamic side, a differentiation was also emerging. One line was the pro-clerical rule, which was conventionally called "fundamentalists." This was what typically supported theocracy. The other was a more moderate view that did not totally alienate itself from the modern notions such as democracy, freedom, modern social theoretical reasoning, and technocracy. The latter groups were not restricting their conception to that of the final authority; only the clergymen did this. They believed that other devoted Moslems could also become leaders of an Islamic state. Since the clergy were identified as those with "turbans" on their heads, the latter were called those with "hats" (*Mo kal la*). This was a nickname that did not necessarily mean that the person had to wear a hat, but only that he was a non-turban-wearer. The controversy, then, was expressed as the dialogue of turban-wearers and hat-wearers. It was an argument on the issue of whether the country should be run strictly by clergy, having the monopoly on sovereignty, or whether there was no ground for such clerical monopoly of leadership. For the supporters of the latter position, Prime Minister Bazargan had emerged as one example of the non-turban wearers who qualified for leadership. Although he was a Moslem intellectual who had been both an active opposition leader and a proponent of the Islamic regime, he had liberal tendencies and was ready to tolerate other points of view. He was, indeed, a clergyman who did not have a turban, would dress in the Western style, was a professor of engineering, was trained in Europe, and was a former activist in the National Front. He very closely represented the bulk of the nonradical Islamic segment of the new middle class.

With the emergence and deepening in the Islamic camp of such a difference of views between fundamentalists and the moderate Moslem groups, the confrontation came closer to a polarization of theocrats vs. the better-educated middle class. The cultural background of their respective differences, therefore, became more pronounced.

Pronounced opposition within the Islamic camp became more frequent, resulting in open opposition by the fundamentalists against those officials who were appointed by the Bazargan cabinet. Bazargan's cabinet and the Islamic groups that supported his views were nicknamed "liberals." This tag was made by certain leftists, who had borrowed it from a Marxist analysis of the revolution. They saw Bazargan's cabinet as the last liberal attempt that would fade away as the Revolution intensified. Therefore, they were working with the pro-clergy groups to root out this so-called liberal element. They were also opposing the appointees of the temporary cabinet and its policies.

The fundamentalists were using the term "liberal" as an immoral tag. However, to them it meant something quite different from the conception of the Marxists. The leftists were using it mainly to characterize people as procapitalists. Being liberal to them meant a bourgeoisie-orientation that would eventually grow into a pro-American tendency. The Shiia fundamentalists, whose cognitive mapping of the society was a moral one, were attacking liberals for their cultural and ideological leniency.

The intensification of the conflicts was increasingly taking the form of cultural repression against those charged with being Western or modern oriented. This was a general category that included political secularism and liberalism as two of its dimensions. Therefore, it was pointing at large strata of people, mostly those of the urban better-educated middle class, as the aim of its repression. The instrument of this repression was mostly the dispatch of fanatic groups for the punishment and harassment of the modern-oriented groups, making their lives difficult by any means available, purging them from the public organizations, and so on. Because of such oppressive measures, and with the equally violent reaction of some of the attacked groups, post-revolutionary Iran was becoming very violent. The oppression was not just political, but was cultural as well. Cultural, academic, and political oppression was becoming the official policy of the new sovereigns.

Following the differentiation of the Islamic camp, even Islamic committees within the organizations experienced a change in the composition of their members. In the new form, many of the better-educated Moslems were either pushed out or began themselves to lose their enthusiasm for further active involvement. In its new form, the Islamic association became a unified pro-clergy grouping, typically membered by the less educated, the Bazaari, and the rural and lower-class employees. They were mostly those who worked at the lower echelon of the organization. However, there still were some, but not many, better educated and upper echelon employees involved with them. The Islamic elements who now were branded as liberals were showing signs of dissension. Some would stand at a distance from the more enthusiastic Islamic images of their earlier days. The ongoing differentiation quite clearly indicated that all spectra of the better educated middle class were under attack and pressure. The secularists were under attack for their non-Islamic political objectives; the moderate Islamic-oriented groups were under attack for their liberal tendencies; the Marxists were under attack because they were thought to be atheists.

As the tension deepened between the two Islamic factions, fundamentalists and liberals, it became quite clear that the latter's days were numbered. With them under attack, the Islamic regime alienated a large category of its own previous middle class supporters. The attack upon the Bazargan cabinet was not just an attack against an Islamic group, but one directed against all force that was identified with the ideals of parliamentary democracy also. Therefore, as Bazargan's camp was getting weaker and weaker, the theocratic group was gaining more control of the state. Increasingly, he and his followers were receiving the same criticism and treatment that were being directed at the rest of the middle class, especially at the modernized ones. Occasionally, he was called pro-American, a proponent of technocracy, and democratic minded.

It was quite clear that the Iranian Revolution was headed toward the dominance of those who intended to crush the power structure of the better educated middle class, subdue them in the state organizations and industrial settings, close down their mass media facilities, and purge their ideas and influence out of the educational materials of the country. Radical Moslems, whose sympathizers were the hundreds of thousands of high school and college students and better educated youth, were also under severe attack from the fundamentalist camps. They were looked at as communists, or "compositionists'' (el te gha ti). Compositionists were accused of confusing and combining Islam and other non-Islamic outlooks. This notion was eventually made a tag for "Mojahedin." They were the outgrowth of a small underground armed unit that was active during the reign of the Shah. They were even cursed as being like the group that had emerged in early days of Islam and killed the Imam Ali, the first of the Shiia Imams. This group was known as a deviant branch of Islam. The fundamentalists, who were making these accusations to other Moslem groups, were preparing to take over the administration of the state and other large organizations. The most difficult places for them to take over were the universities, the educational institutes, the industries, and the mass media.

The takeover of the military and the police was not very difficult. Those organizations had already been weakened. Moreover, the strictly bureaucratic nature had made them highly disciplined. Therefore, all that was needed was to appoint a pro-fundamentalist commander to rule them from above. In most cases, clergymen with no military experience were assigned to command them as ideological leaders. From the top, the chain of command descended to the bottom. The only center of resistance with which they had some difficulty was the lower echelon of the air force, which was a core of technical personnel. They were mostly young people, because these branches of the military service and the skills needed for them were relatively new. They were the ones who had revolted, causing the breakdown of the military structure, and had helped to arm the people. They had claims to the Revolution and were highly respected by those who supported it. Being better educated than most other segments of the armed forces, they were mostly under the influence of modern-minded political and social groups. A good number of them identified with radical groups, both Islamic and Marxist. Despite their significant role in the Revolution, they were not a very large group and only counted as a rather small unit when compared to the sum total of all armed forces, which numbered to a few hundred thousand individuals.

The observations of what the fundamentalists did to take over the rest of the public organizations could be summed up as follows:

1. The first step in getting rid of any individual or group was to publically discredit it. This was called "revealing," or ef sha ga ry. That is, they would publicize hidden facts about the people, such as their earlier connection with the West, or with SAVAK, or whether they had any immoral records. If the person did not have such a bad record, then labeling them as liberals was the least they could do in damage. Such charges would psychologically clear the way for the person, who was given a feeling of guilt, to be thrown out of office. The move would justify itself in the public eye, showing that something was wrong with this person. Under the given circumstances, no one dared to defend such a person any longer, even if the accusations made were unfounded. If someone did defend another person so labeled, they themselves could be charged with similar accusations.

2. The new Islamic associations that were restructured within the organization would begin to harass the people in any way that they could find. In the case of a high

officer, for example, they would not take his orders or deliver his letters. Therefore, in an organization where the division of labor rules, all the lines connected to that person would gradually be cut off. Meanwhile, they would transfer his tasks to someone else whom they did favor. The person would find himself having nothing to do. In case he was a professor or a teacher, he would not be assigned any courses to teach.

3. They would assign one of their men or get a high-placed clergyman to put a pro-clergy appointee into the high office as an assistant to a person that they disliked. At the least, they would call this newcomer a trusted representative of that high clergyman in order to guard against wrongdoing. Then, pressures would be exerted to make the isolated authority cooperate with this person. The isolated one would have no choice but to cooperate. Gradually, the appointed assistant would take over all the tasks and learn some of the basic skills. Then they would strike the final blow and kick the unwanted one out of office. Sometimes, such a dismissal would be done in quite a humiliating way.

4. Upon the installation of some of their own men, the control of the organization would be taken over from two directions. They would move from the bottom through the new Islamic association and from above through the new fundamentalist boss or bosses.

5. They would begin to squeeze those who were in the middle, which were usually the white collar and better-educated middle class. Sometimes, they would take advantage of the political rivalries between such employees. For example, they allowed the leftists to help discredit and purge the liberal-oriented elements, and then they got rid of the leftists themselves.

The nonfundamentalist Islamic groups (liberals, Mojahedin, Ommaties) were also more or less treated like secularists. They were made to feel less secure in their jobs, less attention was paid to them, and they were even made the target of hostile actions.

Following the consolidation of the power and authority of the fundamentalists, a number of changes were taking place. First, the clergy, who had assumed leadership, were being transformed into the rulers. They had managed to take over the strongholds of the better-educated middle class, namely the state bureaucracies and large industrial enterprises.

Second, their followers managed to force upon the employees their own preferred codes of conduct, so that they would see them as the only conduct of which Islam could approve. This policy had turned into unbearable, culturally repressive measures that would dictate how one should dress, how one should behave in public, and how one should associate with others. Their aim was to give these institutions, in their words, "an Islamic look." However, the materialization of such an objective was not quite possible in the first year after the Revolution, for the presence of large numbers of modern-minded employees, many of whom were still in positions of power, would not permit a full-scale cultural dictatorship.

Increasingly, it was becoming clear that a polarization was taking place with fundamentalists on one side and the rest of the employees on the other. Parallel with this trend, the concept of "reactionary" and "fanatic" was finding more widespread usage. The fundamentalists were often referred to as reactionaries, while the accusers would call themselves "progressive." These notions were mostly used by the leftists whose numbers increased considerably after the Revolution.

From the point of view of the fundamentalists, there was not much difference between leftists, liberals, nationalists, and even the moderate Moslems who had intellectual orientations. They were all seen as "non-Islamic." Islam was being interpreted mainly as they would define it. In this definition, the unquestioning obedience toward the ruling clergy was the main criterion.

The psychological mechanism of consolidation of their rule was through use of weeding out unwanted members. This was turning into an instrument of intimidation and repression, a way of dealing with rivals. The Islamic association would make the suggestions or set the pressure, and their implanted boss or "cleaning up" committees would implement their demands. The idea of being weeded out, defamed, accused, or threatened with losing one's source of income had put the employees under a reign of terror. They would not once and for all say who should be kicked out and who was clear of any accusation. Every day they would come up with a new criterion for discrediting people. Therefore, a state of ambivalence, job insecurity, and intimidation prevailed that was used to make the employees comply with the demands of those who manned the "cleaning up" committees. It should be mentioned that the fundamentalists were not the only ones responsible for this reign of psychological pressure and terror. Still, many members of different groups were in key positions and had access to information to "reveal" someone, that is, in a position to find a document and reveal it, showing that the person had done some wrong in the past. For example, it was quite common for some employees to use as evidence a picture of a woman employee that they had been associating with for years as colleague, wherein she would be depicted dancing with some men in a nonconservative dress. The possession of this picture in the hands of the "cleaning up" committee members was enough to make that woman miserable.

Another case was that of showing a person in a ceremony where the Shah was present. In the past, it had been the customary practice to assemble notable people as an audience whenever the Shah was visiting the campus. This attendance was often made mandatory by the high officers of the university. It was common to force the people to bow when the Shah was passing by them. If a person happened to be in such a picture, bowing to the Shah, he would unfortunately be in trouble with the new fundamentalists. Sometimes such a picture would be posted on the wall with some humiliating statements to prove that the person in the picture had been an instrument of the regime. Given the fact that letters of gratitude and appreciation were often sent to encourage high officials during the Shah's regime, it was not difficult to find such a letter in a high level employee's records. If one was found, there was very little a person could do, for at any moment the letter could be revealed and used to kick the person out or put him or her in the state of probation.

The moment that the "cleaning up" committee saw any accusation that seemed to be supported by a document, the accused person's salary would be cut. His or her presence on the job would be forbidden or limited, and it would take months before a decision was made on the case. Many of those employees who did not have any records were still fearful that something would surface that could become the basis of accusations. Such people were also quite careful not to rock the boat, and tried to keep a low profile. This is exactly what certain hardliners who controlled the committees were anticipating. It was a way to intimidate the employees not to ask questions, to mind their own business, and to dissuade their intentions of taking over the seats of power. Almost everyone identified with some political group, therefore the possibility of being victimized by rivalries of political opponents was very high. The main struggle, however, was developing between the fundamentalist and all other groups.

The struggle for power had become highly intensive in the industrial sector. With the industrial employees, the accusations of moral corruption, Westernization, and liberal mindedness were less effective than they had been in educational institutions. They could not be used against those workers and employees who were confronting the Islamic committees. The strength of the leftist influence, as well as that of the higher level technocrats, was strong enough to seriously resist domination by the fundamentalists. Because of the highly technical nature of the work in the industrial bureaucracies, personnel could not be as easily replaced as in the state organizations. In addition, the solidarity of the work force was much stronger than what one ordinarily witnessed in the white-collar sector.

The behavior of the political parties within this context was not at all according to one pattern. The liberals and the nationalists had reservations concerning the fundamentalists' strive for power. However, the Tudeh party had a rather complex behavior. They openly supported the fundamentalists and would not confront them. In their view, people at that stage of political consciousness had chosen these clergymen as their leaders. Therefore, they would not try to go against the wishes of laity. All they wanted was to avoid a confrontation, and to buy time for the consolidation and expansion of their own organization. Thus, they decided that they could use the existing freedom to publish, organize, get rid of rivals, and influence the course of events in the direction that they saw proper. In their view, the clerical leadership included some "progressive" elements, and they would try to help the promotion of these elements.

At the same time, they were putting a heavy emphasis on educating the masses toward socialist political and economic policies. For example, to them it did not matter who got fired from his job or why. What mattered more was to distribute their leaflets about why foreign trade should be nationalized and taken out of the hands of certain big businessmen. They wanted to have the chance to call for land reform, and for anti-Western policies. They tended to narrow their distance with the working class by not confronting them on emotional and ideological issues. By following such a policy, they were less harmed by the Islamic committees. In contrast, certain smaller leftist groups would openly oppose the fundamentalists. The latter would often call these leftists "American Marxists." The strongest resistance to the fundamentalist takeover was by liberal-oriented technocrats and the leftist shiia groups (*Mojahedin*). In their view, the clerical dominance was equal to a takeover of the counterrevolution. They were the ones who, more than anyone else, would call the pro-clergy people "reactionaries."

Nearly one year after the fall of the Shah, it was becoming quite clear that the better-educated middle class and the political forces that they were supporting were rapidly expanding their influence. Being dominant in sensitive positions in the mass media, state organizations, and especially educational institutions, were allowing them to make the best use of whatever political freedom they still enjoyed. With the disintegration of the unity of the Islamic forces, the Islamic committees were not capable of having a large majority of the employees of the organizations behind them. It was in such an atmosphere that the incident of the taking over the American Embassy helped the fundamentalists to overcome some of their difficulties. Probably, this was not their only intention. However, the outcome of this attempt helped those groups that advocated the sovereignty of the clergymen to implement their policies and take over the sensitive organizations that were manned and controlled by the better-educated middle class. When the students, who were loyal to the rule of clergymen, invaded the gates of the American Embassy, those who had been identified as "reactionaries" reemerged as the leading revolutionaries, capable of dumping the modernist and secularist forces all together.[6] They ended the era of middle-class dominance of Iranian administrative systems. It was the beginning of the rule of a new coalition, in which certain clergy and their Bazaari associates were the leaders and large groups from the lower-middle class and urban-lower class were the functionaries.

The takeover of the Embassy had created a lot of mystery in Iranian post-revolutionary politics. There are still some questions that need to be answered, for example, Were the Americans really uninformed that this was going to happen? How seriously were they trying to release their men? What hesitation, if any, did they have about reverting to punitive action in order to force their men's freedom? On the Iranian side, more things are clearly known. The takeover was a pre-planned effort. Students in the University informed us later that prior to the takeover of the Embassy, certain students belonging to the Islamic Republican Party (a pro-clergy group) had had a gathering. They even knew some of those who were involved in this action. The students seemed to have daily information on what was happening inside and outside the American Embassy. One could put together this information and create a theoretical explanation of why this event had happened. I personally knew a number of their ringleaders, who had been my students. One of these leaders I knew from the pre-revolution days, and I was quite familiar with his line of thinking. Earlier, he had told me, "This time, we are not going to repeat the mistakes made in the Constitutional Revolution. We have to put a clergyman at the top of everything." Later, he was assigned to a highly sensitive government post.

When the Americans were taken hostage, it once again provided the Ayatollah with the capacity to speak for the whole nation. Leftists offered their full support of this action. They were doing all they could to get as many people to march to the Embassy site as they could, to lend their support to this action. There were some people who may not have personally approved of it, but the public was emotionally steered to support it. Once again, there were mass gatherings and marches that resembled those of the revolutionary days. Public pressure was so supportive of this action that no one dared to openly speak against it. This support came mainly from the radicals, who saw this as a chance to reorient the Revolution toward an anti-Western and anti-capitalist system. The laity saw it as challenging the most powerful nation in the world, the one that had supported the Shah. The ruling clergy saw it as a chance to gain international recognition as revolutionaries and to silence their opponents. The students who had taken the hostages and their associates saw it as a coup against the liberal-oriented government of Mehdi Bazargan and as a chance to take over the government. In fact, from the very first day that they took over the American Embassy, the students used the mass media to show that some of Bazargan's cabinet members had had American sympathies, and they tried to orient public enthusiasm against what they called "liberals," meaning the Bazargan cabinet and the social class that it represented. It was obvious that this act of taking hostages was not like similar ones that had occainally happened elsewhere in the world, carried out by a small band of radicals. This was an event that was an attempt to confront America with a people in revolution, and in which the Iranian urban lower class and their leadership were trying to become the ruling class. The potential generated by the Iranian Revolution was invested in this confrontation with a superpower.

It could be theorized that when these young men invaded the American Embassy, they ended the era in which the Iranian new middle class dominated administrative systems of the country. In addition, they ended whatever power and authority still rested with the moderate Islamic partners of the regime. An era began in which the clergymen were on their way toward fully commanding the administration of Iran.

With this invasion, the internal strifes once again loosened because it was claimed that the new stage of the Revolution had begun—the stage of face-to-face confrontation with the power that had masterminded the Shah's regime. They began calling the U.S. "The Great Satan." As previously mentioned,

Iran's century-old striving was not simply against autocratic rulers, but against the union of the monarchy and its dependency on foreign powers. The Shah's removal was pictured as the first stage of the Revolution, and in fact, the minor one; confronting the U.S. was claimed to be the more important phase. This was the impression gleaned from the statements of the Ayatollah and his supportive elements. Therefore, those who had attacked them by calling them reactionaries were to an extent disarmed and quieted. Once, even on national television a statement was made asking, "Are we reactionaries who are fighting the U.S. by taking their men hostage?" Apparently, the message was addressed to both the liberals and the leftists.

With the takeover, the streets of Tehran were once again crowded with pro-clergy demonstrations. Now the country was nearly completely controlled, from the occupied American Embassy, by those who had taken the Embassy people as hostages. They would formulate the policies and masses of people outside would approve by shouting their support. The students were obviously not acting on their own, but were under the command of some powerful clergymen and were totally obedient to the Ayatollah. It was, therefore, the group ruling under the Ayatollah's orders who were implementing their own policies through the hostage-taking students.

The fundamentalist students of the "Islamic Associations" who a few weeks earlier had been looked upon by their rivals as reactionaries and fanatics, were now posing as super revolutionaries and were cheered by masses of people whenever they appeared at the gate of the Embassy to be interviewed by reporters. It was this revolutionary image and the public support that they counted on to neutralize the power of their opponents and rivals, and with which they were able to justify their use of oppressive means to take over the state.

The first victim was the cabinet of Bazargan itself. They did all they could to picture this cabinet as the functionary of U.S. policy. They called it the "Brezinski line," referring to the meeting of Bazargan and Brezinski (then head of the U.S. Security Council) in an international meeting. In the University, students who were closely connected to the ones inside the Embassy compound were saying that the hostage takers were talking about forming a new cabinet composed of their favorite candidates. This one would be the cabinet of the new ruling powers—namely fundamentalists.

Now with the leftists on the side of this action, the only groups that were singled out as unhappy with the embassy event were some of the Western-oriented strata. Therefore, some of the liberals and those who had an inclination toward the West were the first to come under attack. Such groups were identified as the modernist middle class, and were the same ones that in most cases had been the occupants of the state and industrial bureaucracies. It was claimed that they supported the United States, but such claims were not based on evidence, but on theoretical grounds. Modernity was identified by Westernization, and Westernization in turn was identified with the United

States. A modern orientation, therefore, was to become the target. For example, a campaign was staged, both by the fundamentalists and certain leftists, not to show American films, which had previously been viewed all over the country. In the University, one of the Marxist professors believed that all Ph.D. degrees issued to Iranians by American universities should be announced as "void," and that those having academic jobs because of these degrees should be dismissed. Another highly prominent professor, who was a sympathizer of one of the major Marxist parties, told me that "Sociology is the science of the bourgeoisie. Now that we have closed the American Embassy and are going to end the U.S. influence, there is no reason why such a subject should be taught."

Even though the leftists were supportive of the students' action, they still received their similar treatment, because for the hostage takers, such support did not mean much. They did not look for partners, but were striving to monopolize the sovereignty. It did not matter much whether or not the leftists were supporting them, they just did not want nonfundamentalists to be in a position of power.

These are examples of how taking over the Embassy helped to crush the power and influence of the modern-oriented middle class. From then on, the Ayatollahs who earlier had risen up to the leading position of the Revolution managed to become its actual sovereigns. In the context of Iranian society, taking over the administrative organs was equal to the dominance of the single most important power structure of the society. With the events of Embassy, Iran's theocracy was consolidated and the administration of the country was passed to another group. This was not an isolated "terrorist" act, as some Westerners may prefer to call it or to think of it. It was the peak of a power struggle for sovereignty in which half a century of intellectual, political, and administrative leadership of the Iranian modernized middle class came to an end.

NOTES

1. Ayatollah Mottahari, in *Iran: A Revolution in Turmoil*, edited by H. Afshar (London: Macmillan, 1985). Mottahari was one of the theoreticians of the "Islamic Government."

2. Sunnis do not follow the Shiia clergy. They have their own religious leaders. Sunni Iranians live mostly on the border regions of Iran. *Turkman, Kurd,* and *Balouch* are the main groups of Iranian Sunni Moslems. The largest of all are the Kurdish people, who number a few million and are the dominant population in northwestern Iran. A smaller group of Kurdish settlers are stationed in many other regions of Iran, such as Ghochan and some rural areas in the central provinces. Turkmans are exclusively concentrated in the Gonbad region with some of them in the north of the province of Khorasan. The Balouch are the main population of a large but lightly populated province in southeastern Iran. All these groups resisted the rule of the Shiia clergy by showing autonomy-seeking tendencies. Such tendencies were relatively weaker with the Balouchi people.

3. Shariat Madar was a Grand Ayatollah from the Turkish speaking province of Azarbaijan. His influence was widespread among all Iranians. He was known to have liberal tendencies. Shariat Madar was discredited by the government controlled mass media of the Islamic regime and was isolated from his followers.

4. Iranian Marxists show deep opposition to the liberal political leaders. In the post-revolutionary era, they managed to inject their anti-liberal tendencies into certain fundamentalist Shiia groups as well. "Death to the Liberal," chanted in many clergy-led gatherings such as the Friday prayer congregation, had become a common practice.

5. This opposition eventually grew into a genocidal policy toward *Mojahedin*, who were first on the list of the Ayatollah Khomeini to be executed if they were proven to have engaged in anti-regime actions. Thousands of *Mojahedin* followers and activists were later put into jail and over a thousand of them, mostly high school and college students, were executed. The reports of these executions were published in Iranian newspapers and broadcasted over the state controlled radio stations. In the mid-1980s such executions could reach as high as 50 per day.

6. The takeover of the U.S. Embassy was manned by a group of students who were directly related to the fundamentalist political group, the Islamic Republican party. In the cabinet that was formed after Mr. Bazargan had resigned, representatives of the hostage-taking student group, known as the "Student followers of the Imam's line," had strong presence. They are still in control of the Ministry of Foreign Affairs. The incident of the takeover of the U.S. Embassy was the beginning of the formation of post-revolution Iranian foreign policy, which involves frequent verbal attacks on the U.S. government.

Conclusion

The Iranian experience provides valuable data and certain insights into some key theoretical issues in sociology. It could contribute to the sociology of modernization, the sociology of revolutions, and the social study of culture and religion.

Since the Iranian Revolution is only a single case and a case that seems to be historically specific, we may be prevented from overgeneralizing based on Iranian findings. However, the event raises certain issues and addresses certain questions that could shed some light on the shortcomings of existing theories. One such shortcoming is in the area of theories of modernization. Theoretical works on modernization were begun by pioneering sociologists and were later pursued by those in communications. As it had begun with the works of earlier theorists such as Daniel Lerner, modernization was viewed as a process that had great social-psychological consequences. What these attempted to do was trace the consequences for the material modernization of a society in terms of the internal (psychological) changes that take place within the individual.[1] They further expanded these concerns in order to learn more about what facilitates or hinders the process of modernization of individuals. Our study of the Iranian case may suggest a need to look at the facilitators and impedances that are of a class and political nature. The breakdown of the individual's internal constraints against modernization, which the existing theorists tend to focus on, is not sufficient to understand both the modernization and countermodernization developments. As the Iranian case clearly shows, modernization is not viewed by the people who are subject to it as a value-free experience. It is understood as favoring certain groups more than others, and therefore becomes a political or even a class-domination process in the eyes of the people. It is this sort of cognitive mapping of modernization that is the key to understanding the cultural and religious revitalization movements that were active in Iran, and may potentially develop in many other Middle Eastern countries. What we propose is not to do away with what has already been accomplished, but to shift toward a more holistic treatment of the subject.

Similar arguments may be made about the theories of revolution. There exists a tendency for certain social theorists to try to reduce revolutionary events to causal models. Moreover, they tend to focus on monocausal explanations. The fact, as the Iranian Revolution seems to suggest, is that it might be futile to look for a single cause. Rather, one may need to favor a holistic approach. Again, it must be asserted that while none of the causal explanations can probably be rejected, even the monocausal ones, they do seem to only show a glimpse of revolutionary events.

If what is presented in this book is to be considered convincing, then we must conclude that a variety of forces and causes are involved in revolution, none exercising the same strength at all times. It is at the different phases of the historic events of a revolution that each one may be brought to light as the main cause of that specific phase.

This issue could also be raised in another way. Why, for instance, should we assume, as many sociologists do, that active participation in a revolution ought to be motivated solely by material interests? Why should there not be other causes, such as the people pursuing some ideological objectives? Why should we not assume that culture and religion are also potential locuses of an impetus toward structural changes of a society? Why should we not have a pluralistic view of these causes and motives that instigate a people to rise to revolution? A proper response to such questions and their implications, in observance of the events, is what is meant by a "holistic approach." To us it appears to be a realistic as well as a reasonable effort to make.

One consequence of this approach is to not have to unjustifiably ignore facts that do not fit our mode of theorization. We do not even have to downplay the significance of such facts that may happen to run counter to our own theoretical way of thinking. In addition, instead of jumping over certain phases by ignoring them or leaving them unexplained in order to get to the historic moment that seems to best fit our own mode of explanation, we might treat each vital phase of a revolutionary build up as it has indeed occurred. It does justice to all who have been involved in the Iranian Revolution and to the historical facts, and it may provide a more comprehensive explanation of the Revolution. In the case of Iran, we have seen a good example of what this suggests. In addition, we leave room open for the anticipation of what may next occur, not needing to conlcude that the Revolution is totally accomplished. We may have reached the end of our list of preconceived causes, but surely the people of that country have not reached the end of their ideas and ideals, as well as those interests for which they are ready to struggle. As long as people exist, there remains the possibility that they will generate major political events. The people may never reach the end of their possible struggle. Thus it may be for the people of Iran. Their case is not closed and may not be closed for a time that no one is able to forecast.

This theoretical issue could be raised about the potential sources of change generated by culture. If culture is viewed as a homogeneous medium, as in most cases it is, then it may closely resemble a static entity, a passive one that could not be the source of major social changes. However, from the way it has been treated in this book, a different conception develops. What makes the Iranian culture and Shiiaism a potential ground for the generation of political forces is the dualism that is embedded in it. It is not just a series of justifications, historically formed by the interests of the ruling classes; nor is its content all anti-ruling class sentiments. It is both. The dynamism that could make culture and religion two important sources of change arises from this very fact of dualism. In the case of the Revolution, it was the anti-ruling class elements of Iranian culture and Shiia Islam that became the seedbed of radicalism that represented itself as revitalization movements. Such movements may well parallel other drives, such as those caused by material and group interests. For certain strata of people, the impetus could quite reasonably be cultural or religious movements, and nothing more. I am convinced that for many Iranians this was so. Surely, there were and still are many Iranians, acting and sounding as radical as any other "anti-imperialist" and "anti-ruling class" activists, who still sincerely believe that they revolted to vitalize their religion, that Shiia revitalization is indeed a revolutionary act, that the Revolution was definitely for Islam, and that they are ready to sacrifice their lives for that cause. For this category of people, ideologies, motives, supportive sentiments for revolutionary actions, and the ideals for which they have striven all have originated from their religion and culture.

NOTE

1. W. E. Moore, and N. Smelser, eds., *Modernization of Traditional Societies* (Englewood Cliffs, NJ: Prentice Hall, 1966); D. Lerner, *The Passing of the Traditional Society* (Glenco, IL: Free Press, 1958); and J. Malcolm, *History of Persia* (London: Murray, 1829).

Appendix: Tables

Table 1
Literacy Rate in Rural and Urban Iran (percentages)

	1956	1966	1976
Urban	34.6	50.4	65.2
Rural	6.1	15.1	29.7

Source: Salnameh Amary (farci) (Tehran: Markaz Amar
e Iran, 1985), p. 112.

Table 2
Rainfall and Humidity in Cities of Iran, 1982

	Annual Rainfall (in mm)	Relative Humidity (in percent)
Tehran	217	41
Shiraz	311	41
Kerman	93	33
Bakhtaran	435	53
Rasht	1514	84
Anzali	1870	84

Note: Tehran, Shiraz, and Kerman are typical of arid regions,
Bakhtaran is in a semi-arid and pastoral region, and
Rasht and Anzali are in the province of Gilan on the
coast of the Caspian Sea.

Source: Salnameh Amary (farci) (Tehran: Markaz Amar e Iran,
1985), p. 39.

179

Bibliography

The following books about Iran are available in English. Some of them contain similar information to what I originally used for my readings in farci.

Abrahamian, E. *Iran: Between Two Revolutions.* Princeton: Princeton University, 1982.

_____. "The Guerilla Movement in Iran, 1963-77." In *Iran: A Revolution in Turmoil*, edited by H. Afshar. London: Macmillan, 1985.

Afshar, H, ed. *Iran: A Revolution in Turmoil.* London: Macmillan, 1985.

Akhavi, S. *Religion and Politics in Contemporary Iran.* Albany: State University of New York, 1980.

Al e Ahmad, J. *Plagued by the West*, translated by Paul Sprachman. New York: Caravan Books, 1982.

Algar, Hamid. *Religion and State In Iran, 1785-1906.* Berkeley and Los Angeles: University of California, 1969.

Amnesty International. Briefing: Iran. London: Amnesty International Publications, November 1976.

Arjomand, Said Amir. *The Shadow of God and the Hidden Immam: Religion, Political Order, and Societal Change in Shi'ite Iran from the Beginning to 1890.* Chicago: University of Chicago, 1984.

Avery, Peter. *Modern Iran.* New York: Praeger, 1965.

Ayatollah Mottahari. "The Nature of the Islamic Revolution." In *Iran: A Revolution in Turmoil*, edited by H. Afshar. London: Macmillan, 1985.

Banani, A. *The Modernization of Iran, 1921-1941.* Stanford: Stanford University, 1961.

Behrangi, Samad. *The Little Black Fish and Other Modern Persian Stories*, translated by Eric and Mary Hooglund. Washington, D.C.: Three Continent, 1976.

Bill, James A. *The Politics of Iran: Group, Classes, and Modernization.* Columbus, OH: Merill, 1972.

Binder, L. *Iran: Political Development in a Changing Society.* Berkeley and Los Angeles: University of California, 1962.

Browne, E. *The Persian Revolution of 1905-1909*. London: Cambridge University, 1910.

Cottam, R. *Nationalism in Iran*. Pittsburgh: University of Pittsburgh, 1964.

Documents on the Pahlavi Reign of Terror in Iran [Eyewitness reports and newspaper articles]. Frankfurt, W. Germany: The Documentation Center of the Federation of Iranian Students-National Union, n.d.

Fatemi, F. *The U.S.S.R. in Iran*. New Jersey: A. S. Barnes, 1980.

Fischer, M. *Iran: From Religious Dispute to Revolution*. Cambridge: Harvard University Press, 1980.

Green, J. *Revolution in Iran: The Politics of Countermobilization*. New York: Praeger, 1982.

Imam Khomeini. *Islam and Revolution*, translated and annotated by Hamid Algar. Berkeley: Mizan Press, 1981.

Issawi, C., ed. *The Economic History of Iran, 1800-1914*. Chicago: University of Chicago, 1971.

Kazemi, F. *Poverty and Revolution in Iran*. New York: New York University, 1940.

Keddie, Nikki R. *Religion and Rebellion in Iran: The Tobacco Protest of 1891-1892*. London: Cass, 1966.

————. *Sayyid Jamal al-Din "al-Afghani."* Berkeley and Los Angeles: University of California, 1972.

Lerner, D. *The Passing of the Traditional Society*. Glenco, IL: Free Press, 1958.

Malcolm, J. *History of Persia*. London: Murray, 1829.

Moore, W. E., and N. Smelser. *Modernization of Traditional Societies*. Englewood Cliffs, NJ: Prentice-Hall, 1966.

Neshat, G. *The Origin of Modern Reform In Iran, 1870-80*. Urbana: University of Illinois, 1982.

Perry, John R. *Karim Khan Zand: A History of Iran 1747-1779*. Center for Middle Eastern Studies, no. 12. Chicago: University of Chicago, 1979.

Ramazani, R. K. *The Foreign Policy of Iran: A Developing Nation in World Affairs 1500-1941*. Charlottesville: University of Virginia, 1966.

Roosevelt, K. "How the CIA Brought the Shah to Power." *Washington Post*, May 6, 1979.

————. *Countercoup: The Struggle for the Control of Iran*. New York: McGraw-Hill, 1979.

Saikal, A. *The Rise and Fall of the Shah*. Princeton: Princeton University, 1980.

Savory, R. *Iran under the Safavids*. Cambridge: Cambridge University, 1980.

Shariati, Ali. *Collected Works (farci)*. Tehran: Hoseini yeh Ershad, 1970-1980.

————. *Islamic View of Man*, translated by A. A. Rusti. Houston: Islamic Free Press, 1974.

————. *On the Society of Islam*, translated by H. Algar. Berkeley: Mizan Press, 1979.

Upton, J. *The History of Modern Iran: An Interpretation*. Cambridge: Harvard University, 1968.

Wilber, Donald N. *Contemporary Iran*. New York: Praeger, 1963.

————. *Reza Shah Pahlavi: The Resurrection and Reconstruction of Iran*. New York: Exposition Press, 1975.

Wittfogel, K. A. *Oriental Despotism: A Comparative Study of Total Power*. New York: Random House, 1981.

Zabih, Sepehr. *The Communist Movement in Iran.* Berkeley and Los Angeles: University of California, 1966.
_____. *The Mossadegh Era: Roots of the Iranian Revolution.* Chicago: Lake View Press, 1982.

Index

ABOUT THE AUTHOR

MOHAMMAD M. SALEHI was a member of the faculty of sociology at the National University of Iran for more than a decade. In Iran he published a number of sociology textbooks and papers. He was also active in team research on industrial studies and planning for the country. Recently, he came to the United States. He is currently advancing his quantitative knowledge and skills for social research and at the same time is finalizing reports of some of the social studies he had undertaken in Iran. He holds an engineering degree from Purdue University and a Ph.D. in Sociology from the Michigan State University. He has taught sociology at a number of American universities.